"Perry and Tom not only understand every nuance of the technical aspects of getting Facebook ads to work for your business, they also understand the psychology behind what works and what doesn't when it comes to advertising online. If you're looking for an über-effective way to master the art of driving traffic to your offers through paid advertising, get this book—it truly is the ultimate guide!"

—Mari Smith, co-author of *Facebook Marketing: An Hour a Day*
and author of *The New Relationship Marketing*

"Aw, the whole thing makes my head hurt. But other than puffery about 600-million customers, Perry's an honest man in a field rife with charlatans. If anybody can make practical sense of Facebook for marketers, it's Perry. He has his finger on its truth—as advertising media not social media. He also realizes there is a short window of time during which it offers greatest opportunity. He identified this with Google AdWords. Now this book shows how to capitalize on ideal timing with this media. Finally, he is a well-disciplined direct-response practitioner who holds this accountable for ROI. I bestow my 'No B.S. blessing.'"

—Dan S. Kennedy, legendary direct marketing advisor
and author of the *NO B.S.* book series, www.NoBSBooks.com

"*Ultimate Guide to Facebook Advertising* just might be your ultimate guide to earning a ton of money with this social media phenomenon. What you don't know about Facebook could hurt you and what you will learn about Facebook from this book definitely will help you. It's a fun and easy read and a surefire way to seriously increase your income."

—Jay Conrad Levinson, The Father of Guerrilla Marketing,
author of *Guerrilla Marketing* series of books—over 21 million sold; now in 62 languages

"Facebook advertising appears simple, but it's trickier than search engine marketing. In this book, Perry Marshall and Tom Meloche teach you secret of "Right Angle Marketing"—selling based on who people are and what they identify with. This is entirely different from Yahoo! or Google. They help you determine how to prioritize Facebook within your particular marketing mix. Then they take you by the hand and lead you through the minefield, showing you the tools, bidding techniques, and sales cycles of Facebook ads. Without their help, the odds are stacked against you. With their help, your chances of success are excellent."

—Alex Mandossian, Heritage House Publishing, author of *The Business Podcasting Bible*

"Perry Marshall has done more to de-mystify Google AdWords for business owners than any person on earth. With this book, he's done the same for Facebook. If you want to cut through the smoke quickly and make money advertising on Facebook, this is the book to read."

—Ken McCarthy, The System Seminar, Tivoli NY

"The irony of living in the Information Age is that good info has gotten harder to come by. The lame stuff still manages to clog the pipes, causing chaos and preventing you from discovering the legit specifics that can actually help you in your quest for business success and a bigger bottom line. Perry Marshall has been a first-stop, one-stop resource for the best possible advice on making AdWords work since Google unleashed it on the marketing community . . . and now, Perry's new tome on Facebook's astonishing (and yet-to-be-fully-tapped) power to reach gazillions of targeted, eager prospects (most of whom you'd never even know existed, otherwise) is the first and probably the only book you need to be one of those early adopters who score fastest. Perry's books are always essential. This one is perhaps more so than usual."

—John Carlton, the most respected and ripped-off veteran copywriter on the web

"Perry Marshall is amazing! He reinvented himself from engineer to white paper expert to become the world's leading expert in Google Adwords. Now with his secret weapon, Tom Meloche, he's reinvented himself again, this time as the guru in Facebook advertising . . . through which, he points out, you can access 600 million customers in 10 minutes."

—Bob Bly, author of over 60 books including *Complete Idiot's Guide to Direct Marketing*, *The Online Copywriter's Handbook*, and *Public Relations Kit for Dummies*

"One of the things I love about Perry is that he always shoot from the hip. *Ultimate Guide to Facebook Advertising* is written with no holds barred, which means that all the 'juicy' tips that might get left out of other, similar books are all in this book. It's more than just a tactical 'how to.' It goes into the psychological aspects of ad writing specifically suited for Facebook and gives all kinds of practical advice for fan pages. So for anyone who really wants to get serious about Facebook advertising, this book is definitely a must read."

—Shelley Ellis, contextual advertising expert, www.ContentNetworkInsider.com

"Perry Marshall is a terrific writer who makes wonderful use of stories and analogies to illustrate a concept. He does this exceptionally well in the chapter on ad copy writing, 'The Power of Hidden Psychological Triggers.' That chapter alone is worth the price of this book."

"Many companies have tried Facebook ads and failed for one simple reason: they treated Facebook advertising like search advertising.

"Facebook is social advertising. Social advertising is about understanding and reaching the user. Not the user's behavior; but the actual person. This is where the book shines. It walks you through strategies of reaching your target audience based upon the person's social profile so that you aren't just accumulating 'Likes,' but actually gaining new customers.

"I'd recommend this book to anyone who is advertising, or wants to advertise, on Facebook. Social advertising is unique from most other types of advertising, and this book will teach you the concepts and how-tos you must understand so that your Facebook ads increase your overall profits."

—Brad Geddes, author of *Advanced Google AdWords*

"Perry Marshall led the pack with Google AdWords back in 2006. He's still leading the pack today with Ultimate Guide to Facebook Advertising. Perry and Tom Meloche combine 'insider' knowledge of marketing on Facebook with proven marketing fundamentals for a powerful one-two punch that delivers results. Perry doesn't just theorize about how Facebook marketing works, he does it himself, and he's worked with thousands of others to hone his knowledge of this emerging landscape. If you're thinking of marketing on Facebook, or if you're already doing it, you'd be crazy to not get *Ultimate Guide to Facebook Advertising*."

—Clate Mask, president, InfusionSoft

"Hands down, I have never seen a more comprehensive in-depth study of successful Facebook advertising than what you are holding in your hands. Perry has done it again, he's extracted the 'gold' within this amazing system of advertising that every astute marketer should devour and implement."

—Ari Galper, founder and CEO, Unlock The Game, www.UnlockTheGame.com

"Perry Marshall delivers, AGAIN! This book is guaranteed to take you from an advertising novice to social media marketing expert. You will learn how to adopt a social media mindset and how integrate it into your marketing funnel. This book not only teaches you how to understand your prospect's social environment, Perry guides you through the technical process of setting up your ads, and . . . most importantly, how to nurture your prospects into customers while building trust in your brand."

—Rich Schefren, Founder and CEO, Strategic Profits

ULTIMATE GUIDE TO FACEBOOK ADVERTISING

*How to Access
600 Million Customers
in 10 Minutes*

PERRY MARSHALL AND THOMAS MELOCHE

EP
Entrepreneur.
Press

Ryan Shea, Publisher
Cover design: Beth Hansen-Winter
Composition and production: Eliot House Productions

This publication is designed to provide accurate and authoritative information in regard to the subject matter covered. It is sold with the understanding that the publisher is not engaged in rendering legal, accounting, or other professional services. If legal advice or other expert assistance is required, the services of a competent professional person should be sought.

Library of Congress Cataloging-in-Publication Data
Marshall, Perry.
     Ultimate guide to facebook advertising: how to access 600 million customers in 10 minutes/
by Perry Marshall and Thomas Meloche.
     p. cm.
     ISBN-13: 978-1-59918-430-2 (alk. paper)
     ISBN-10: 1-59918-430-3 (alk. paper)
     1. Facebook (Electronic resource) 2. Internet advertising. I. Meloche, Thomas. II. Title.
HF6146.I58.M37 2011
659.14'4—dc23   2011022064

Printed in the United States of America

15 14 13 12   10 9 8 7 6 5 4 3 2 1

Contents

Preface

TIRED OF SOCIAL MARKETING?

Have you already failed once at Facebook marketing? Have you spent months tweeting, blogging, posting videos, and updating status messages without putting an additional dollar in your pocket? Are you worn out on social marketing? Don't despair, this book is not about "tweeting your way to fame and fortune."

It's not about blogging for 12 cents an hour. And it's not about posting Facebook status messages with no objective other than the desperate hope of somehow attracting tons of fans and becoming rich and famous.

The Ultimate Guide to Google AdWords *by Perry Marshall is the world's most popular book on Google Ads. This book is the sister text for Facebook advertisers. You can get a free introductory course on Google at www.perrymarshall.com/google/.*

Have you been trying "social marketing" and finding yourself worn out, tired, and broke? Then this book is for you. It is about advertising, paid advertising. Paying for a click and getting more money as a result. Specifically, it is about paying for advertising on one of the greatest advertising platforms ever created—Facebook. Learn to play the game of paid Facebook advertising well and your life will never be the same.

IS THIS BOOK FOR YOU?

Can paid advertising on Facebook get more money into your pocket? Bring more customers through your door? Is it worth the time? Should you start today?

This book addresses your bottom line. Facebook changed the rules for selling online. And for some businesses, Facebook is not only a place where you should advertise, it is the place where you should advertise *first*. A dramatic shift.

For 10 years, whenever people asked us about where to start marketing on the internet, we had a simple proven answer: Google AdWords. Smart businesses learned how to refine marketing funnels, craft calls to action, and set baselines first with Google AdWords. Perry Marshall wrote the number-one-selling book on Google advertising. Google was fast, effective, and reliable, and always the easiest place to start.

Was.

But Google grew more competitive. Then Facebook advertising broke the rules. Facebook provides a different and powerful new channel to reach customers. Some businesses should start with Facebook. Alternately, Facebook paid advertising may not be a good place for your business at all. This book will help you decide which path to take and show you if paid advertising on Facebook is right for your business.

If you decide Facebook advertising is for you, this book will teach you how to write and bid ads and how to turn your clicks into sales. We will tell you if you are better off starting with Facebook paid advertising, before AdWords or other search-and-content advertising, and we will show you how to squeeze the maximum value out of your hard-earned advertising dollars.

THE FACEBOOK MIND FREAK

Paid advertising on Facebook requires a fundamentally different mind-set from search-engine marketing on Google, Yahoo!, or Bing. Top-level achievers in paid search advertising may also dominate Facebook, but if you use the same approach as you do in search, you will likely grow discouraged, fail, and miss the real Facebook opportunity.

There is a life-changing benefit waiting for those who learn how to advertise on Facebook. The techniques you will learn in this book on sociographic targeting and right angle marketing are the grad school of advertising. This book will help you take your advertising techniques to an entirely new level.

And, you can use what you learn from Facebook on your other advertising campaigns. One technique alone reliably improved opt-ins 11% on a traditional landing page—with one extra sentence in the third paragraph! This technique requires the data Facebook freely provides but you won't find any other place.

IS FACEBOOK PAID ADVERTISING RIGHT FOR ME?

This book will help you decide within a few minutes if paid advertising on Facebook could provide a large source of traffic for your business. Our self-assessment makes it totally clear if paid Facebook advertising will be a good source for leads. We also provide a second assessment—"Should I Start First on Facebook?"—to determine if you are better off using Facebook advertising as one of your first ways to advertise your product.

Sorry Google AdWords, you are no longer the default first choice for paid advertising! This is a good thing. Businesses everywhere should be delighted to have solid alternatives. It helps every business owner sleep easier to have multiple sources of customers.

If Facebook paid advertising is a good fit for your business, we will teach you how to get your first ad in front of up to 600 million Facebook users in less than 10 minutes.

You will discover how to build an effective end-to-end marketing and sales campaign using Facebook pages and how to turn that first click into an actual sale and maybe even a relationship that lasts for years.

There are many reports in Facebook to help you track your progress. The reports guard the secrets for generating cash in the Facebook machine; when studied carefully, they reveal amazing ways you can minimize the cost of your clicks.

Not only do we teach you where these reports are and how to read them, we also teach you why you should care.

WARNING FOR ADWORDS EXPERTS

Facebook advertising adds a devilish twist to pay-per-click advertising. So it's just tricky enough to confound even the AdWords professionals, catch them by surprise, and sidetrack their efforts.

Even worse, those who have AdWords experience are uniquely vulnerable to making certain Facebook advertising mistakes. Of course, if you learned proper AdWords techniques from us, your mistakes should be small, measurable, and easy to recognize.

If you did not learn how to manage risks properly in AdWords, launching online marketing campaigns in Facebook may lead to tragic results. Tragedy, of course, is wasting your money. But if you give up early, you may miss the real opportunities Facebook offers.

To understand the difference between Google AdWords and Facebook advertising, just ask 10 people why they go to Google:

"To find things," is the answer that comes back almost exclusively.

"How do you use it?" you may ask.

"I just type in what I am looking for in the little box."

Everyone understands Google. It is how you find things, like looking up a word in a printed dictionary or searching for a business listing in the old Yellow Pages. People go to Google because they have a specific itch they are trying to scratch, and they believe Google will do a better job than anyone else at helping them scratch it.

Now, ask 10 different people why they go to Facebook:

"Check up on friends."

"Look at pictures."

"To post interesting articles to friends."

"I don't know."

"Just because I am a lonesome old widower."

"I'm not getting anything out of it."

"I just wish it made more sense."

"Just to see if anything interesting is there."

"Because I am bored."

"To play FarmVille."

You will get almost as many different answers as you have people answering. This is a fundamental shift that we examine in detail in Chapter 6, "Selling on the Front Porch," where we discuss new ways to think about advertising when done in Facebook. It is a dramatic change from Google search and even Google Display Network advertising (although as the Display Network offers more retargeting opportunities, the two become more similar).

So search-engine hotshots, pay attention. We will warn you that you need to pay close attention when a major change of thinking is required.

THIS BOOK IS NOT A BLOW-BY-BLOW TUTORIAL

Facebook is a living experiment that changes almost daily in subtle and substantial ways. It would be impossible in printed media to capture an accurate tutorial of how to use Facebook.

Therefore, this book is not a hand-holding, color-by-numbers tutorial.

It is not a step-by-step guide on how to set up a Facebook account, build a Facebook page, or even set up a Facebook ad.

You will not get page after page of screen shots showing how to do basic operations. A tutorial in a book on Facebook would be out of date before the ink dried on the paper because Facebook changes the details of how things work that frequently.

However, if you are totally new to Facebook, Perry offers you special support in the form of videos providing detailed descriptions of how to complete basic operations such as:

· Setting up an account
· Creating a Facebook ad
· Reviewing advertising reports
· Creating Facebook pages
· Posting status messages
· Reviewing Facebook page reports

These online videos will be updated as Facebook changes the interface and behavior of these fundamental activities. **Access to the tutorials can be found at http://www.perrymarshall.com/fbtoolbox/.**

Chapter One

Facebook's Move to Rule the World

IT ALL STARTED IN A COLLEGE DORM ROOM. WHY THAT MATTERS TO YOU

Facebook was founded in Mark Zuckerberg's Harvard University dorm room by Mark, his roommates, and friends. It was not built for you, the advertiser. They did not have you in mind. They were not trying to meet your needs. They were not interested in providing you "clicks."

It was February 2004 when "The Facebook" launched, and Mark and his classmates had no idea what they

> "*When you give everyone a voice and give people power, the system usually ends up in a really good place. So, what we view our role as, is giving people that power.*"
>
> —MARK ZUCKERBERG

were doing, or how important it would be. They certainly could not imagine that their simple tool would be instrumental in toppling dictators before even eight years would pass.

Instead, they were simply making a cool, digital place for Harvard students to see and connect to other Harvard students. Real connections. Real names, real people, real pictures, and real Harvard email addresses required to register.

It was a place to connect with the college version of "friends"—the studious guy sitting next to you in physics or the slender girl in calculus. A place to really connect, without anonymous, fake, user names that had come to dominate most use of the internet. A place to meet without the expectation of committing to a "date." It grew.

Within 30 days, more than half of Harvard's undergrads had become members. It grew some more.

First to other Boston colleges, the Ivy League, and Stanford University. Then to other universities across the country and around the world. Then to high school networks and a few select companies.

Two and a half years after it was launched, in September 2006, Facebook finally opened the floodgates when it opened service to anyone over the age of 13 with a valid email address. Facebook has continued to grow at a phenomenal rate:

- August 2008: 100 million members.
- April 2009: 200 million members.
- February 2010: 400 million members.

As of this writing, Facebook is moving rapidly toward its goal of one billion members, and the company is valued in the tens of billions of dollars.

The founders of Facebook created history. They redefined what it means to interact on a global scale. They created a massive social graph of how the world is connected: whose friends, parents, brothers, cousins are friends with whom, and on and on.

Facebook knows what its members look like, think, enjoy, and visit because they are the world's largest

- photo-sharing site,
- thought-sharing site,
- liking site,
- linking site.

It is possible, even with Google's gargantuan lead, that Facebook eventually will become the world's largest advertising site, especially as the internet goes mobile.

Facebook reports that 50% of its active users log on to the site on any given day. The average user has 130 friends and is connected to 80 community pages. Collectively, "Facebookers" create more than 300 billion pieces of new content each and every month. There are now 70 translations of the site available, and 70% of Facebook users live outside the United States.

As exciting as all this is, it is important for advertisers to remember that Facebook did not build the site for us, the advertisers. They built it for themselves.

The hottest, young, college graduates Facebook hires from the world's top universities don't say, "I want to work at Facebook to help them maximize ad revenue." Oh, Facebook will get around to that concept eventually, but seriously, it is not what the site's creators are focused on.

And they probably won't really even begin to care about dramatically increasing advertising revenue until after Facebook has gone public. As long as Mark Zuckerberg controls the board of directors, Facebook will have a focused vision. Although temporarily inconvenient for advertisers, this focus actually works to our advantage because Facebook will last. The best thing that ever happened for advertisers was that Facebook was not acquired by Microsoft or Google.

While other companies focus on growing revenue, Facebook focuses on growing vision, improving the product, and supporting the user base. Mark Zuckerberg refers to his core vision as extending the "social graph," a mapping on a global scale of "everyone and how they're related."

Mark plans to change the world. Who knows, a world truly connected by a social graph may stun the imagination. It might end dictatorships in the Middle East. Perhaps someday Facebook will end war? That's a long way from a college dorm room. And perhaps grandiose and foolish to suggest that extending the social graph could help bring about the end of war. But it may help, and the possibility of ending war is a lot more motivational to a fresh, young staff than the idea of maximizing ad revenue.

But regardless of why Zuckerberg built Facebook or what high ideals his staffers may hold, the personal demographic information Facebook collects is tremendously valuable to us advertisers. Spend a little time advertising on Facebook, and you notice new ways both you and Facebook could make more money.

It could dramatically increase its advertising revenue and our clicks, all without being an affront to their members.

Facebook is not stupid.

It is more closely connected with its advertisers than any other platform on the planet. Facebook visionaries already have years' worth of additional ideas to implement. How do we know this? We see the ideas publicly volunteered every day on Facebook pages by Facebook advertisers.

Welcome to socially developed advertising software. As Facebook designers support these features, we advertisers are hungry to suggest more—"Instead of just letting me send an ad to users on their birthdays, how about you let me advertise to their friends and family 30 days before the birthday?" The opportunities are endless.

We advertisers are anxious to provide Facebook with more revenue. Why don't Facebook engineers improve their advertising engine? This is a question you will be asking within a few hours of advertising on Facebook. Don't despair. It will get better. Facebook advertising is not the end for Facebook, it is the means. It is a way to pay the bills, keep those catered meals coming, and provide cool toys to play with. Eventually, Facebook will get around to the tools we really need.

Adult supervision at Facebook is minimal, which is probably why it is so absolutely brilliant. The company almost exclusively hires fresh, college graduates. The brightest college grads on the planet, but still fresh, college graduates.

These are the smart kids, smarter than you, smarter than us.

They have never had a "real" job outside of Facebook.

They have never tried to live off revenue generated by an ad.

They do not feel your pain.

Remember that. It is really important.

To use Facebook's paid advertising tools effectively, it is important to understand just how much its creators and designers are not really trying to help you. Fortunately, they do need cash, and we do need clicks, so we can get some great work done together. We focus on the clicks, and they focus on changing the world.

THE NEWS OF FACEBOOK'S DEATH IS GREATLY EXAGGERATED

Almost every month I've read some article by some technology pundit predicting Facebook's doom. They drip with clever insights into why Facebook's phenomenal success will soon end. Competitive product, Google+, privacy fears, user fatigue, unwelcome interface changes, too many users, a highly fictional Hollywood movie, and inane comparisons to Myspace are freely offered. The list of reasons Facebook will fail goes on and on and on.

The pundits point out real problems and real risks. But they don't "get" Facebook. The big disappointments in the competitive space are not indicators of Facebook's future. It is foolish to project the relative failure of Friendster and Myspace onto Facebook—relative failure because a lot of people would love to fail in the same manner as the founders of Myspace.

Facebook is unique. And continuing to ignore the changes it represents to advertisers and to world leaders is a serious underestimation.

If you've been hoping that Facebook will just go away so you can stay focused on how you have always attracted clicks and customers, don't delude yourself into ignoring it any longer. Betting against Facebook is like betting on the Yellow Pages making a comeback. You really just don't understand the situation.

Facebook has the potential, the real potential, to be highly relevant for decades to come. Our rule of thumb is the founder's rule: when you have a dynamic and visionary founder running a business, better to bet on that business continuing to be a success for as long as you see that founder at the helm.

We suggest that as long as you see Mark Zuckerberg engaged at Facebook, you should plan on Facebook being a dynamic and growing, competitive place to advertise.

Oh, Mark was born in 1984.

He will probably be around for a long, long time.

1984? It turns out that little brother is the one who's watching you.

ONE TOOL TO RULE THEM ALL, AND IN THE FACEBOOK BIND THEM

> One Tool to rule them all,
> One Tool to find them,
> One Tool to bring them all
> and in the Facebook bind them.

The poem should haunt Google. Facebook is actively creating one tool to bind the entire internet together. And Facebook, not Google, is in charge.

Facebook has extended its reach in ways that boggle the mind, and the company does it so well, with so little fuss, hardship, or fanfare, that you hardly notice it is happening. As an advertiser on Facebook, you need to be aware of these changes because they can make you a fortune.

First, it provides the Facebook Platform, a way for software developers outside of Facebook to create new applications that run "inside" of Facebook, seamlessly. Folks, that's what FarmVille is, a third-party application running entirely within the Facebook world.

More than 2.5 million developers from more than 190 countries have now built more than 550,00 applications running inside of Facebook. Bay Partners created an investment fund specifically for companies creating Facebook applications. And every day, Facebook users install 20 million of these applications.

But wait, there's more!

Facebook provides Facebook Connect, which quietly accomplishes what other companies for years tried and failed to do. Facebook Connect becomes your internet identity.

Literally.

Over 2.5 million different websites across the world now allow you to log in to their services with a single click, using your real identity from Facebook. With this service, Facebook makes creating an account on their service dramatically more compelling. Their users now need to manage only one identity, one user name and one password, not hundreds. Most of the top 100 internet sites now let Facebook users log in with a simple click.

Facebook Connect also lets you extend directly into your website the core Facebook functionality, including Friends, Likes, Comments, and Reviews.

Fast. Easy. Secure.

But wait, there's more!

Facebook built Facebook Mobile and more than 200 million cellphone users have installed it on their cell phones. These users are potentially connected to Facebook 24/7. Facebook reports that mobile users are more than twice as active as nonmobile users. Facebook is deploying an advertising model for local businesses to advertise to customers who are literally next door, "Come on over for a 10% special discount. Good for the next 30 minutes!"

Facebook Places lets Facebook users announce where they are and see where their friends are. Friday nights in the big city need never be lonely again. Friends share where they have been, what they have liked, and where they will be, so you can meet up while the night is young.

But wait, there's more!

Facebook is now set up to be your email provider. You can now have a real identity Facebook email address: your.name@Facebook.com.

But wait, there's more!

Facebook is extending the social graph even deeper into their partners' websites, so your website pages can be "liked" like a Facebook page. These likes automatically enter the news feed of your Facebook community.

But wait, there's more!

Facebook has a payment system, Facebook Credits, to allow you to buy and sell digital goods and services in Facebook's virtual currency. Credits could potentially lead to "higher conversion rates, more paying users, and greater net revenue," at least according to Facebook. Credits are mainly used for games, but it is easy to imagine that Facebook may expand this system into larger and larger financial transactions.

Soon, for some of you entrepreneurs reading this book, your entire business may reside entirely within Facebook.

One tool to rule them all, and in the Facebook bind them.

YOUR MISSION, SHOULD YOU CHOOSE TO ACCEPT IT

So what do you do with all of this information about Facebook? Simple. Your mission is to buy a click for $1 and to turn it into $2.

Your mission is to make more profit from your $2 than your competitors.

This is your mission, and it has moved to Facebook. It is a new platform but a very old mission.

The rest is just strategy and tactics. Many existing strategies and tactics that we have taught for years to Google advertisers work directly in Facebook. You need to understand your sales funnel, craft a compelling ad, have a focused goal for your landing page, and track and follow up with your leads and your customers. More important, you want to do this automatically.

We will teach you the strategy and tactics required to fulfill your mission: to get those clicks, and to turn them into customers.

Some tactics, especially those built around keywords and bidding strategies, have changed dramatically for Facebook. Don't worry, we will show you the secrets we have found to be successful in Facebook.

Your Mission, a Penny at a Time

Those with a little more math background may appreciate how powerful your fundamental mission is. Depending on the size of your market, your mission may also be stated as, "Your mission is to buy a click for $1 and to reliably and repeatedly turn it into $.01 worth of pure profit."

This is how professional gamblers think. If they can find a game where betting a dollar nets them a penny, they are in heaven. They sit there for hours and hours playing round after round trying to bet as much as possible to earn that 1% net.

They even have a name for it; they call it "grinding." The best part about grinding when you're a digital marketer is that you do not have to actually sit at a table in a smoke-filled room. Digital grinding happens in that area of the web now called the "cloud," and clouds are much nicer than smoke-filled rooms.

Also, you do not have to live in Vegas. In the online world, the game comes to you.

Think about this for a moment: a 1% net return on an investment that may be achieved within a matter of minutes from when the investment was made. What is the return on a dollar on an annual basis that can return 1% every 3 minutes? The figure is so large it makes even Goldman Sachs blush. A penny, if there are enough clicks available, is worth a fortune.

Entire empires are built on a one percent net profit.

Don't despise making a penny, especially if you can make it reliably and repeatedly.

Instead, focus on how to make a lot more pennies. Focus on how to get a lot more clicks.

Perhaps it is on Facebook?

For your sake, we hope so. Because advertising on Facebook is actually a lot of fun.

For some advertisers, using Facebook paid advertising to find new customers is also stunningly easy. The next chapter provides a link to a quiz where you can find out if you are one of the lucky ones. Facebook advertising may be a great fit that will cause new customers to fall into your lap.

Chapter Two

Is Facebook for Me?

WILL EVERY BUSINESS BENEFIT FROM ADVERTISING ON FACEBOOK

Facebook offers so many opportunities to reach customers with specialized advertising that almost every business can benefit from some form of paid advertising on Facebook, even if it spends only a few dollars a week.

However, it is one thing to use paid Facebook advertising sparingly—for example to tell your fans about an event—and quite another to commit to making Facebook a significant source of leads or traffic for your business. This chapter is about determining if Facebook ads can be a significant source of leads for your business.

> "*How important will Facebook be in your marketing mix? Score yourself from 1-10 at www.IsFBforMe.com*"

ARE YOU A LOCAL BUSINESS WITH A PHYSICAL LOCATION?

Does your business have a doorknob that customers turn? If so, then Facebook is for you. Dentists, doctors, lawyers, veterinarians, physical trainers, gyms, specialty shops, cupcake stores, specialty groceries, beer and wine shops, restaurants, mechanics, theaters, and music venues are highly likely to benefit from locally targeted Facebook campaigns, which may cost as little as $100 to $200 a month.

Facebook allows you to advertise to people who live within a few miles of your location, to advertise directly to your known customers, and to advertise directly to your customers' friends who live nearby. These features, and the nature of Facebook, make Facebook a great candidate to fill your advertising needs.

Facebook is amazing for selling locally because Facebook makes it easy to get your message in front of your local market demographic even before your target audience has begun searching for your particular product or service.

DOES YOUR BUSINESS HARMONIZE WITH FACEBOOK?

I suspect it is possible to successfully sell almost any product or service on Facebook. However, it is clear that some products sell on Facebook like magic and others are really, really difficult to sell there. The interesting question for your business is "How easy will it be to sell on Facebook?"

Some types of products or services are a natural fit for selling on Facebook. So natural that you can set up a campaign and start finding new customers in a few short minutes. Other types of products and services will be a harder sale. And, quite frankly, Facebook may not be a good channel for purchasing clicks until you have exhausted easier channels.

Where does your business fall? I've created an entire website, IsFB4ME.com, to help you answer that question. The site asks you 10 short questions about your business and results in a score from 1–10 that you can use to better understand how your business fits with Facebook.

The more the following statements describe your product or service, the more Facebook is for you.

Our Stuff Is Unique

Facebook is for you if you sell unique or personalized products. Facebook is the worldwide capital of individual expression. It's the perfect place to sell customized and personalied products, items that express a person's own tastes and preferences. It is also a great way to engage potential customers on a human-to-human level.

You will not maximize Facebook's marketing potential if you are selling products that could be listed in the "commodity" category or if your customer can easily find your product at big-box retailers and national chains. If people can easily buy your product elsewhere, or can compare prices easily online, then selling your product profitably on Facebook will be difficult. When you advertise on Facebook, always lead with those products that are most unusual, unique, and eye-catching.

Facebook is the place to sell products that don't carry an expected price. If your customers know exactly what your product should cost, you probably should not be selling it on Facebook. Sell unique products, where the value is determined by the customer's desire to have something interesting, not by the price.

We Sell to Consumers

Facebook is for you if you sell to consumers not businesses. Facebook is a place for individuals to connect with friends and family. It is best used by businesses as a place to find and connect to individuals and individual consumers. It is not a good place to sell to other businesses. Although corporations have pages on Facebook, their presence there is as a sales presence to market to consumers, not as a purchasing presence to buy from your business.

Facebook can be effective in selling to buyers at small companies with only a few employees because most of those companies blend business and personal life. But the larger the client you are seeking to sell to, the harder it will be to use Facebook. Many larger companies actively block Facebook use within the company. These companies might even punish or dismiss employees for spending time on Facebook at work. Facebook is not exactly the location to try to close a deal.

We Sell Fun Products

Facebook is for you if your products are fun. It is a great place to sell events, memberships, experiences, personal improvement, travel, and entertainment. Facebook is fun! It is a place where people go to connect, to play, and to socialize. It is a place to feel, express opinions, and display emotions.

Facebook is a great place to advertise products that are fun and appeal to a person's core identity, which is why a membership in a group or a club is a great sales opportunity on Facebook. Events, travel, and entertainment are full of fun and positive emotions. These subjects are naturally social, and people love to ask "Where have you been?", "What have you seen?," and "Where do you want to go?"

If you provide personal improvement products, especially anything that's new, trendy, hip, or cool, Facebook is also a great fit. If your product involves some form of training, accent the social advantages more than the academic aspects, such as how learning a new language can make travel more fun.

On the flip side, if your product is technical, academic, complex, or requires deep thought, it may be hard to sell on Facebook. It can be done, but you will need to create additional materials outside of Facebook to get your buyer educated on the benefits of your product. You will likely need to create videos, tutorials, and automated emails and have a formal plan to deliver them.

We Harmonize With Identity, Personal Beliefs, and Convictions

Facebook is for you if your business harmonizes with a person's identity—political affiliations, religious convictions, beliefs, or social movements. On Facebook, it's a significant advantage if your company and your target customer share beliefs religiously, politically, or socially.

Regardless of whether your company leans right or left or whatever, there are lots of people who may be predisposed to do business with you for that particular leaning. And you should take advantage of it. There are very simple ways you can target your customers on Facebook and communicate with them in ways that connect to the things they care about.

For a rich set of Facebook tools, videos and tutorials, register at www.perrymarshall.com/fbtoolbox/.

If you appeal to a variety of such backgrounds, then you can design specific marketing campaigns to cater to each of those preferences. You may have different pockets of people within your customer database, and the better you understand those pockets, the more you can target your ads, and the more you can sell.

If the shared beliefs aren't immediately obvious, don't give up. You might want to survey your customers and see if you can identify any political, social, or religious preferences. Better yet, get your customers to "like" your Facebook page and then review their profiles for "likes and interests" and the summary reports that Facebook provides.

You may find shared beliefs and convictions are held by many of your customers only after many sales, when you know your customers better. These factors may well shape what you say to your customers so you can deepen the emotional bond they share with you.

PERRY MARSHALL'S FACEBOOK QUIZ

To make it easier for you to understand how well Facebook paid advertising may work for your business, take the www.IsFB4me.com 10-question quiz. It will give you a score from 1 to 10, with the higher score representing a better potential outcome for Facebook advertising. Record your score below.

Scan QR code to go to www.IsFB4Me.com

My score _____

What Your Score Means

   1: *Danger.* See if you can get your money back for this book.

2–3: *Caution.* If your final score is 2 or 3, then finding new leads and customers through paid advertising on Facebook is likely to be difficult, time-consuming, and expensive. If you are a small company or a startup, it may be a losing proposition, and you should focus your advertising dollars elsewhere to find new leads and customers.

   However, you should probably still use some Facebook paid advertising to feature events, market to existing customers, and collect customer and lead demographics. Facebook is an amazing tool simply for what it can teach you about your own customers, such as their age, gender, location, affiliations, favorite books, favorite music, favorite movies, political affiliations, and other likes and interests. Buying some Facebook advertising may be useful just to help you collect this data.

4–5: *Helpful.* If your final score is 4 or 5, then paid advertising on Facebook has the potential to bring you more customers, but it will take a bit of work, and it probably should not be your primary source of traffic. The biggest benefit of being on Facebook is to provide you another channel to connect to existing customers and to collect detailed customer demographics.

6–7: *Significant.* If your final score is 6 or 7, then you are definitely in the Facebook sweet spot. Facebook paid advertising may be a new way for you to attract significantly more traffic to your website. In addition, at least for the next few years, you may be able to get this traffic very affordably.

8–10: *Jackpot.* If your final score is 8 to 10, then you have hit the Facebook jackpot. It is possible that Facebook paid advertising may even become your number-one traffic source.

   If you scored 6 or above, you should devour every word of this book.

   If you scored 5 or lower, there is still a lot of useful content for you here, but some chapters will be less important because you likely will be spending only tens of dollars, not tens of thousands of dollars, on Facebook ads. Read extra carefully Chapters 17, 18, and 19.

Sample Scores

At the beginning of the chapter, we suggested some types of local businesses that might do well selling themselves or their products on Facebook. Now you know why we're able to make that statement. We score these business types at 7.5 or higher every time: dentists, doctors, personal lawyers, veterinarians, physical trainers, gyms, specialty shops, restaurants, mechanics, theaters, and music venues.

- Dentist: Score 8
- Vinyl Records-Only Store: Score 8.4
- Musical Venue that Hosts Events: Score 9.2
- Summer Day Camp with Religious Affiliations: Score 9.6
- Selling Industrial Network Cards: Score 3.6 (Perry's previous job)
- Selling Automated Tutors to Home-Schooling Families: Score 8.4 (Tom's education business)
- Selling Hipster T-Shirts: 6
- Manufacturer of cardboard boxes: 4.4

SHOULD YOU ADVERTISE ON FACEBOOK?

Facebook is changing the texture of online advertising. For the first time in more than a decade, I actually advise some of my clients to start paying for advertising on Facebook before—or even instead of—using Google AdWords.

Is this sacrilegious?

Not at all. If you have been following our advice, you know we are not Google fanatics, we are pragmatic marketers. We will take a cost-effective click from wherever we can get it. If Facebook makes it easier than Google, then bless 'em. I will use their tool until the next guy comes along. There is always a next guy. So if you are starting a new venture or just starting digital marketing, should you consider using Facebook first as your initial source of traffic?

Are you a local business and did you score above 9 on the "Is Facebook for Me" quiz? YES—start first with paid ads on Facebook.

Are you a national online business, did you score an 8 or higher on the quiz, and do you have a strong affiliation with a belief or movement that people identify themselves with on Facebook? YES—start first with paid ads on Facebook.

Are you a local professional with finite capacity and did you score an 8 or higher on the quiz? YES—start first with paid ads on Facebook. You may be able to generate all of your business just with Facebook advertising, and you will save yourself the learning curve of Google AdWords tools.

Please understand, "starting" is simply a matter of building a Facebook page and running ads for a week or two. I am not advising you to never use other advertising channels. In fact, except for the case of the professional who may get fully booked and not be interested in adding more business, I expect everyone to develop multiple sources of clicks and leads.

TO NOT DO SO IS STUPID.

If starting first on Facebook is recommended, that's because it will probably be easier for you to hone your message, build your funnel, and capture your market's demographics on Facebook than anywhere else. So take advantage of it.

It took 10 years, but the world finally has an advertising channel that is a better place for some businesses to start than Google AdWords.

Congratulations, Facebook.

FACEBOOK WAS FOR ME—TOM'S STORY

I am a Facebook fanatic. I've built an entire software company from the ground up using Facebook ads to sell our product. The ads are simple, powerful, and affordable. However, I didn't start my advertising with Facebook in mind.

I designed a software tool for accelerated learning called HomeSchoolAdvantage. It was ready for beta users, and I needed to drive a few hundred of them to the site to kick the tires and see if they would take it out for a spin. I created an awesome landing page to convert leads to trial users, and I was ready for clicks.

Because I had prior success driving traffic with Google AdWords, I started there. Google, however, was doing all sorts of snaky things, "Oh, you want a click? That's $2 to $3." After a time, of course, that comes down to $1, then $0.50, but then they've given me an amazingly low "quality score."

I was a "home-school" tutoring service selling to "home-schoolers" by advertising on the keyword "homeschool"; my URL is "HomeSchoolAdvantage.com." You would think it would be a good match.

Not so, said the great and mighty Google.

Now, I was willing to arm-wrestle with Google bots to convince them I was a good advertising fit and should receive cheaper clicks and a higher score. I could have tried to convince Google bots I was "quality" by placing articles, blog posts,

---

FACEBOOK WAS FOR ME—TOM'S STORY, continued

and content outside of the pay-wall—all my hard work was behind the pay-wall. I could have done some tricks with my keywords, I could have done all these things, but they all require a lot of work.

Or

I had been on Facebook, so I thought perhaps I could try this new Facebook advertising thingy and see how it worked. I put up my first ad.

Magic.

Facebook immediately drove clicks to my existing landing page and never stopped. No weird quality score. No exorbitant pricing scheme. No struggle.

I was hooked. I immediately saw all sorts of conversions coming in, coming in for 40% less than I was paying on Google, and I wasn't arm-wrestling the system to drive the clicks.

Awesome.

I was an entrepreneur launching a highly speculative software venture where the typical failure rate is more than 90%. I was already spending all of my time, creative energy, and money trying to change the world. I needed to put my energy into listening to my customers and responding to their needs, not arm-wrestling Google bots over quality score.

I turned Google AdWords off and left it off—FOR AN ENTIRE YEAR.

Sure, Google is still part of my long-term strategy, but it moved from spot Number 1 to spot Number 4. Here is my new world order:

1. Facebook ads
2. Email blasts to paid lists
3. Button and banner ads on home-school websites
4. Google AdWords

I found an alternative for what I was initially trying to achieve on Google with Facebook.

FACEBOOK WAS FOR ME—TOM'S STORY, continued

I got the leads I needed for my beta test for $4,100 not the $20,000 I had budgeted. And, I built an entire, interconnected community of fans on Facebook for

free—after I moved my landing pages to Facebook pages! Because I charged to use the beta HomeSchoolAdvantage service and the advertising was so affordable, my beta campaign broke even. As a bonus, my Facebook community offers suggestions, provides feedback, and continually attracts more customers.

I purchased 15.5 million impressions and 11,000 clicks in my beta program for about 37 cents a click. I spent less than 1 hour a week managing the campaigns. Do you have any idea how amazing this is?

I used Facebook for this project because it was easier.

I used Facebook for my next project because it was better. Read on, you'll see what I mean. Is Facebook for me? You bet it is, I scored an 8.4!

One last note, and this is very, very important: I did not initially focus on the "social media" aspect of Facebook. Yes, "liking," posting, and interacting with people on my fan page has proven to be important over time. But all of this is nearly useless unless and until you have the ability to steadily and reliably get targeted traffic to your website or fan page.

If you want to build a real business that makes money, most of the advice you find in "social media" books demands enormous amounts of manual labor from you, at best. And much of that advice is woefully ineffective. If you want to build a real business that makes money, invest $1 in advertising, acquire a customer, and get $2 back. It's faster, it's easier, and it's the most reliable way to grow a company.

Chapter Three

A Few Fundamentals

LEARN THE VOCABULARY TO UNDERSTAND THE TOOL

There are a few fundamentals you, the Facebook advertiser, must know before you begin spending your hard-earned cash. These terms and definitions are so important that you really should understand them comfortably and completely before giving Facebook your credit card and telling them to have at it.

The rest of this book assumes you know this vocabulary hands down. So if you are totally new to pay-per-click or pay-per-view advertising, pay extra close attention.

> *"First master the fundamentals."*
>
> —LARRY BIRD

Please don't skip this chapter if online advertising is totally new to you. It is actually important that you understand everything in this chapter 100% before you purchase your first ad. A quiz at the end of this chapter will test if you can score 100%. Take the quiz. We will not grade you—the marketplace will. The penalty for failing is a hefty bill from Facebook with no pesos in your bank account to show for it.

This chapter isn't the final discussion on these topics, just the first wave.

ADS

An ad in Facebook is content displayed to Facebook users at an advertiser's specific request (see Figure 3.1).

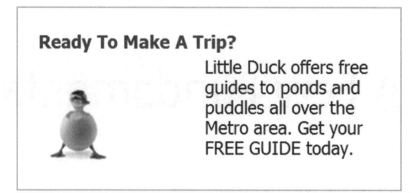

FIGURE 3.1–A Facebook Ad Displayed Horizontally

These ads are frequently seen in the right-hand column of your Facebook wall, profile, and photo pages. Up to five different ads may show at one time. Of course, where ads are displayed, what they are called, how they work, how they are presented, and how many are shown at a time are subject to change at any time.

Every time an ad is displayed on a Facebook page, a user could potentially read the ad. Facebook calls that an impression. An impression is an opportunity for someone to see your ad. If the ad seen in Figure 3.1 had 1.4 million impressions, then the ad had 1.4 million opportunities to be seen.

Impressions does not mean separate people have had the chance to see the ad, which has not in fact been shown to 1.4 million people. The estimated reach for this ad is reported by Facebook to be 200,000 people. The estimated reach is the number of Facebook users who meet the criteria the advertiser has selected for people the advertiser wants to see the ad.

If an ad has 1.4 million impressions and an estimated reach of 200,000 people, we know that, on average, each of those 200,000 people has had seven opportunities to see the ad.

Most people do not click on an ad on the first impression. As users browse Facebook, moving from page to page, from their wall to their profile to their friend's wall, to their pictures to business pages, the same ads are displayed multiple times.

If the ad title—the top line of the ad—is good and the ad image is compelling, the ad may eventually capture the attention of a Facebook browser, who then may actually read the ad's body text. (See Figure 3.2).

FIGURE 3.2–Ad Title, Image, and Body Text

If the ad interests the user enough, then the user actually clicks on the ad and is taken to a new destination specified by the advertiser.

Facebook captures and reports the number of times all users have clicked on each ad. They cleverly name this clicks.

HOW WELL IS MY AD WORKING?

One of the first questions everyone asks is "How well is my ad working?" This question is actually trickier than it first seems because there are many measures of working:

- Does the ad encourage the users to click?
- Will users do the next step we want them to after clicking?
- Will users ever purchase from us?
- Will users stop buying stuff from the other guy?

All four of these questions may be different ways to define "working." Facebook helps us track and answer the first question, "Does the ad encourage the users to click?" You will learn secrets to answering the remaining questions in later chapters.

Facebook reports how well an ad encourages a user to click, in a statistic called the click-through rate (CTR). This rate identifies how many impressions it takes, on average, before a user clicks on the ad.

CTR is clicks divided by impressions (clicks/impressions). (10 clicks/1,000 impressions = 1%.)

If your ad has had 1,000 total impressions and users have clicked on the ad 10 times, then your CTR is 1%.

The ad in Figure 3.3 had 376,409 impressions leading to 344 clicks. What is its CTR? Don't peek at the answer. Seriously, calculate this yourself at least once.

Finger Painting Adventure

Free finger painting project ideas. Seven fun-at-home projects for rainy weekends. Click for free video.

FIGURE 3.3–Calculate the CTR for this Ad

Did you get 0.091%? If not, do the math again.

The formula: 344 clicks/376,409 impressions = 0.091% CTR.

If you are still having trouble getting the math right, don't fret. Facebook reports the impressions and the clicks and calculates the CTR automatically. But it is important that you understand what the click-through rate means.

Landing Pages

When users click on an ad, where do they go? The page that is displayed after a user clicks on an ad is called a landing page. The advertiser specifies the landing page when the ad is created in a field called destination URL.

You can send a user who clicks on an ad anywhere that does not violate Facebook's landing page policies. You may send users to your own web page or you may send users to other locations within Facebook—such as a Facebook page, event, application or group.

Paying for Ads

Facebook does not display ads out of the goodness of its heart; it wants cold, hard cash. You have to provide a credit card before Facebook will even think of displaying your ad. Once they have your payment information, they let you create an ad. During this process they ask if you want to bid for clicks or for impressions.

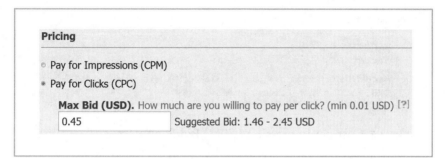

Pricing

○ Pay for Impressions (CPM)

⦿ Pay for Clicks (CPC)

Max Bid (USD). How much are you willing to pay per click? (min 0.01 USD) [?]

0.45   Suggested Bid: 1.46 - 2.45 USD

FIGURE 3.4–Pay for Clicks (CPC) Bidding Selected

If you choose to bid for clicks, you will be charged only if a user clicks on the ad. You can specify the amount your are willing to pay for a click, the cost-per-click (CPC), starting at one cent per click. If you say that you are willing to pay 45 cents for a click, then that is the most you will be charged for a click.

Technically, you are bidding on the ad space, so what you enter in a field labeled Max Bid is the maximum amount you are willing to pay for the click. You are bidding against other advertisers who are unseen and unknown, and you do not really know what they are bidding.

From your perspective, the bid word is a bit of a sham. Initially, the higher your bid the more likely your ad will be displayed. After a few thousand impressions, additional factors weigh in to affect the cost of your ad, including the click-through rate and whether users "like" or complain about your ad.

The good news? Facebook reserves the right to "lower the price" you pay per click. You read that right! They will actually charge you less than you bid, and lucky for you, they do this all the time.

Cost per Impression (CPM)

You may also select to bid on impressions instead of clicks (see Figure 3.5). You actually bid what you are willing to pay for 1,000 impressions of your ad. This is called pay per view (PPV). The advertiser is paying for someone to view the ad whether or not the user clicks on the ad. PPV is frequently associated with brand advertising. If the goal is only to get the user to see the brand name and not to get a click, then PPV is the advertisers' first choice. Of course, we think not trying to get a click is nearly always a mistake in digital advertising.

In the Facebook interface, pay per view is labeled CPM, short for cost per thousand impressions. You are thinking, "M? What is the M for?" Do you remember your Latin?

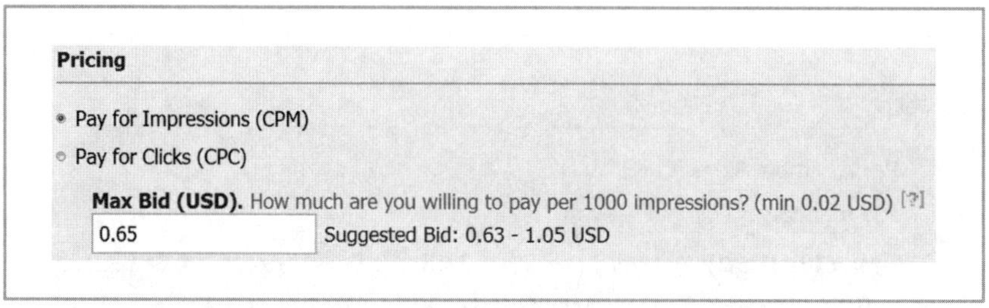

Pricing

* Pay for Impressions (CPM)
○ Pay for Clicks (CPC)

Max Bid (USD). How much are you willing to pay per 1000 impressions? (min 0.02 USD) [?]

0.65 · Suggested Bid: 0.63 - 1.05 USD

FIGURE 3.5–Cost per Impression (CPM) Bidding Selected

Mille means 1,000 in Latin.

M is 1,000 in Roman numerals.

Our word millennium means a span of 1,000 years.

CPM stands for cost per M impressions (M = 1,000). Get used to that crazy little "M." It is not going away.

You can tell Facebook that you are willing to pay simply to have it display your ad 1,000 times whether or not anyone clicks on the ad.

Did you notice that if you bid CPC you can still calculate CPM, and if you bid CPM you can still calculate CPC? In fact, no matter which way you choose to bid, Facebook will calculate and display both results for you. Bidding strategy is covered in greater detail in later chapters. If we covered it all now, you might run screaming from the room and that would not help anybody.

Progress Reporting

Facebook provides extensive reporting for each ad that tells the impressions for the ad (Imp), the clicks for the ad, the CTR (%), the average CPC, the average CPM, and the total amount spent. Before you continue reading the rest of this book, you should be comfortable looking at the following report in Figure 3.6 and explaining what each of the numbers and labels mean.

Date Range ?	Campaign ?	Ad Name	Impressions ?	Clicks ?	CTR ?	CPC ?	CPM ?	Spent ?
06/09/2011-06/15/2011	Campaign Name	Ad Name	77,563	37	0.048%	0.74	0.35	27.52

FIGURE 3.6–Basic Advertising Report

Reach, Frequency, and Ad Fatigue

Ads display on Facebook multiple times to the same user. The number of individual people who have seen your ad during a specific period of time is reported by Facebook as reach. The average number of times each indivual user has seen your ad is reported as frequency. If you run your ad long enough, your actual reach will approach your estimated reach. Facebook displays the relationship between reach and estimated reach in a graphic. Reach is displayed as a smaller circle inside of a larger estimated reach circle.

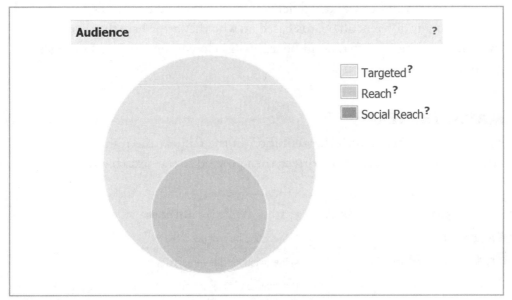

FIGURE 3.7–Relationship between Reach and Estimated Reach

Eventually, an ad may have a frequency of 30 or more. An ad with a frequency of 30 has been displayed to each individual reached user 30 times. Even if the ad is excellent, the users still get tired of seeing it, and they stop clicking on it.

This is called ad fatigue—your prospects stop clicking on an ad as the frequency gets high simply because they have grown tired of seeing it.

Have you ever watched a television commercial and really enjoyed it? Perhaps you thought it was funny, clever, or emotionally moving. Later, after seeing the same commercial over and over and over and over again—you slowly begin to hate it. If you have had that experience, then you have experienced ad fatigue firsthand.

Get a Fast Snapshot of Other Facebook Advertisers with Ad Board

The Facebook "ad board" is a page in Facebook where you can see ads that have recently been displayed to you. Your ad board can be seen by typing in the following URL while you are logged into Facebook:

http://www.Facebook.com/ads/adboard/

Examine your ad board to see the different types of ads other people have created to try to sell to you. It is a great place to see a large number of different ads all together. Ask your friends and co-workers to let you look at their ad boards. Different people will have totally different ad boards based on who they are, where they live, and what they like. Looking at different ad boards will help you understand how Facebook customizes its ads for the individual.

MATCH THE TERM

Match the term below with the definition in the table at the right. When you are absolutely sure every answer is correct, then proceed to the next chapter.

Term	Match	Definition
A. Ad board		Abbreviation for cost per click
B. Average cost per click		Abbreviation for click-through rate
C. Average cost per thousand impressions		The number of times the ads in this campaign have been shown to users on the site.
D. Clicks		The web address where a user is taken when they click on an ad.
E. Click-through rate (%)		A name for that page where users are taken when they click on an ad.
F. CPC		The number of Facebook users who match the criteria to see this ad. The potential number of Facebook users who may see an ad.
G. CPM		The maximum amount you're willing to spend on an ad per click (CPC) or thousand impressions (CPM).
H. CTR		The number of times users have clicked on the ads in this campaign.
I. Destination URL		Abbreviation of cost per thousand ad impressions.

Term	Match	Definition
J. Estimated reach		The amount spent on an ad or group of ads divided by the number of clicks the ads received.
K. Fatigue		The amount spent on an ad or group of ads divided by the number of thousand impressions the ads received.
L. Frequency		A location in Facebook where you can see ads that have been recently displayed to you.
M. Impressions		The number of individual people who have seen your ad during a specific period of time.
N. Landing page		The average number of times each individual user has seen your ad.
O. Max Bid		A rate calculated as the number of clicks divided by the number of impressions.
P. Reach		A word used to describe what happens to an ad that no longer gets the same high CTR that it once achieved. Usually comes as a result of the ad being displayed too many times to the users.

You are looking for the answer key aren't you? If you have to look for the answer key, then you do not know the terms well enough. Go back and read the entire chapter again.

*F*or a rich set of Facebook tools, videos and tutorials, register at www.perrymarshall.com/fbtoolbox/.

Fatigue
Prospects
Impressions

Chapter Four

10 Minutes to Your First Ad

10 MINUTES TO REACH 250,000 PEOPLE

"250,000 people?" You are thinking, "I thought Facebook was going to help me reach over a billion people!"

It may be true that Facebook could reach a billion people with your advertising message. But be serious, you can't afford to target a billion people. Do you know what is more exciting than advertising to a billion random people across the planet? Advertising to 250,000 people who are highly likely to buy your product. By the time you finish this chapter, you will be ready to reach that first 250,000.

> "*Doing business without advertising is like winking at a girl in the dark. You know what you are doing, but nobody else does.*"
>
> —STEUART HENDERSON BRITT

FACEBOOK CAN'T AFFORD TO TAKE SIX BILLION QUESTIONS THIS YEAR

The Facebook Help Center is your one and only, real, Facebook friend. And it is not much of a friend. It's like being friends with the sexiest girl in high school who doesn't return your calls, and secretly thinks she can do better. Type in the following URL to go on your first date:

https://www.facebook.com/help/

Facebook Help Center offers advice on:

· Using Facebook
· Facebook apps and features
· Ads and business solutions.

This book is about Facebook ads, so if you want the official latest and greatest scoop on features, rules, and regulations, review the "Ads and Business Solutions" links from the Help Center. They can help clear up a lot of your questions. But they will also generate even more questions that you will probably never get answered.

Do you know how to tell if you are talking to a true Facebook expert? They qualify all of their answers with, "The last time I checked," even if they last checked yesterday. Facebook changes continually, so don't get too comfortable just because you did something once before. Instead, learn to be comfortable poking around the interface, clicking on question marks, and reading help text. Questions marks indicate help text is available.

If you look at other people's accounts you may encounter entirely different features within the ad interface than you see in your account. There is no "one" ad interface Facebook is supporting at any point in time. You need to be comfortable with always learning. The first time you use the advertising interface (or when something changes) click on lots and lots of question marks, the ones that look like this: [?]. They give pithy little descriptions of what you are looking at, as seen in Figure 4.1 below.

Facebook does have several locations where you can submit a question to the Help Center staff. After you submit the question, you are directed to the Help Center. If the question strikes an interest, someone may even get back to you.

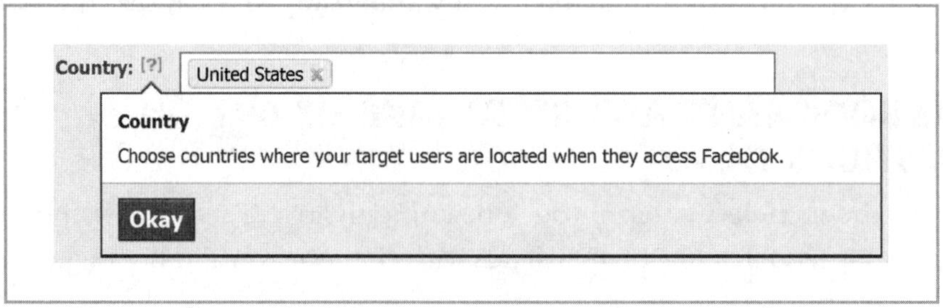

FIGURE 4.1–Clicking on the Question Mark Displays a Description of the Country Field

When you have 600 million free users you cannot afford to take phone calls to answer most people's mind-numbingly stupid questions. One of the reasons Facebook ads are so affordable is because they are basically self-service. Facebook, for the most part, doesn't care to talk with you unless you are spending lots and lots of money and need help spending more money. By then, you will probably already know the Facebook ad system better than the rep taking your call.

SET UP YOUR ACCOUNT

To run Facebook ads you need an account. If you already have a user account Facebook wants you to use that. If you do not already have a user account, you may create a user or a business account.

Do not create a fictitious user account. That is a great way to get banned from Facebook.

Remember the story that Facebook was created in a dorm room? Did you wonder why it was told? Because it matters! Facebook currently has absolutely insane policies regarding business accounts. In Facebook's mind, there should be one account for every person on the planet, and that is it. No need for an account that is attached to a business.

Yes. Facebook does offer business accounts. But if you already have a Facebook account you are prohibited from creating a business account without permission. Fill out their form and ask for permission, everyone who asks nicely will get the help they need. Do not violate the current terms of service, which requires contacting Facebook, since it may get you banned from the site.

Whether you create a business account to run your ads or you run them from your personal account, you need an account to run ads. Read the following Facebook Help Center sections if you need help creating an account:

· Sign up
· Business accounts

Facebook did implement the help system correctly. You do not have to be logged in to access help!

If you have to manage multiple accounts, you need permission from Facebook.

FIND THE ADS MANAGER

There are many different ways to find the ads manager. If you scroll to the bottom of your Facebook home or profile page, you will see the menu like the one shown in Figure 4.2. Select "Advertising" to go to the ads manager.

FIGURE 4.2–Click "Advertising" to Go to Ads Manager

You can also reach the ads manager by clicking on the Ads link in your menu on the left-hand side of your page as seen in Figure 4.3.

FIGURE 4.3–Click Ads Menu to Go to Ads Manager

Clicking on a button labeled "Create an Ad," as shown in Figure 4.4, on the Facebook Advertising Page also takes you to the ads manager.

FIGURE 4.4–Press Button to Go to Ads Manager

Finally, you can also type in the following URL to go directly to the ads manager:

http://www.facebook.com/advertising/

From within the advertising page, select "Create an Ad" to start designing your ad.

CREATE YOUR FIRST AD

To understand ads quickly, create an ad and run a $10 experiment. To get your first ad produced and executing, you will skip setting many of the fields in the Facebook form. As you get more comfortable with running ads, you will intelligently set more and more of the fields.

Take a brief look through all of these steps here to get a lay of the land. Most of this book is dedicated to explaining these settings in detail so you can master the capabilities they offer. There is a lot here, and a lot to digest, but before we dig into the details, it is good to have an overview of everything you need to design and launch an effective ad campaign.

STEP 1: DESIGN THE AD

The first step to creating a new ad is to "design your ad." Design includes selecting the destination for the ad and writing the ad copy, as seen in Figure 4.5. This is the fun part and the part you get to focus on first.

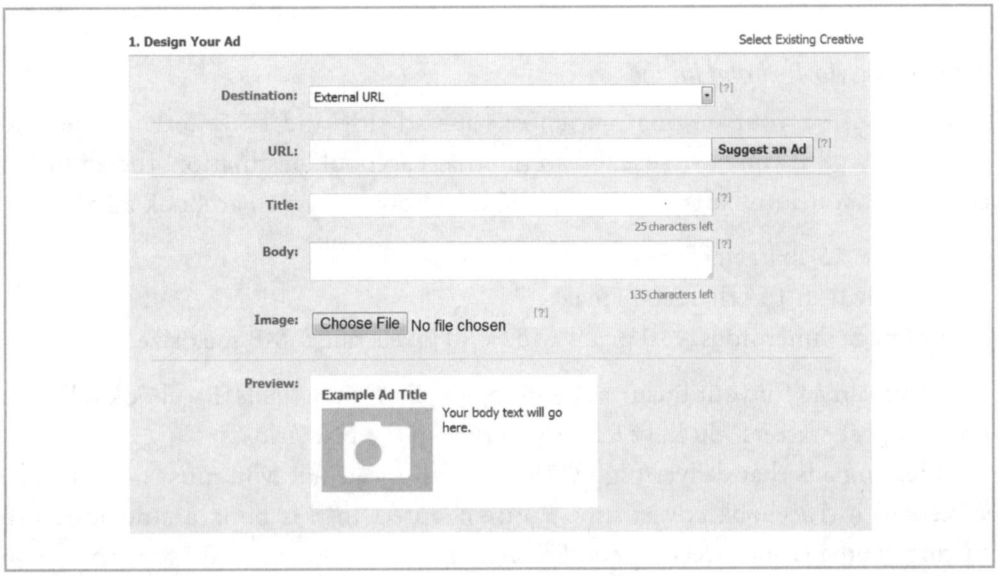

FIGURE 4.5–Design Your Ad

Enter the Destination

Designate whether the destination for a click will be an external URL or an internal Facebook destination. Internal Facebook destinations include:

· Pages
· Groups
· Events
· Apps

You may only select an internal Facebook destination for which you are an administrator. If you meet the qualification to advertise to an internal destination, that choice will automatically appear in a pop-up list for you to select.

Facebook changes the input fields displayed to you based on your destination. To avoid wasting effort, set your destination first, before filling in the other fields.

For example, if you select "External URL" as your destination, you are prompted to enter a specific, external, destination URL. If you select "Facebook Page" as your destination, you do not enter a destination URL, instead you select the specific tab in your Facebook account to use as the landing page.

It you are running your first ad and do not have a Facebook account yet, then select external URL and enter in the destination URL for a landing page on your website.

Entering the Ad Text and Image

After you select your destination, enter your ad title and body text and upload your ad image. If you have selected an internal Facebook destination, the ad title is entered for you automatically. The required components of a Facebook ad are:

- Title: 25 characters max
- Body text: 135 characters max
- Image dimensions: 110 pixels wide x 80 pixels tall, 5 MB max size.

Create an ad for your business by filling in all of these fields. Facebook tells you how many characters you have left as you type in the text fields.

Creating ads that deliver high CTR is an advanced skill you must master to be successful in Facebook advertising. Entire chapters in this book are dedicated to writing good ads and selecting good images. For the moment, write something you think will trigger your target audience to really want to click on your ad!

Facebook provides a cheat for an external URL. You can press a button titled "Suggest An Ad," and Facebook will automatically generate an ad based on text and images it finds on the destination page. If you press this button and use the ad suggested, we will send the ad fairy to you with instructions to treat you unkindly.

Don't use their suggestions! You are permitted to press the button once—but only just for fun.

Facebook displays a preview of the ad like the one shown in Figure 4.6 as you are creating it.

STEP 2: TARGET THE AD

The second step to creating your Facebook ad is to select the Facebook users who will see the ad. Facebook calls this "targeting" your ad. The first four targeting

FIGURE 4.6–A Preview of Your Ad Displays Instantly

selections displayed for external URL destinations are "location," "demographics," "interests," and "connections on Facebook," as seen in Figure 4.7. You may see different targeting fields depending on the destination selected in Step 1.

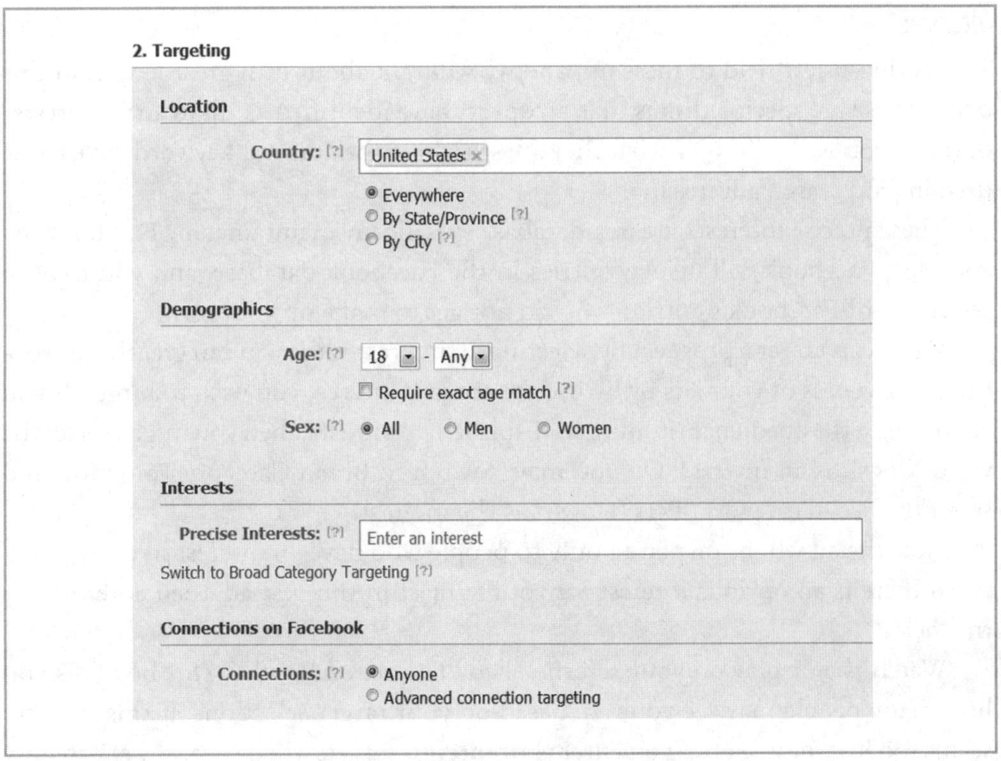

2. Targeting

Location

Country: [?]   United States ×

    ● Everywhere
    ○ By State/Province [?]
    ○ By City [?]

Demographics

Age: [?]   18 ▾ - Any ▾

    ☐ Require exact age match [?]

Sex: [?]   ● All   ○ Men   ○ Women

Interests

Precise Interests: [?]   Enter an interest

Switch to Broad Category Targeting [?]

Connections on Facebook

Connections: [?]   ● Anyone
    ○ Advanced connection targeting

FIGURE 4.7–First Four Targets

Location

You may select for your ad to be displayed only to Facebook users living in certain countries, states, provinces, or cities. If you do not choose a target, the selection defaults to everyone in your country.

Target the area where your prospects are located and don't display it anywhere else. If you are a local business, target your local city in your ads. If you are a national business, target your home country in your first test ad.

Do not try to target everyone everywhere in just one ad. If your country is large, target your home state or province in your first test ad.

Demographics

You may select that your ad be displayed to Facebook users of a certain age or sex. The selection defaults to everyone 18 years old or older. If you know you are selling to a specific demographic—say, women between the ages of 20 and 45—then enter that in your first test ad. Otherwise, use the default settings.

Interests

This is the easiest field to mess up, and we will talk about it in great length in this book. These are specific things that prospects have identified as "likes and interests" in their profiles. IT IS NOT what they are searching for. It is not keywords like those used in paid search advertising.

These precise interests are in a database specifically maintained by Facebook. As you type, Facebook will display entries in the Facebook database, and you have to select one of Facebook's entries—you do not get to make up your own!

If you can target a prospect by selecting an interest, then you can greatly improve the effectiveness of your ads by listing the specific interest you wish to target. If you are running the obedience training ad displayed previously, then you might select the word "dogs" as an interest. Or, you may "Switch to Broad Category Targeting"and select the broad category "Pets (Dogs)" as the interest.

Now the ad will be displayed only to people who have an interest in dogs.

If there is an obvious interest for your subject in this test ad, then enter it into this field.

Watch the display on your screen called "Estimated Reach." This box tells you how many people may see your ad, based on your target selections. If this number seems too low for you after you enter your interest targets, then try another category or leave this field blank for your first test ad.

Connections on Facebook

Connections allows you to specifically include or exclude people connected to pages, events, groups, or apps for which you are an administrator. This is a powerful feature we will discuss in detail later. If you are building your first test ad, leave the default selections for now.

Advanced Targeting Options

Facebook offers advanced targeting options. For your first test ad we suggest you leave these fields set to their defaults. Options available in advanced targeting are seen in Figure 4.8 in two categories: "advanced demographics" and "education and work."

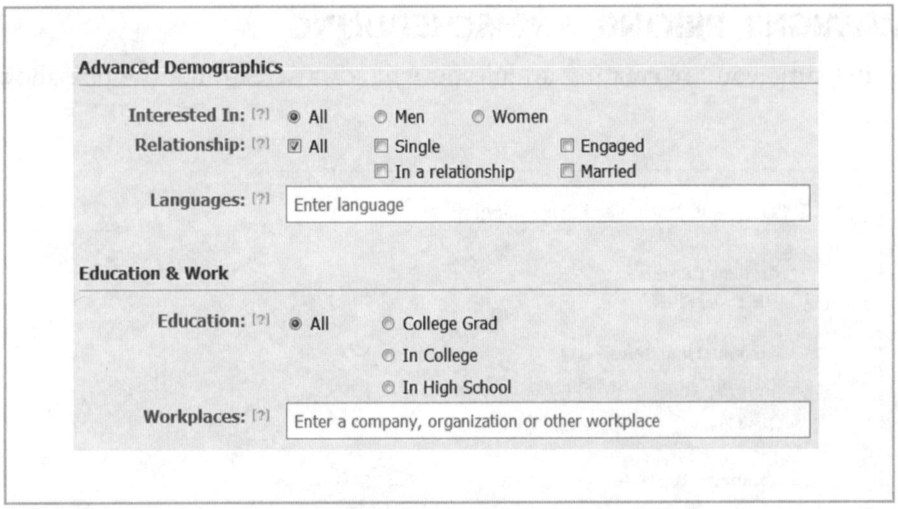

FIGURE 4.8–Advanced Targeting Options

Advanced demographics targets people interested in meeting men or women, in a relationship (single, married, engaged, etc.), using a specific language in Facebook (French, Spanish, German, etc.).

Education and work targets people with specific education levels, degrees, and graduation dates; specific employers.

A SIMPLE STRATEGY TO INCREASE CTR

A simple strategy to dramatically reduce the cost of ads in Facebook is to break your target audience into different highly-targeted groups. Be hyper-specific in your ad targeting and then write ads to appeal to those exact target groups.

If you wanted to advertise to people who liked "Bing Crosby," "Frank Sinatra," and "Dean Martin," you could list all of those names in the interests field of just one ad and that one ad would display to fans of Bing Crosby, Frank Sinatra, and Dean Martin.

However, it is dramatically more effective to write three ads, one for each artist. One ad for "Bing Crosby," one ad for "Frank Sinatra," and one ad for "Dean Martin." The image, headline, and body text of each ad will be specific to each artist.

This type of highly targeted ad is more work, but the work pays off in noticeably higher CTR.

This type of highly targeted ad is the secret of Facebook advertising success.

CAMPAIGNS, PRICING, AND SCHEDULING

The first time you are creating an ad you will see a screen like the one shown in Figure 4.9.

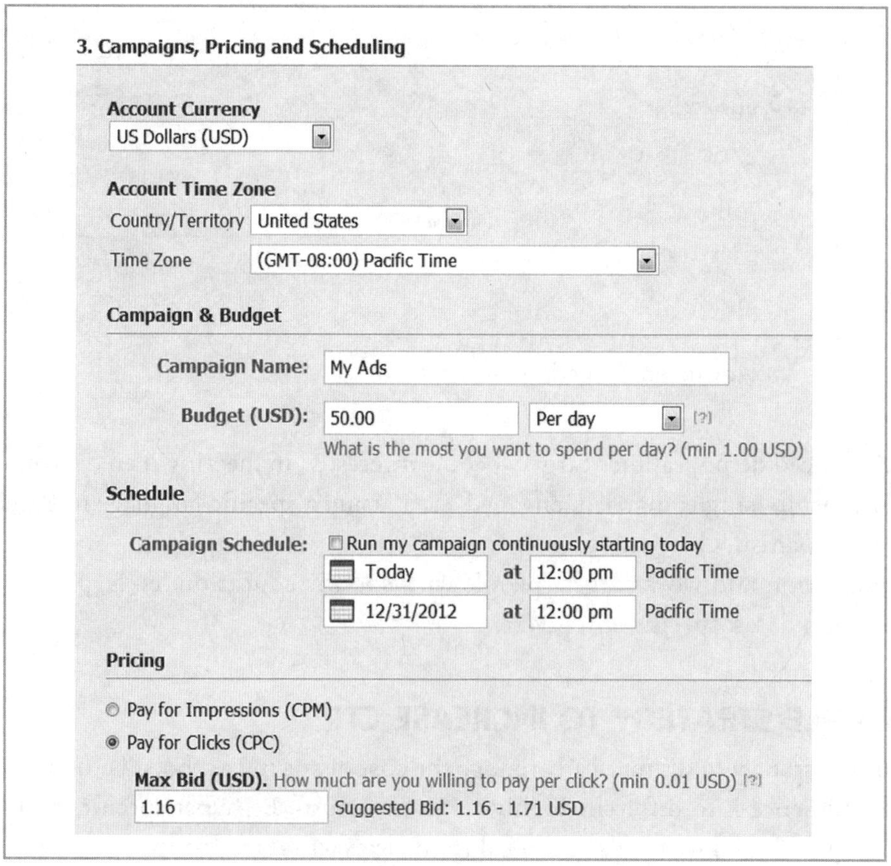

FIGURE 4.9–Campaigns, Pricing, and Scheduling

When first setting up your account, you will be asked to set:

- *Account Currency*: What type of dollars you are bidding and paying in.
- *Country/Territory*: Where the account is located. This may impact you for tax reporting purposes.
- *Time Zone*: Budgets can be run on a daily basis, setting your time actually impacts how Facebook will optimize itself for daily ad spends. In the United States, if you are advertising on the west coast, you may wish to set your time zone as Pacific Time. If you select Eastern Time, your campaigns will be optimized for daily spending ending at midnight Eastern Time, only 9 P.M. Pacific Time.

Campaign and Budget

Ads run in the context of a named campaign. Campaigns are important because you set and manage budgets at the campaign level. For a test ad, create a campaign name and set a very low "Lifetime Budget," only $10. With a lifetime budget, this is the most you will ever spend on your test ad.

Schedule

Facebook supports some ad scheduling. You can set:

- Date and Time Campaign Begins
- Date and Time Campaign Ends

If you set "Lifetime Budget," you are not allowed to select the item "Run my campaign continuously starting today." If this is selected for you, unselect it or change your budget to "Lifetime."

Pricing

In later chapters, we will show you how to think about CPC and CPM bidding. To get your trial ad started, bid the ad CPC, and set your max bid for two cents higher than the lowest recommended bid.

This way, if your ad sucks and nobody clicks, you will not pay anything.

Facebook offers a "Suggested Bid" mode where it handles all the bidding automatically for you. Don't use that. That is like giving the keys to the Lamborghini to teenage Facebook robots.

PLACING YOUR ORDER

Place your order after you have carefully reviewed your settings. Check to make sure you have a low daily budget, a specified advertising end date, and a reasonable bid (near the bottom of the suggested range).

The ads are reviewed by real people. It may take a few minutes to a day or more before a submitted ad is approved for display. It is always a good idea when first getting started to review the Facebook ad policies to make sure your ad and landing pages meet the Facebook requirements.

For a demonstration video of setting up this ad, visit www.perrymarshall.com/fbtoolbox/ and watch the demonstration tutorials.

Select a Funding Source

If this is your very first ad, after you select "Place Order" Facebook will ask you to select a funding source for this ad campaign. As shown in Figure 4.10, you may pay via credit card or directly from your PayPal account. Facebook will not run your ad until you provide a valid payment source.

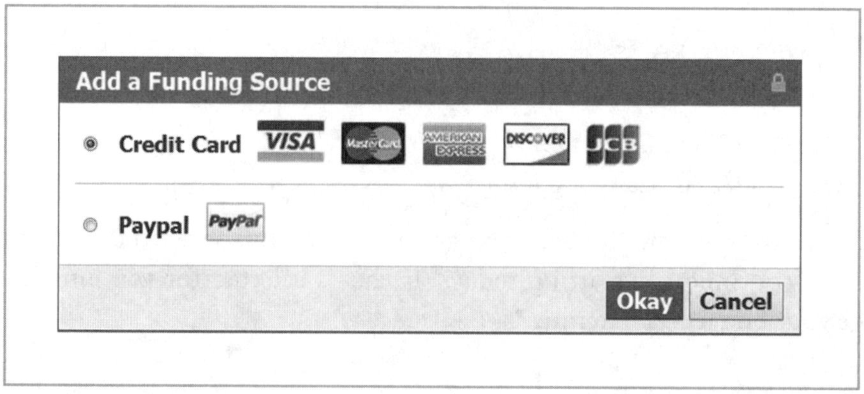

FIGURE 4.10–Options to Pay for the Ad

Now that Facebook has your credit card, pray that the advertising gods smile mercifully upon you. Oh, and batten down the hatches.

Reviewing Your Campaigns

After the ad has been ordered and the payment form specified, you wait for the ad to be approved. You can check your status on your ad manager screen:

http://www.facebook.com/ads/manage/.

Facebook displays all sorts of status information on this screen, including:

- When your ad was approved or rejected
- How much you have spent today
- The basic status of all your campaigns—when they start, when they end, budget, and what was spent today

If you panic, you can pause your campaigns at any time and stop spending money.

You May Never See Your Ad Displayed on Your Account

Facebook is not like search advertising where you can search on your keyword and see your ad displayed. If you do not match your own targeting profile, you will not see your ad displayed on your Facebook account.

You can, however, see what your ad would look like on your profile page. When looking at your ad, click on the button that says "View on Profile." You will see what your ad would look like displayed on your profile page.

Chapter Five

Batten Down the Hatches

DON'T CLICK "PLACE ORDER" YET: FIRST, BATTEN DOWN THE HATCHES!

A batten is a thin strip of solid material, typically made from wood, plastic or metal. It serves many uses, for example being inserted into the edge of a sail to keep it flat and catching the wind.

You have likely heard the phrase, now an idiom, "batten down the hatches." Perhaps you saw it in an old sailing movie. It is usually shouted as a ship heads into a storm as a warning to secure the hatches heading below. They need to be closed tight to prevent water from filling and then sinking the ship.

> "*It is not the ship so much as the skillful sailing that assures the prosperous voyage.*"
>
> —George William Curtis

Batten down the hatches to prepare for imminent disaster or emergency, on a ship, or in your Facebook advertising campaigns.

Many digital advertisers have sailed into the storm without battening down the hatches. We usually hear a story that goes something like this: "I created my new Facebook advertising campaign, and before I knew it spent $3,000 on clicks but only received $60 in sales."

That user forgot to batten down the hatches.

Unfortunately, for small businesses $3,000 is a lot of money to waste. Even worse, if the small business advertiser gets discouraged and stops trying, that $3,000 wasted may even be the end of the business.

Don't let this happen to you. Starting a new ad campaign is a tricky business. You are sailing into unknown waters. Giving Facebook your credit card and permission to charge at will is like adding a hurricane to those unknown waters.

You must batten down the hatches!

A lot of people mistakenly believe that selecting CPC (cost-per-click) bidding instead of CPM (cost-per-impression) bidding is battening down the hatches. It isn't. Our friend in the example above used pay per click, spent $3,000 and only received $60 in sales. Pay per click doesn't protect you from the storm. So what does?

DURATION AND BUDGET BATTENS

Facebook proves you two solid tools for battening down the hatches. The tools are called duration and budget. Duration and budget are currently set when the ad in a campaign is first created. They can be reset at any time at the campaign level. All of the ads in the campaign will share the one budget.

The first batten Facebook provides is budget, as seen in Figure 5.1. You can set your budget "per day" or as a "lifetime budget" when you first create the ad. Set a low daily or lifetime budget to avoid a catastrophic overspend.

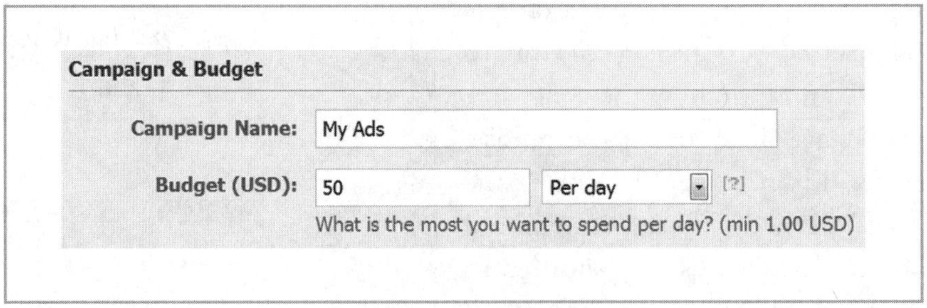

Campaign & Budget

Campaign Name: My Ads

Budget (USD): 50   Per day   [?]
What is the most you want to spend per day? (min 1.00 USD)

FIGURE 5.1–Creating a Campaign Name and Budget

If you select "per day," you are telling Facebook you are willing to spend that much money over a 24-hour, calendar day. Facebook may or may not charge you up to the budget amount of money each day the campaign runs. It may serve your ads at any time throughout the day.

Daily budget is how much you will allow Facebook to charge on your credit card for that campaign, each and every day. Think carefully about this number. Add all of your daily budget numbers together to understand your exposure to daily credit card charges by Facebook.

Although three tiny campaigns with $10 daily budgets seems small, think of receiving a $30 charge each day for 31 days. You could have a $930 advertising expense exposure in just one month from only three tiny campaigns.

Also notice that Facebook provided a default daily budget of $50 in the example above. Care to calculate your monthly exposure if you run three tiny campaigns with a $50 daily spending limit? As high as $4,500 a month! This adds up fast, so pay attention and batten down the hatches.

Fortunately, there is another hatch we can batten to control daily budgets; that batten is duration. We can use duration to start and stop campaigns at specific dates and times.

Beginners may notice that Facebook might throttle your daily spend. However, as your ads run successfully and you develop a history of paying your bills, you will be allowed to spend more and more each day.

Another batten Facebook provides for controlling your budget is a lifetime budget. You may tell Facebook to stop running the ad campaign when it has reached your lifetime budget.

If you choose "lifetime budget," then Facebook claims it will distribute your ad "throughout the duration of the campaign." The implication is it will try to distribute the budget evenly across the days, but there is no guarantee that this will be the case, so be careful about setting a large lifetime budget. Better, at least initially, to manage a daily budget with short durations.

How Long to Batten Down

Duration is how long you are willing to let a Facebook ad campaign run without stopping. Duration defaults to unlimited. That is correct—if you do not intervene, the campaign defaults to running forever. If you do not change the duration, then Facebook reserves for itself the right to keep charging your credit card day after day after day after day, without end—at least if you set a daily budget. Clearly, we need to batten this down.

If you select daily budget, set short campaign durations.

The first thing to do when battening down duration is to uncheck the box, "Run my campaign continuously starting today," as seen in Figure 5.2. This is a lovely feature Facebook offers to maximize your risk. Click here, run your ads continuously, potentially forever, with no expiration date!

Schedule

Campaign Schedule: ☑ Run my campaign continuously starting today

FIGURE 5.2–Schedule Defaults to Running Forever

All this option does is put you at infinite risk. Our advice—immediately uncheck that box, and never willingly check that box. (Note: You cannot check the box if you set a lifetime budget.)

Set your campaign schedule (the duration is the time between the start date and the end date) to run for a reasonably short period of time. We suggest using daily budgets and setting duration to two or three days at most.

You can extend the duration any time you like, and it does not require your ad to be reviewed again by Facebook, so your ad starts running again instantly if you set a new end date after it timed out. Check your campaign twice a day. If things are going well and your duration is almost over, extend your duration another day or two. It only takes five minutes to check your statistics and update duration, so spend the time and keep on top of the performance of your campaign.

Batten Down Total Exposure

The question here is simple. After you have battened down daily budget and duration, what is your total exposure? Is this an amount you are willing to lose in two days in a failed experiment?

We frequently start new campaigns at $10 a day, but sometimes go higher based on what we need to bid for clicks. The key is, we are managing risk by keeping this daily spend down to the level we are actually willing to simply lose each day over the duration of the experiment.

Extending Duration and Budget

Once you are sure the campaign is working, you can crank the budget up higher. But still think of it as what you are willing to lose. You should look at increasing budget and duration in terms of risk.

In one case, we knew our ads and landing pages fundamentally worked and our short-term goal was not financial; it was simply to drive a few beta testers to a new software product each day. We set the daily spend at $50 and the duration at 30 days. We were willing to lose $1,500 to try to get beta testers.

In other cases, where the goal of an ad is clearly to deliver more profit and we know the ad is working, we crank the daily spend up to maximum and collect as much cash as possible as fast as possible, because we never know when the game will change and the gold vein will end. If your ad is making money and you can keep up with the orders, spend as much as Facebook will let you each day and set the duration to be one day at a time. If the daily spend is high, we manage our risk on a day-by-day basis.

Heading Into a Storm

To not properly batten down budget and duration is to sail into the hurricane with all of your hatches fully open. You risk sinking your entire business. Until you know that every dollar you spend in Facebook advertising is truly delivering at least a penny in net profits, you must set a low budget and a short duration. We mean net profits—the money left over after paying all of your expenses!

Make no mistake. Handing Facebook, Google, Microsoft, or any other online advertising company your credit card and saying "bill me whenever someone sees or clicks on my ad and do this forever" is basically insane. It is giving them carte blanche. It is taking the battens, breaking them into little pieces, and throwing them overboard right before the hurricane strikes.

Do you get the idea?

Batten down the hatches instead by setting spending limits and short campaign durations.

YOUR AD CAMPAIGN IS NOT A ROTISSERIE CHICKEN

When talking about ads, it is hard for us not to think about rotisserie chicken. Why? Because Ron Popeil of Ronco Inc. sold close to a billion dollars worth of "Showtime Rotisseries" using TV direct sales using the catch phrase, "Set it and forget it."

I bet if we yelled "Set it" in a crowd we could still get a few people to yell "and forget it" back at us. The ad's phrase brilliance not withstanding, your ad campaign is not a rotisserie chicken.

Do not "set it and forget it."

In fact, when you are just starting a new campaign, we suggest you look in on it within 60 minutes of it first activating. The first few hours, as the ads get impressions, you actually have an opportunity to immediately reduce your bids and look for unintended consequences.

Reducing bids is treated nicely by Facebook; that change does not require you to wait for a reviewer to approve the change. Unfortunately, changing from CPC bidding to CPM bidding does currently trigger a manual review. This is unfortunate because if an ad performs well in terms of CPC we might immediately change it to CPM bidding.

Review every ad at least every one to two hours the first day. Once the campaigns are running, they should be reviewed at least at the beginning and the end of every day.

RUNNING IN THE DARK

You can produce dramatic results from digital advertising campaigns. It is what makes this business so rewarding. But you shouldn't expect to get dramatic results from your first ad. Discovering how real customers will actually respond to a new ad is always walking in the dark.

It is dark!
So we walk.

Tiny and measured steps. After each step, we measure and validate our results. Our goal is not to write the best ad on our first attempt. Our goal is to refine an approach to advertising that will improve, using natural selection, until it produces winning ads.

The key to creating great ads is to learn to run experiments with specific goals in mind. Then, gather real data to prove whether the experiment is a success.

Relentlessly test your ad ideas. Let data (specifically click-through-rate and conversion rate) tell you which ideas are best. Develop an approach to advertising that says experiments are the norm. Everything is always an experiment. Build the experiment, collect the data, and then analyze the results. If the experiment worked, do more of it. If it failed, learn from it and move on.

Sometimes you win, and sometimes you lose. Keep the winners; throw away the losers, and then start the process over again.

Experiment, gather data, analyze, repeat. Again and again and again. Society keeps changing, customers keep changing, technology keeps changing, so you keep experimenting.

Do you want to know the secret of successful digital advertisers? They aim tiny and miss small. And, as a result, they learn a lot very quickly.

WHY AIM TINY?

A low daily budget is one example. If the budget is small and the ad was a mistake, we lose $10 and move on. But any changes to our sales funnel—from the original ad to the final processing of a credit card—can be done in tiny increments.

Change one small thing and see if your ad or landing page improves. Take a working ad and change only the image. Does the ad get a better response? If so, keep the change; if not, change it back or try something else. Take a working ad and change the headline. Does the ad get a better response? Change the call to action. Does the ad get a better response? Change the demographic targeted age. Does the ad get a better response?

Over time, you get smarter and smarter by testing lots of tiny changes and watching the CTR. In Facebook, you will also need to make tiny changes just to stop the ad from fatiguing.

Discovering how real customers actually respond to a new ad or making a tiny change to an existing ad is throwing darts in a blizzard. You set low budgets and low limits because it is hazy. You walk in tiny and measured steps because you can't see clearly. The more data shines light on the project, the faster you can go.

Eventually, when you really think your ad and your sales funnel is working, you turn the spigot on full blast and run the ad continuously for as long as possible. The data will tell you when you can do this, and you do not need to guess.

What is most important is not any specific ad you write or response you get. What is important is that you have a reliable process you can follow to eventually deliver results; a process that strives to help you make decisions based on real data and understand why you see the results you see.

If one change to an ad makes the CTR (click-through rate) go up, and another change to an ad makes the CTR go down, you want to understand why (if possible), because that will help you make better guesses in the future on what to test next.

Understanding why gives you the ability to get more of the desired results in future tests.

Understanding why is truly understanding your customer.

It may be necessary to test 20 different variations or more on a single Facebook ad to get optimal performance from the ad. Do it quickly. Don't spend a year to figure out how to improve your conversion rate. If you spend a year finding an optimization that could have been found in a month, then you have lost eleven months of financial gain. A very costly 11 months!

Throwing darts in a blizzard is a great way to get injured. You need to use your testing, analysis, and arithmetic skills. You need real skills in digital marketing. By the time you read and implement all of the strategies and tactics in this book, you will have them.

Chapter Six

Selling on the Front Porch

WHERE SELLING MEETS SOCIAL

Imagine you live in a small town in a big, old house on Main Street. The house has a large front porch that extends its entire length and even wraps around the side. People in town walk up and down the street to see what's going on, to meet and chat with friends and neighbors, and perhaps to stroll to the library or the theater.

You are sitting on your front porch as people walk by on a warm, summer evening. You sit quietly, sipping lemonade, commenting on the heat, and playing checkers with your neighbor. Many of the people who walk by wave or say hello. Some even stop, lean on the rail, and visit for a while, talking about nothing in particular but sharing news: births, weddings, deaths, local gossip—who is in a new relationship or who is arguing with whom.

A few of those who pass by even join you, finding a seat on the front porch to watch others walk by. You welcome them with a fresh glass of lemonade and a snickerdoodle cookie.

> "*Let us make a special effort to stop communicating with each other, so we can have some conversation.*"
>
> —MARK TWAIN

Those who join you on the porch also see friends passing by. Sometimes they invite their friends to join them on the porch. They may sit together on a swinging bench and talk for a while, sharing pictures just picked up at the Five and Dime, and telling tall tales. Some folks walking by shout a quick hello and a short bit of news without even slowing their pace.

This casual, dynamic, social environment is Facebook.

Facebook is where people connect with friends, family, and acquaintances. Facebook is the new town square. People do not go to the town square to search for the answers to a problem or to buy life insurance. They go to meet people, to see and to be seen, to interact.

Facebook is not about what people are doing right now, it is about who people are: what they like, what they believe in, and with whom they like to associate. Facebook is where people share announcements, opinions, and insights not for any particular objective, but just to share. To connect. To be alive.

People do not go to Facebook to search for the answer to a problem. Or to find a product. Or to learn about your service. The front-porch experience is about connecting and exchanging—exchanging things as simple as a poke or as unexpectedly world-changing as the suicidal death of Mohamed Bouazizi on a Tunisian street that soon spread revolution to the entire Middle East.

Can you sell on the front porch?

Absolutely.

What you are about to learn is nothing new. People have been selling from their version of a front porch for centuries. What is important to recognize is that the front porch is not the market; it is not the boardroom; it is not the mall. You do not conduct business on the front porch in the same way you do in these other locations.

Learn this lesson and you crack the code to effective Facebook advertising.

THIS IS NOT YOUR FATHER'S ADWORDS

Selling on the front porch is not that same as selling with Google AdWords. AdWords is an absolutely amazing tool produced by Google to display ads in Google search and across the internet. (A free short course on AdWords is available at www.perrymarshall.com/google/.) However, those who have extensive experience with AdWords may find Facebook advertising a little frustrating.

You may have had a thrilling and positive experience selling on Google. Then you take those exact same ads to Facebook and flop. What happened? Facebook looks almost the same, but looks are deceiving in this case. Facebook is not AdWords.

Try a real-world example. Bring up one window for Google and another window for Facebook. We are going to pretend that we are users interested in buying a guitar. In Google type in the word "guitar" and press "enter."

Instantly, Google shows natural search results related to guitar. We describe Google search as the "Yellow Pages" when we are talking to older people. It is where you go to look things up. When we say "Yellow Pages" to younger people, they look at us funny and say "Oh, you mean like Google."

As Google delivers links to textual information about guitars, it also simultaneously displays ads related to guitars.

When looking at a screen full of information related to their Google inquiry, most users probably don't recognize what is a search result and what is an ad. If Google does its job well, users shouldn't care because the search results and the ads are of equal interest to them.

These ads are purchased by advertisers who specifically request that their ads be displayed when the word "guitar" is entered into the search bar. A simple concept, right? If someone types in a specific word or phrase you want to advertise to, then Google displays your ad associated with that key word or phrase. Simple.

Now go to Facebook.

Facebook also has a search feature, but it is primarily focused on searching Facebook, Facebook pages, your friends, likes, and interests. Facebook is not focused on searching the entire internet for you. It is NOT the Yellow Pages or Google.

In Facebook type in the word "guitar" and press "enter."

Notice anything interesting about the ads shown in Figure 6.1?

Not a single ad about guitars!

Not a lot of choices, either!

The ads you see at the right-hand side of the page in Facebook are not ads based on what you are doing right now, which is searching the word "guitar." Rather they are ads focused on who you are as a person: your age, your sex, your marital status, and the pages, TV shows, and other things you're into.

In Google you get to sell to the specific need that the user is digitally shouting at you. The user is saying "Hey, I am thinking about a 'guitar' right now," and you, as the advertiser, get to shout back, "Hey, I've got great deals on guitars."

No so on Facebook.

If you were to stand on your front porch and yell at everyone walking down the street that "I have a great deal on car insurance," some people might stop by and talk with you, but most would start walking down the other side of the street.

So is there an effective way to sell on the front porch?

FIGURE 6.1–Not a Single Ad about Guitars

You bet there is. It all begins with adding value, and with a snickerdoodle, a glass of lemonade, and a game of checkers.

ADD VALUE BEFORE YOU RECEIVE A DIME

Selling on the front porch is about engaging people where they are, based on their personal likes and interests. People stop by the front porch because they see something they find interesting and want to learn more. This is what makes Facebook such a great tool for advertising products related to art, beliefs, music, culture, health, fitness, or anything that appeals to personal interests.

If you were selling pottery on the front porch, how would you approach it?

For starters, if you want to sell pottery on the front porch, you begin by having incredibly interesting pottery in plain view. You choose pieces that stop people in their tracks and cause them to come up onto the porch and see what they are. You engage people on your front porch. You make them smarter about pottery. You answer their questions about pottery, and you converse about art, artists, clay, and kilns.

You may even have a pottery wheel on the front porch where you demonstrate how a pot is made. When people stop by for lemonade and snickerdoodles, you invite them to try the wheel for themselves. There's nothing like trying to make a pot yourself to appreciate why you might be willing to pay $150 or more for amazing pieces of pottery art made by hand, a piece of pottery you can cherish for years to come.

Selling on the front porch is about adding value and engaging the customers so that they want to spend time on the front porch.

If they spend enough time, see the products, learn about them, and do so in a way that engages and entertains . . . guess what? They stop by the front porch the next time they are in town. The more people stop at the front porch, the more people hang around, the more people learn about pottery, and the more they want to own a nice piece of pottery themselves.

Done correctly, the entire process doesn't even feel like selling. Why? Because it isn't selling; it is being social. It is a natural extension of your customers' old (or even newfound) interest in pottery. They ultimately ask you, "How much does this one cost? I really love it."

This scenario is real, and it has real and very practical applications in Facebook.

If you are trying to sell pottery on Facebook, do not drive your users to a page that says, "Buy this pot right now for only $150." If they are not interested in buying a pot right then (and Facebook users are not shopping), then you will miss the real opportunity and will probably not sell enough pots to pay for the ads.

So what might you do instead? It depends on your Unique Selling Proposition (USP). Your USP is the front porch story you tell about why your product or service is so special. Unique is the critical word in USP. You have to display something unique—something that nobody else offers, does, or promises. Tell your front porch visitors stories about your USP.

It may be a story about quality, service, a satisfaction guarantee, or even artistry. Is there

- Something you can guarantee uniquely?
- An experience your customer will have with you that he or she will have nowhere else?
- Something memorable to tell them that nobody else is saying?

You may be continually refining your USP as your business develops.

Once you have your USP, you must craft interesting and engaging content that reflects your USP. Are you selling pottery as an investment? Art form? Dinner plates? Are you selling to twenty-something hipsters? Forty-something professionals? For each one of these, you may craft a different front porch experience.

Can you name a magician who lived more than 100 years ago? Did you say Harry Houdini? Houdini was the master of the USP. In his case, a USP was a new illusion that nobody had ever seen before. Houdini was a marketing genius. You can probably name one of his USPs more than 100 years after it was introduced. Can you name one of his illusions? Did you think of the Chinese water torture cell?

His USPs worked, and he attracted large audiences. Of course, other magicians were always copying him and ripping off his ideas. Can you name any of those other magicians? No. Being first with a string of USPs is a powerful advantage. Don't worry about being copied, worry about being great.

If you are selling beautifully hand-crafted pottery for 40-something professionals to give as gifts, you may offer visitors to your porch a free guide to the 15 most stunning pieces of pottery you have ever seen. You may talk about how the pieces are made, why they are special, and why discriminating individuals might enjoy such a magnificent piece of pottery.

Pictures, videos, cartoons, testimonials—all about pottery—support your front porch conversation and validate your USP. We always encourage capturing your visitors' email address through at least one special offer that only comes via email.

Do you have a piece of pottery that is so exceptional that visitors to your front porch would urge their friends walking by to stop and see that piece? Is it beautiful, provocative, or funny? If so, then feature it and encourage your visitors to invite their friends to engage.

PLAYING WITH CUSTOMERS: A NEW WAY TO ENGAGE

Do you have 1,000 friends on your Facebook page but almost no interaction from them? It is probably because you are not playing with them. Playing leads to interaction, interaction leads to information, information leads to interest, and interest leads to sales. This is the way of the front porch.

One of the simplest forms of play is asking a trivia question. It works on the front porch, and it works in Facebook. In our chapter on Facebook pages, we will tell you how a few trivia questions can provide you with thousands and thousands of additional free impressions for your brand—impressions on important status messages, not just trivia!

BEING FRIENDLY, TRULY FRIENDLY

Selling on the front porch is not new. For years I have been encouraging my clients to engage their customers with a website with a strong landing page offering relevant conversation and value-added information.

I encourage my students not to focus initially on their products or service offerings but to first provide free information around their products and services. If the potential customers request more information around the product or service and we collect their contact information, then we have a lot more space to work with them until they are ready for a sale.

The goal, once you pay for a click, is to begin to build a relationship with a customer. One where they like you, appreciate your expertise, and actively desire to purchase from you.

Ten years ago, I said if you are selling ink for a commercial printer, first offer your potential clients a free paper (now perhaps a free video) on how to save money on ink. Include every good suggestion you can find on how to save money on ink without mentioning your product or service. Only in the last point might you note that you sell high-quality commercial ink for 35% less than your nearest competitor.

This strategy works precisely because it is not just a tactic, but is a way to demonstrate that you are actually there to help. You are not out to make a quick buck but to build a relationship. You are selling on the front porch.

The conversation built around helping your prospect find ways to save on ink could be followed with a series of messages in an email auto-responder that describe other ways to get more value in the printing process, saving paper, saving electricity, etc. Adding value for your customers, making them want to visit your Facebook page or open your email, is key.

Eventually, when they want ink, guess who they will think of first.

"IS THIS THE RICHARD SHERIDAN?"

Richard Sheridan, founder of Menlo Innovations, runs a now world-renowned shop that does custom software development using lean and agile techniques. Sheridan wasn't always world renowned. When he was first setting up shop in his basement in 2001, he and his partners turned on the TV and watched the attack on the World Trade Center. New business, no office, no customers, undercapitalized—and an economy that had turned itself off.

In early 2002, Richard and his team started implementing front porch techniques for their very specialized B2B products: high-end training, consulting, and software development using agile software development techniques.

They put together an information campaign with the specific purpose of telling every secret they know about agile software development. They wrote papers, made public speeches, sent emails, and provided literally thousands of free hours of training. And they attracted readers from more than 100 countries within their first year.

Of course, they also had an AdWords campaign, a dedicated website landing page, and an auto-responder. They didn't sell—they chatted on the front porch about software, process, and what they had learned. Anyone who ordered their papers received dozens of emails, often highly technical, containing every bit of good advice Menlo could provide. FREE.

One day Richard Sheridan answered the phone. "Hello, Menlo Innovations, Rich Sheridan speaking."

"Rich Sheridan. THE Rich Sheridan? We've been reading your papers. Can you come on down here and talk to us?"

Care to guess who called?

Care to guess who knew his name?

Care to guess who already considered Rich Sheridan a somebody who was interesting to talk to?

"IS THIS THE RICHARD SHERIDAN?", continued

It was Coca-Cola. "The Coca-Cola Company" on the other end of the phone was excited to reach "The Rich Sheridan."

Would you like your prospects to call you too?

Then master selling on the front porch. Harness the fundamental principles that have been working for millennia, because they have never been more true than they are in Facebook. The fundamentals don't change. The tools and tactics change; the strategy remains.

Engage your customers with value-added experience so they enjoy hanging out on your front porch. Get as many leads as possible on your front porch, playing checkers, eating snickerdoodles, and occasionally even learning something interesting or important. When the time comes to purchase a product or service, who do you think they will be most inclined to buy from?

Your version of Coca-Cola may soon be calling you, too.

Chapter Seven

Targeting

DRAMATICALLY REDUCE ADVERTISING COSTS THOUGH TARGETING

Imagine you have an Austin-based pottery craft business where parents bring children to create and decorate pottery crafts, especially for birthday parties. Now imagine you can advertise to different groups to drum up business for your pottery store. These groups are:

1. Every person in the world.
2. Every person in the United States.
3. Every person in Austin, Texas.
4. Every female in Austin, Texas.
5. Every married female in Austin, Texas.
6. Every married female in Austin, Texas, between the ages of 25 and 50.
7. Every married female in Austin, Texas, between the ages of 25 and 50, who has children and is planning a birthday party.

Which of these groups would you prefer to advertise to first?

> *"People don't notice ads, they notice what interests them and sometimes it's an ad."*
>
> —Howard Gossage

Which group will cost the least amount of advertising money per sale?

Targeting every person in the world—Group 1—may lead to some local sales. However, the cost to advertise to everyone in the world will probably bankrupt you. You need to be smarter about how to spend your advertising dollars. You want to spend your dollars getting the right message in front of the right person so you can make a sale profitable.

This is the nature of targeting—focusing our ads to groups we can reach and sell to with the least amount of money. It is also reasonable to believe that if we advertise to Group 7 we will get a much higher click-through rate (CTR) at a much lower cost per click than if we advertise to Group 1. We save money by advertising to fewer people, and we save money by advertising to the right people.

It is obvious to most who might be running an Austin-based pottery shop that it is better to advertise to every married female in Austin, Texas, between the ages of 25 and 50, who has children, and is planning a birthday party—Group 7—than to every person in the world.

It is not quite as obvious to those same shop owners that it would probably be better to advertise to every married female in Austin, Texas, between the ages of 25 and 50—Group 6—before they advertise to every married female in Austin, Texas—Group 5. But the reason is the same.

It is reasonable to expect that it will be more cost effective to advertise to Group 6, and Group 6 will return a higher profit than advertising to Group 5. The higher the profit margin, the better. Of course, you need to gather data to prove that advertising to Group 6 delivers more profit than Group 5, but, fortunately, Facebook helps you gather the data required to see if this is true.

There are names for various types of targeting:

· geographic (where someone lives)
· demographic (who someone is)
· psychographic (what someone thinks: their interests, activities, and opinions)

We will explore all three of these areas to describe how to target your ads and reduce the cost of acquiring customers.

In addition, Facebook offers a unique fourth targeting area—sociographic. Sociographic targeting finds customers based on the social graph, how people are connected. Sociographic targeting aims at people based on who they know.

ESTIMATED REACH

Explaining accurately how targeting works in Facebook is difficult. At last count there were over two dozen different controls in the Facebook targeting interface. We

FIGURE 7.1–Estimated Reach for All People in the United States Age 18 and Older

know. Sounds way too tricky. Fortunately, Facebook provides an easy way for you to understand who you are targeting in a display called "estimated reach."

Estimated reach displays the number of people who may see your ad, and the selection criteria used to target those people. In Figure 7.1, we see the estimated reach for targeting everyone in the United States age 18 and older.

Estimated reach recalculates in real time as you adjust your targeting criteria. This makes it not only easy to use but also fun to use. In the example, if I restrict my target to just California, estimated reach updates its totals automatically, as seen in Figure 7.2.

FIGURE 7.2–Estimated Reach for All People in the State of California Age 18 and Older

So instead of trying to teach first-order logic in this book to help you understand how targeting works, I am going to suggest you play with a sample ad using all of the targeting features and watch how each of the changes you make affects the estimated reach.

Some changes will raise the number, some will lower it. The best way to learn how and why is by playing with the tool. Seriously, you should spend at least an hour watching how the numbers move based on changes you make to targeting until you are comfortable you understand what is happening.

In addition, the estimated reach display can help you do market research. If you are thinking of building a store in Ann Arbor, Michigan, that will appeal to married women between the ages of 30 to 40, Facebook can tell you in a few seconds through the estimated reach tool how many of those customers have self-identified in Facebook (see Figure 7.3).

FIGURE 7.3–Married Women in Ann Arbor, Michigan, between the Ages of 30 and 40

You can reach these almost 13,000 women on Facebook. Use them for market research now. Ask them if they would shop at your store. They are readily reachable to you and welcome a front porch conversation. Talk to them about what items they would like to see available. Offer discounts and coupons for great suggestions.

By the time your store opens, you should already have many people in your target market anxiously awaiting your opening-day extravaganza.

GEOGRAPHIC TARGETING—WHERE SOMEONE LIVES

Facebook lets you advertise to people based on where they live. You can target people by

· country or countries,
· state or states,
· city or cities,
· city and surrounding cities.

These choices are about where your target users are when they actually access Facebook. The users may be from the United States, but if they are traveling and accessing Facebook from Canada, they will be shown ads for people who have been targeted in Canada.

Your choices for state/province are limited by your country selections. If you have selected only the United States, you will not have the opportunity to select the city of London, England, although you can select London, Alabama, and its 480 Facebook users.

Similarly, your city choices are limited by your state/province selections. These limits help ensure you are actually selecting the cities and states you intended to select. You can always reach all cities, states, and provinces you would like by adding more countries and adding more states and provinces. It is my personal rule that advertising to different countries always occurs in separate ads. I never target two different countries in the same ad.

If you select that you are targeting by city, then you have the option to extend your ad to people living within some distance of the city, so good target users are not lost because they are a few miles outside of city limits.

Geographic targeting is obviously valuable for most local brick-and-mortar businesses. If most of your customers are walk-in visitors who drive 10 miles or less to your store, then target the smallest geographic area possible within a 10-mile radius of your business. This reduces your number of impressions, slashes your ad cost, and gets your ads in front of someone who is more likely to visit your store and buy your products. Proximity is convenience.

If your store is in Miami, then geographic targeting will look something like Figure 7.4

Estimated reach for this selection (see Figure 7.5) tells you that this choice targets over 1.5 million people.

These are the more obvious cases of why a business may want to use geographic targeting. But what if your business is online? What if your business has customers

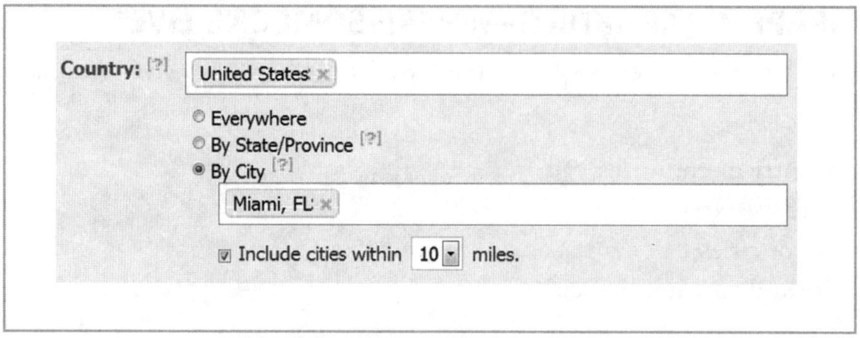

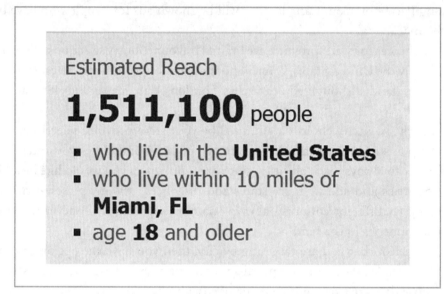

FIGURE 7.4–Targeting Users in Miami, Florida, and Cities within 10 Miles of Miami

Estimated Reach

1,511,100 people

- who live in the **United States**
- who live within 10 miles of **Miami, FL**
- age **18** and older

FIGURE 7.5–Estimated Reach of People Age 18 and Older within 10 Miles of Miami, Florida

all across the United States and Canada? All across the world? Is there a reason to use geographic targeting if your business is global in reach? You bet there is, and it is a mistake to not use it, even if you sell "everywhere."

Geographically Target to Localize Your Ad

Surprisingly to many people new to geographic targeting, it is still useful to use geographic targeting even if you sell nationally or internationally. For example, if you are selling to customers in the United States and Canada, it may still be helpful to create ads targeted specifically for each of the 50 states and 10 provinces. Why? Because people respond better to an ad that lists by name their state or province.

People respond better to an ad where the image features a local landmark. This is called creating a localized ad.

Say you are in the business of making the world's best pecan pie, and most of your business is by mail order. You package and ship pecan pie overnight anywhere in the United States and Canada. Which ad body text do you think converts better in Texas?

Texans love Momma Bakers Pecan Pie

or

Everybody loves Momma Bakers Pecan Pie

In Texas, I'll bet on "Texans love Momma Bakers Pecan Pie" every time.

Even if you are selling everywhere in the United States, you will benefit from specific geographic targeting that localizes your ads, increases CTR, and improves profits.

The ad "Texans love Momma Bakers Pecan Pie" should include a picture of somebody in a cowboy hat. The same product in Connecticut may have an ad that says "True sailors love Momma Bakers Pecan Pie," and features an image of a sailboat.

Localizing your ad copy should improve response rates dramatically. Even if your ad doesn't specifically mention Texas, it is not unusual for an ad that performs great in Texas to totally fail in Maine, and vice verse. Different regions have different cultures, different vocabularies, and different interests. Appeal to local appetites and interests.

Some regions call all soft drinks "soda," others call it "pop," and some areas call all soft drinks "Coke." In some regions, you actually hear people ask "What type of Coke do you want?" Marketers must be aware of these differences, and recognize you need different messages to cost effectively sell the same product in different places.

Sell Where It Sells

There is another reason you may do more focused geographical targeting. Even though you want to sell your product to everybody everywhere, you may not be selling everywhere equally. I strongly encourage you to look at your sales data to determine if there are distinct patterns to where your products sell best. Sell where you sell and stop wasting money advertising in places where you do not sell.

At first you may not know where you will sell, so you may set your ad to target everywhere in the United States as seen in Figure 7.6.

As you sell, you may begin to notice some interesting trends, like 80% of your paying customers coming from only two states—California and New Hampshire.

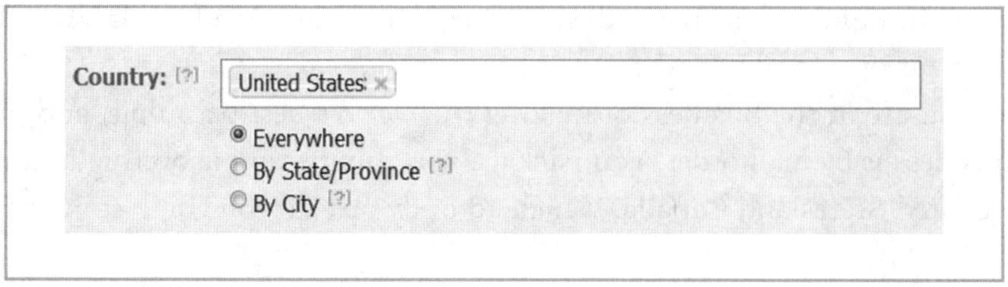

FIGURE 7.6–Targeting Everywhere in the United States

You don't need to know why they come from these two states—though it would be good to try to figure out—you just need to know that they do come from these two states.

Suppose targeting all the United States provides an estimated reach of 150 million. If I detect that 80% of my paying customers come from California and New Hampshire, I target just these two states, limiting the estimated reach to 20 million people.

The money saved by advertising to 20 million people instead of 150 million people makes the entire business dramatically more profitable. Geographic targeting is that powerful.

Identify regions with a disproportionally high number of customers and advertise more in those regions. Identify regions with a disproportionally low number of customers and stop advertising in those regions altogether.

It sounds tricky and like an awful lot of work to figure out where your online customers are geographically. Fortunately, Facebook reports make it easy to determine your hot and cold spots, and you do well to take advantage of that knowledge—use geographical targeting.

DEMOGRAPHIC TARGETING—WHO SOMEONE IS

Facebook lets you advertise to people based on who they are. Figure 7.7 shows how you can target people's basic demographics specifically:

· Age
· Sex

For demographic targeting, selecting both age and sex is what is known as a "logical and" operation. That is, both must be true, the age and the sex must match for someone to be considered a target. We warned you some logic was required to understand targeting. To get a feel for the operation, just play with age and sex and watch the estimated reach change.

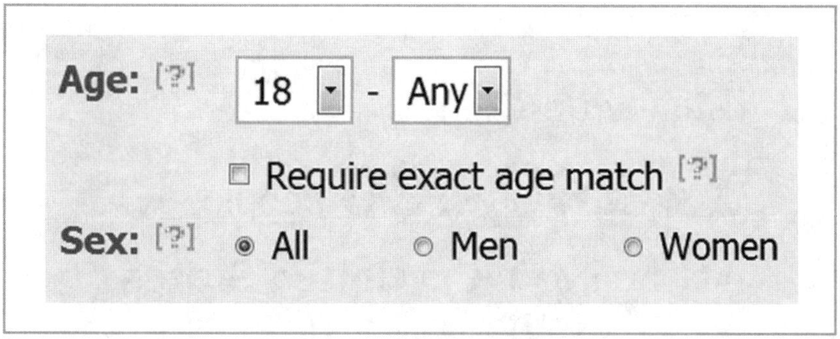

Age: [?]   18 ▾   -   Any ▾

☐ Require exact age match [?]

Sex: [?]   ◉ All   ○ Men   ○ Women

FIGURE 7.7–Basic Demographic Targeting

Estimated Reach

150,497,460 people

■ who live in the **United States**

FIGURE 7.8–Everyone in the United States

Estimated Reach

81,401,780 people

■ who live in the **United States**
■ who are **female**

FIGURE 7.9–Females in the United States

FIGURE 7.10–Females in the United States Who Are 35

TARGETING AGE RANGES

Facebook allows you to target an age range. You can specify the beginning and end of each range with an exact number, or chose "any" for "any age."

If you are not sure what age range will purchase your products, start with a broad range and see who clicks on your ads. Facebook reports tell you the age range of who is clicking on your ads most frequently. Once you know this, narrow your age selection or break the one ad into multiple ads targeting different age groups.

Only go after the lower performing age groups when the higher performing groups have been exhausted. Depending on the size of your target market, you may be able to determine the most responsive age groups in a few hours to a few days.

Very little in targeting by age demographics is exact. And remember, Facebook knows peoples' birthdays. Hence, Facebook provides an additional option called "Require Exact Age Match." If this is selected, Facebook restricts your target to the exact age range.

If "Require Exact Age Match" is selected and you requested targets ages 30 to 45, then a person outside of that age range by just one day will not see your ad. If this is what you want, select "Require Exact Age Match"; otherwise, make sure not to choose this.

If you do not select "Require Exact Age Match," then Facebook displays your ad to more people. Watch estimated reach to see how this option affects your target.

Facebook reports tell you the ages of users who click on your ads. You do not have to guess. If most of your customers are females between the ages of 25 and 45, then target that group first. It provides the least expensive sales.

Cohorts

Cohorts is a term used to describe a "group of individuals (within some population definition) who experience the same event within the same time interval." People in the same age group tend to share many similar experiences, tastes, goals, and values shaped by events they experience together, especially in impressionable years.

People may be especially influenced in making purchasing decisions throughout their entire lifetimes with emotional connections to times, events, and songs from early adulthood. Popular cohort terms include "the greatest generation," "baby boomers," and "Gen X."

If you came of age in the Great Depression, you probably think differently than someone who came of age during the Vietnam War. Depression-era folks may be more moved by the message of "saving for a rainy day." Those who came of age during the free-love 1960s may respond better to a message of "everyone is your brother."

Targeting cohorts is about selecting age groups that may respond to very different appeals in the ad images and copy. In part, this is because people's common experiences shape their emotional responses to advertising.

If you sell to a broad range, you may choose to target cohorts in order to customize your ad copy and your sales channel to better appeal to the group's unique psychographics.

ADVANCED DEMOGRAPHICS

Facebook also allows you to target users using some additional data fields currently labeled "advanced demographics." Advanced demographics include interested in, relationship, and languages, as seen in Figure 7.11.

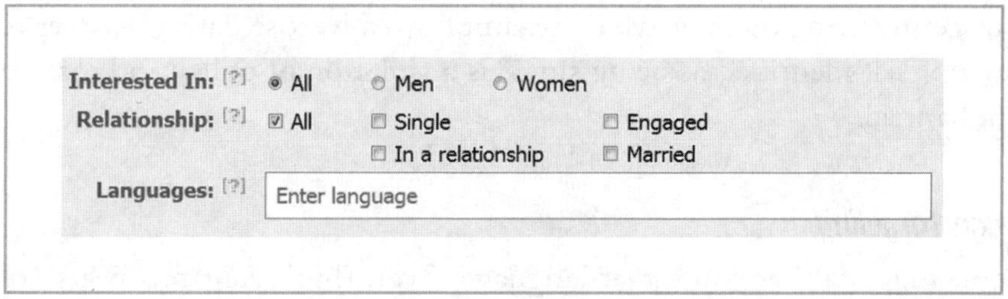

FIGURE 7.11–Advanced Demographics Control Panel

"Interested In" Targeting

The meaning of the field "interested in" is not defined by Facebook when it is selected by the users, and hence it is undefined in the minds of many users. More than half the users leave these fields unchecked. Many people use it to indicate sexual attraction. So if you are targeting users based on sexual attraction, you may consider testing "sex" and "interested in" in a variety of combinations.

Ultimately, people may indicate interest for any of a number of reasons, according to Facebook Help Center, including friendship, dating, a relationship, or just for networking. To basically ignore this targeting option and target all answers and nonanswers alike, select "All."

Relationship Targeting

It is possible to target people who have specifically identified themselves as being single, engaged, in a relationship, or married. If you select more than one, then it targets each category you have selected at the same time. In Figure 7.12 we are targeting people who are "in a relationship" or "married."

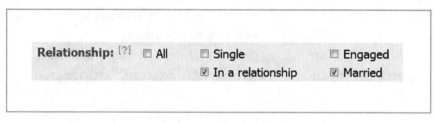

FIGURE 7.12–Targeting People "In a Relationship" or "Married"

Facebook expresses in the estimated reach display the nature of your selection in an English phrase to help make this clear. For example, the above selection is displayed in estimated reach as shown in Figure 7.13.

Read the advertising policies again carefully to ensure you are not violating them when targeting using these fields. For example, to advertise dating services to users who are not self-identified as being single is a violation of policy and may get your account banned.

Language Targeting

Facebook suggests that you target language if you think your prospects are using Facebook in a language other than the most common language for the area you targeted.

If you are writing ads in English and targeting English speakers in the United States, then there is no reason to use the language targeting feature.

However, if you are writing ads in Spanish and targeting Spanish speakers in the United States, then set the language option to Spanish. This will target people in

FIGURE 7.13–Targeting People "In a Relationship" or "Married"

the United States who use Facebook in Spanish—a great audience for your Spanish ad. Figure 7.14 shows us targeting Spanish speakers in the United States who use Facebook in Spanish.

If you are targeting English speakers in the United States, then there is no need to enter anything in this field.

In California, where there is a large Spanish-speaking population, you have some interesting choices. If you do not want your ad shown to people who use Facebook in Spanish, then enter English into the language field. This will remove the more than one million users in California who use Facebook in Spanish.

Estimated reach, as always, is your friend. Watch how estimated reach changes while you play with language selection to understand the impact of your choices on the size of your target group.

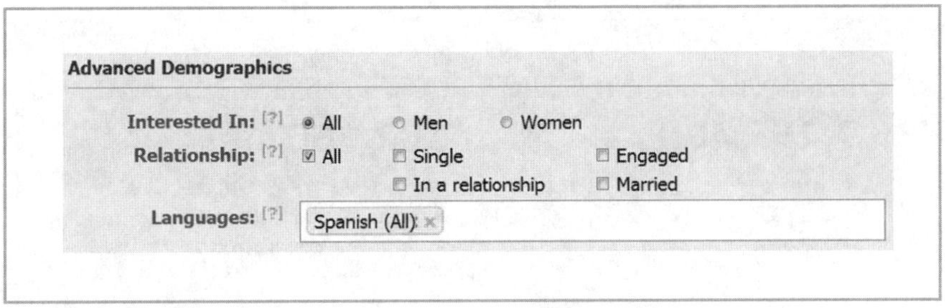

FIGURE 7.14–Targeting People Who Speak Spanish

PSYCHOGRAPHIC PROFILING

In marketing, "psychographics" is used to describe the interests, activities, and opinions of a target group.

Psychographics describes the type of thinking going on in someone's head. Needless to say, understanding the psychographics of a target audience is a tremendous advantage to you. Psychographic targeting in Facebook is provided through an interface called "interests."

When people "like" something on Facebook, it becomes a part of their psychographic profile. In addition, when people create a profile, they may identify their religious views and political views. They also often identify their likes in terms of favorite music, books, movies, television shows, and games. They may identify sports they play or their favorite teams and athletes.

"Interests" is incredibly powerful. It is so powerful that I've included additional chapters on how to use this field effectively. To start, we will use a simple example. Say you are selling a new cookbook. You could place in the "precise interests" field the term "cooking."

Facebook identifies several million people who have self-identified as liking cooking. This seems like a good place to start, advertising to the people who specifically like cooking! Of course, you could also create another campaign you target specifically to people who like cookbooks.

This is a much smaller group at 100,000 people, as illustrated in Figure 7.15, but it is people who specifically like COOKBOOKS. I know who I would try to advertise to first. At the very least, I would put these two different psychographics into two different ads.

A word of caution about psychographic targeting: to capture legitimate prospects with an interest in cooking will likely require using dozens of different psychographic target words. Psychographic target words are not keywords and, surprisingly, they are not direct matches for specific pages. Psychographic targeting

Estimated Reach [?]

7,265,480 people
- who live in the **United States**
- age **18** and older
- who like **cooking**

Estimated Reach [?]

102,980 people
- who live in the **United States**
- age **18** and older
- who like **cookbooks**

FIGURE 7.15–Estimated Reach of Cooking and Cookbooks Psychographics

deserves extra chapters because it's vastly different from keyword targeting used in search-engine ads. You do not understand how this psychographic targeting actually works in Facebook. Perhaps nobody does. Not even Facebook.

I believe Facebook could double its revenue simply by making better psychographic-targeting algorithms. It is already trying by introducing categories. However, until Facebook innovators get the kinks worked out, approach Facebook psychographic profiling with the following thought:

Facebook is trying to hide really good prospects from me.

This means you need to do more research to find the good prospects. Because, intentional or not, this is exactly what is happening.

Facebook Targets User Identity Not User Search

To illustrate how different psychographic targeting ("likes and interests") is from keyword targeting in search advertising, we will run a little experiment. Type in the phrase "agile guitar" in the Google search box and see the ads triggered by the search. Not surprisingly, they feature guitars! You see something like:

Guitars Galore
100s of guitars at low prices!
Compare offers, save with us.
www.stupidlylowpricedguitars.com

The agile guitar search term was instantly sold to advertisers by Google, and the user instantly sees guitar ads. Not so in Facebook. In Facebook, if you search on agile guitars, you will probably not see a single ad about guitars or even music. Instead you may see something like the ad shown in Figure 7.16.

FIGURE 7.16–Facebook May Show this Ad When Searching for "Agile Guitars"

Yes, it is that absurd. I can't even tell you the types of ads you might see. Why? Because your Facebook ads are totally customized to your geographic, psychographic, demographic, and sociographic profiles, not to what you are searching on "right now."

Ads in Facebook are totally different for everybody, based on who they are, not what they are searching for or doing at this specific instant.

If the user does not have agile guitars in their "likes and interests," then they will not be served ads on guitars, even if all they ever did in Facebook was search on the term.

If, however, you previously liked a page called agile guitars, you may be shown ads about guitars at any time. Facebook doesn't wait for you to search on terms to show you ads. Facebook knows you have interests and shows you ads based on those interests all the time.

Facebook-Suggested "Likes and Interests"

To get started targeting on "precise interests," jump right into the advertising interface and begin entering whatever terms are appropriate for your target psychographic. For example, if your prospects love reading Stephen King or horror novels, then simply type in the words Stephen King in precise interests when targeting your ad.

Facebook makes immediate suggestions for additional targets, as seen in Figure 7.17. In this example, Facebook mainly suggests other authors also liked by people who like Stephen King.

You should split these other authors into separate ads so you can target the ad's headline or body text to the specific author.

If you start typing in "horror" in precise interests you will notice something else interesting about psychographic targeting. Facebook displays a menu of interests available containing the word horror, as seen in Figure 7.18.

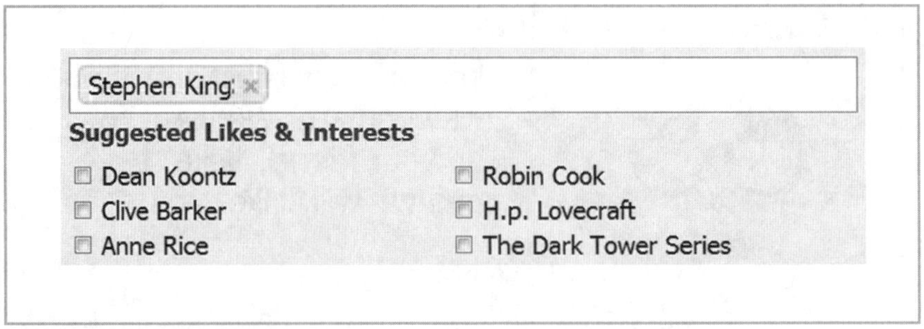

FIGURE 7.17–Additional Suggested Authors if Your Prospects Like Stephen King

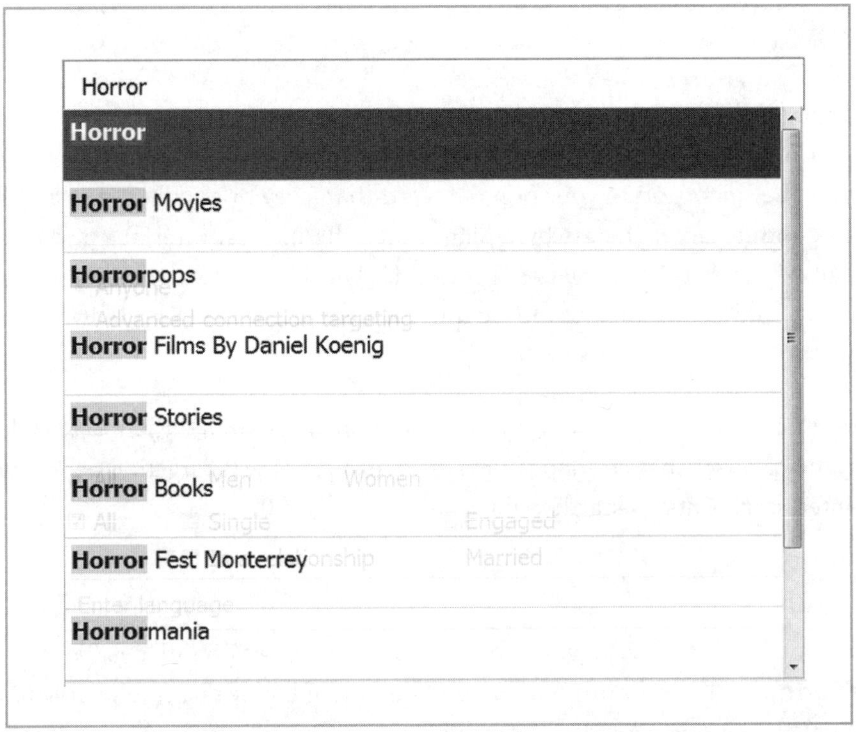

FIGURE 7.18–You Must Select a Psychographic Target from the Pop-Up

You can select psychographic "horror" targets only from the pop-up menu. If a target does not appear in the pop-up, then it is not available. Again, you may not want to include all of the listed selections in the same ad campaign.

If you want to test an ad or dip your toe into Facebook, you can stop looking for more targets and do a quick test immediately. Once you know your ad works, and if you want to reach more people, you will use more Facebook tools to find more interests to expand your expected reach.

Targeting by Broad Categories

Facebook allows you to target broad categories instead of precise interests. The broad categories are identified and created by Facebook and are limited. However, expect more and more categories to be added over time. These broad category targets accumulate a large number of precise interests into one convenient bundle. It is also where specific targeting for people based on their birthday has been located.

You cannot combine broad categories and precise interests. However, you can select multiple broad categories at one time. Our suggestion: Never select more than one broad category in the same ad.

It appears that Facebook does not want to immediately overwhelm you with selections, but there are more possible choices of targets that incorporate your original word than they originally suggest. When I work with a target, I start by typing it into the interest interface and selecting all of the relevant targets suggested by Facebook. I watch the estimated reach tool to try to understand how many people are being added with each suggestion.

Next, I do an alphabet search. What is an alphabet search? It is a way to look for other phrases that contain your target word. Say I was targeting people with an interest in "Cats." I start typing

"Cats A"

Facebook immediately suggests to me "Cats Are Better Than Dogs" and "Cats Are Purrrfect." I select both of them and add more highly targeted people to my campaign. Continue working your way through the alphabet, searching for likes and interests that use cats as a root:

Cats B—eight more suggestions

Cats C—seven more suggestions

Facebook always selects the top of the list, so to add its top suggestion quickly just press the enter key.

At the end of this exercise, for one project I added an additional 160,000 highly targeted people. If all I had done was enter in the original target word and Facebook's original suggestions, I would have reached only 41,000 people. This is a huge difference. Facebook likes and interests are a bit harder to track down and use than keywords in other advertising systems. Still, just a few more minutes of alphabet search can extend your reach four times!

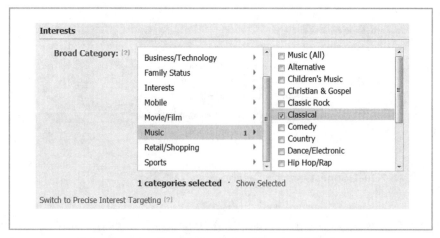

FIGURE 7.19–Selecting the Broad Category Classical Music

SOCIOGRAPHIC TARGETING

Sociographic targeting is about a prospect's relationships. The prospect has a relationship with you because they "liked" your page. The prosect has relationships with other people they "friended."

Sociographic targeting is the 21st century's most interesting advance in advertising. Facebook places this amazing innovation under the simple title, "Connections on Facebook."

"Connections on Facebook" allows you to target prospects based on which of your pages, groups, apps, or events they are, or are not, connected to. Perhaps never before in the history of direct marketing has such an advancement and innovation been so casually introduced nor so universally ignored—until now.

This laser-guided missile of direct marketing looks plain, innocent, and innocuous. Instead, it is a total game changer. If Facebook continues to be successful in making its site a fun place for people of the world to log into every day, this type of advertising will become a major tool used by every business, large and small. All because of the simple idea of identifying "friends" and "likes."

The connections on Facebook interface is currently simple, as see in Figure 7.20.

If you select "anyone," you are choosing not to use the connections feature.

If you select "advanced con-nection targeting" then Alice, you have dived into the rabbit hole. And the limits of your adventure are purely those of your imagination.

When you type suggestions in the fields, "target users who are connected to" or "target users who are not already connected to," Facebook shows a pop-up list of the

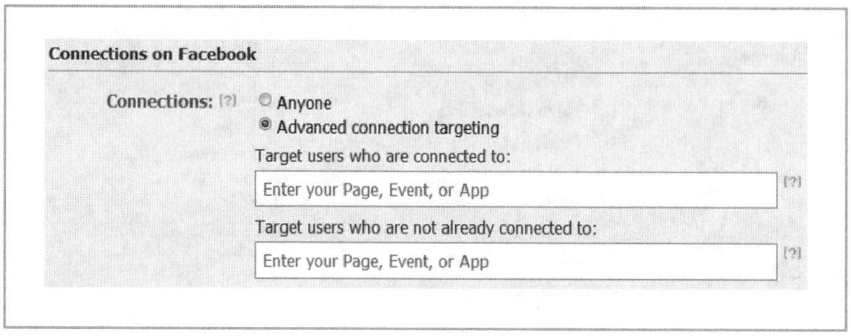

FIGURE 7.20–Connections on Facebook

pages, events, and apps you administrate. You can only select as connections pages, events and apps you administrate.

Facebook created a whole new category of advertising—sociographic advertising: advertisements based on visible, social graph connections.

Every business benefits from this new type of advertising. It makes traditional media prices to reach out to existing and past customers look like a joke. For small businesses, this type of advertising is a game changer. A small shop can now reach all of its customers with a highly affordable, custom message.

Using CPM (cost per impression) bidding, you can potentially remind ALL of your existing customers of your brand and your presence for less than the cost of a few postage stamps!

> *A*ny business who gets its regular customers to "like" a page can now get a custom advertisement in front of those customers for literally fractions of a penny, simply by running an ad that targets users who are connected to its Facebook page.

For this feature alone, EVERY SMALL BUSINESS WITH CUSTOMERS SHOULD HAVE A PAGE ON FACEBOOK.

Please note that while email is free and Facebook ads cost money, email has an annoyance factor. Facebook ads can be ignored, but rarely is anyone annoyed by them.

Only You Can Directly Target Your Fans

If you administrate a page, group, event, or app, then only you and your fellow administrators can directly target those fans with an ad.

It is not obvious this is the case. It sometimes feels like you can target the fans of any page directly. You cannot. Remember when I said "Facebook is trying to hide your best prospects from you?" This is a perfect example of that. Just because you can select a psychographic word that matches letter-for-letter the name of someone's Facebook page, does not mean you have directly targeted their fans.

Psychographics do not target user pages directly. A page may share the same name as a psychographic target, but the psychographic target does not directly target that page's fans.

How does Facebook sort this all out? Who knows.

Confused? You should be. It is confusing. The important thing to recognize is that although we look for pages to find good potential psychographic targets, unless we are the administrators of a page, event, or app, we cannot directly target fans of that page, event, or apps.

Do the math yourself watching estimated reach. The page someone else created you thought you were directly targeting, you were not directly targeting. Let me say this again. As it currently stands, only the administrators of a page can directly target the fans of their page with direct advertising.

So build your page of your fans. For the moment, anyway, they really are your fans to target.

Exclude Your Fans From Ads—Save Money

If you administrate a page, group, event, or app, then only you and your fellow administrators can directly exclude those fans from an ad.

If you are advertising to 500,000 people a message that tries to get them to be fans of your Facebook page, you may choose to exclude those people who are already fans of your page, event, or app.

This saves you money. I do it frequently with most of my ads.

To exclude existing fans, simply select your page name in the field called "target users who are not already connected to."

It costs money to display your ads. This field allows you to exclude from your ads those who have already responded and "liked" your page.

If you have multiple pages and multiple offers, you can cleverly combine both of these fields to selectively target fans of one of your pages, events, or apps and try to make them fans of a second page, event, or app. Any business—local or national—can use this feature to capture a group of leads and then continually target them for new products and special offers that are featured on other Facebook pages.

You Can Directly Target the Friends of Your Fans

If you choose as your destination a Facebook page, Facebook provides you with another powerful option: The option to specifically show ads to the "friends of the fans" of your page.

When your target "friend of the fans" of your page, prospects who see the ad also see the names of their friends who have liked the ad. You get immediate street cred for your ad and for your page.

Local businesses who target "friends of fans" in their local area, now have an amazing tool to expand their brand presence.

National businesses who target "friends of fans" can try to identify people who may secretly fit their psychographic profile because of people they associate with.

EDUCATION AND WORK TARGETING

You may target prospects based on their level of education and where they work, as seen in Figure 7.21.

Many Facebook users have not filled out these fields in their profiles. However, Facebook continues to improve their profiles by slowly enticing more and more users to enter this type of "resume" information.

Because the fields are optional, you may need to look for more ways to reach these targets in the short term. Lack of matching on an educational or work target does not mean unmatched prospects do not have the education specified, or do not work at the company. It may simply mean they did not fill in this information in their profiles.

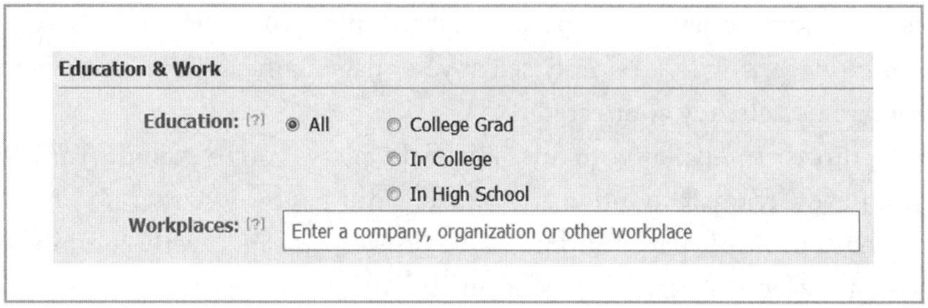

FIGURE 7.21–Education and Work Targeting

Education

The educational targeting can be brilliantly specific. You can target electrical engineering students at Berkeley who are graduating in specific years (see Figure 7.22). Why would you would want to reach these estimated 220 people with a custom message? If you were recruiting in the Bay area, it might be interesting to realize you could reach them for one or two dollars. It might also be a great way to advertise a campus group.

You can specifically target people who have education at the following levels:

· All levels
· College grad
· In college
· In high school

If your prospects are college grads, you can further target specific colleges and majors. If they are in college you can target colleges, majors, and expected graduation years. These targets are better for those currently in college, or high school. They are more likely to have entered this information accurately.

FIGURE 7.22–Connections on Facebook

Targeting Based on Where Someone Works

Facebook allows you to advertise directly to someone based on where they work. This addition to targeting opens up dramatic new, potential, B2B opportunities for Facebook ads. The work field allows you to target people who work at:

- Companies
- Societies
- Other workplaces

Trying to get a brand message established with employees of Ford Motor Company? Targeting white-collar workers? You can target with an ad those who self-identify as working at Ford Motor Company who also have a college degree (see Figure 7.23).

A CPM campaign would allow you to put a message in front of these employees 20 or 30 times for less than one business lunch. Have your click lead to a well-produced, animated video, and your prospects will be calling you.

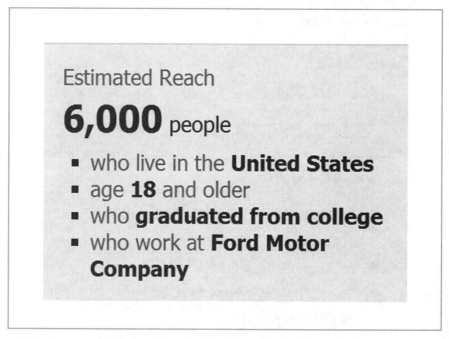

FIGURE 7.23–Targeting People with a College Degree Who Work at Ford Motor Company

MORE TARGETING IS ON ITS WAY

Facebook socially connects to its advertisers. You can be assured that it has hundreds of new features already suggested to improve targeting. Many will be added over the coming weeks, months, and years. The fundamentals, however, remain the same. You save money and have more effective ads by getting them in front of the right people.

There are an unlimited number of new targeting ideas that could be supported by the data Facebook collects. Facebook has to balance the interests of its advertisers with the privacy concerns of its users. As long as the users find the targeting a benefit and not a drawback, expect to see more and more targeting opportunities.

Someday it may be possible to advertise birthday party information to a mother, 30 days before her daughter's birthday, or flowers to a husband two weeks before his wife's birthday. You get the idea. Facebook has the potential to offer an unlimited number of specific interesting marketing targets. This will be fun.

ADVERTISING AND TARGETING REPORTS

It would be remiss to talk about targeting without requiring you to turn on the essential reports you need to evaluate your targeting choices. You should turn on these reports, which you can schedule in advance to run daily or weekly.

Set up now to have these reports generated automatically for you each week. To find the reports, go to your advertising management page. The "reports" menu is on the left side (see in Figure 7.24). Facebook has moved most navigation to the left hand side so always look there first for navigation and features.

Select the "scheduled reports" menu item and schedule a copy of each report Facebook currently offers. The scheduled reports dialogue looks like Figure 7.25. Initially use the default settings, name each report after its name, and have a copy emailed to you. These reports provide you with essential data for improving targeting over time.

Develop the habit of reviewing these reports to understand how your targeting works. These reports contain the answers to important questions about your ads:

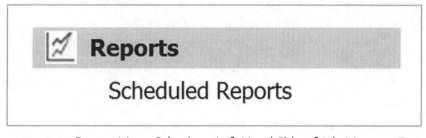

FIGURE 7.24–Report Menu Selection—Left-Hand Side of Ads Manager Page

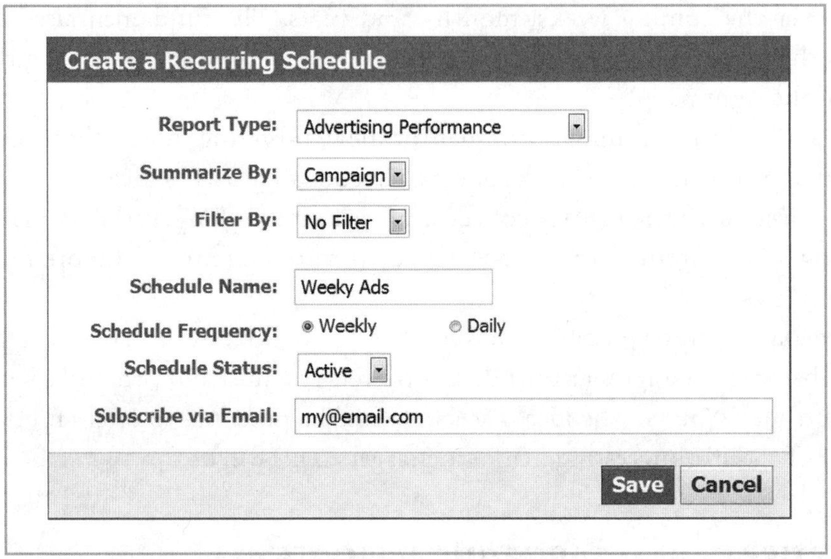

FIGURE 7.25–Dialogue to Create a Recurring Report

· What ads are getting clicks? See the "advertising performance report."
· Who is clicking in the ads? See the "responder demographics report."
· How long does it take to convert? See the "conversion by impression time reports."

Chapter Eight

That Quirky Little Image Is Everything

DRAMATICALLY IMPROVE YOUR CLICK-THROUGH RATES WITH BETTER IMAGES

Image is everything, at least for your Facebook ads. The ads are formatted by Facebook to project an image of the site as a friendly and social place. Facebook's goal is to have the ads "seamlessly integrate into the Facebook experience." Of course, your goal is a little different. You want to interrupt the users, force them to look at your ad, capture their interest, and compel them to click.

> "*The secret of all effective originality in advertising is not the creation of new and tricky words and pictures, but one of putting familiar words and pictures into new relationships.*"
>
> —LEO BURNETT

To stand out, you have to interrupt whatever the users were going to do and have them focus on you—your ad, your landing page. There are really only a few tools to help your ad stand out, the biggest being your ad image. Perhaps 80% of the click-effectiveness of your ad will be determined by the image you choose and the headline you provide for that image, with 70% coming from the image alone.

Images are so important to your ad that you should never fully convince yourself you really know what you are doing when you choose them. Instead, select and test lots of images and never stop trying new ones.

CAPTURE ATTENTION WITH YOUR IMAGE

The image should interrupt your target customer and make him want to look further at the ad. It has to catch the eye of the Facebook user and make her want to read your headline and your ad text.

So what images are more inclined to interrupt?

Well, clearly, overtly sexual images interrupt almost everyone. However, overtly sexual images that show "excessive amounts of skin, cleavage, or imply nudity" are forbidden by Facebook.

However, context is everything. So if you are selling swimsuits or beach vacations, bikinis are entirely in order, as shown in Figure 8.1. And we have seen some very clever necklace ads that feature their product draped over a very pronounced bust line.

FIGURE 8.1–Is This an Excessive Amount of Skin? Only Facebook Knows for Sure

Sexual images interrupt because they trigger our subconscious. To recognize images that have the potential to make a bigger impact, you should get into the habit of observing your own emotional reactions to images. If you are looking at 10 images on a page, which of the 10 immediately grabs your attention? Pay attention to your own physical reaction to an image, as that reaction may also indicate an attraction for your target audience.

Look for images that provoke your "lizard brain." Does the image stand out in the crowd and make you want to look more? We are looking for the same attraction as generated by sexual images but in images that are not forbidden by Facebook.

Here is the weird thing: if someone hunts up 10 images for you to consider for an ad, it is highly likely the image you do not like is the image that will perform best. Why? Because that image created in you an emotional response. It captured you emotionally enough to say, "I do not like that, Sam I am!"

That Seuss character could spot green eggs and ham a mile away. Put up an image with green eggs and ham on it and that guy could not help but click on it. If you don't like an image, chances are other people will not like that image, which means it will interrupt them and force them to look at it.

Images you strongly like or dislike, that make you go AWWWW, or laugh, or go "What on earth is that?" are the images you want to try first.

Use whatever tools you can to interrupt your audience, to get them to look. You get them to look first because of the image, then they read the headline, then they read the body text, and then, perhaps they click. And it may all happen in less than one second. If you get a positive or negative visceral response to an image, then that image interrupted you, too; it just may be a keeper.

USE PICTURES OF PEOPLE

Facebook is all about people, so look for images that include pictures of people. Pictures of people are the backbone and lifeblood of Facebook, and they make great images to include in your ad campaigns.

The following observations continually test true:

- Men look at women.
- Women look at women.
- Women also look at children.

No matter who you are targeting, it is hard to go wrong with pictures of women.

Selling to Married People?

Test pictures of happily married couples doing adventurous activities together. Capture both the happy couple and the sense of adventure. Or, pictures of what? We hope you said "angry couples," which will likely interrupt even better than pictures of happy couples.

Selling to Moms?

Test pictures of kids. Cute kids, dirty kids, happy kids, and what else? We hope you said "crying or screaming kids." Pictures of crying and screaming kids evoke a strong emotional reaction that interrupts. The crying child in Figure 8.2 was a very successful image for me that I still use today.

If you are looking at lots of pictures of kids, the crying kids are just like green eggs and ham—you spot them a mile away. Every mom immediately relates to a crying kid: "Yes, please, help me get this kid to stop crying!"

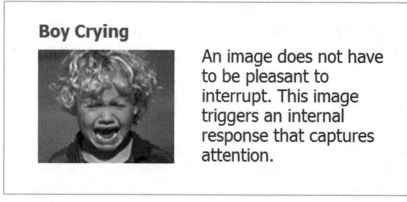

FIGURE 8.2–Images You Do Not Like May Be Great Triggers

Selling to Patients?

Test pictures of doctors. Or, at least, busty models pretending to be doctors wearing white coats and stethoscopes. I might even test a picture of a doctor who looks like they just survived a zombie apocalypse. I bet, at least, that picture would get your attention and the text wrote to support it would be fun. Don't spend too much time on it though, because it may get banned.

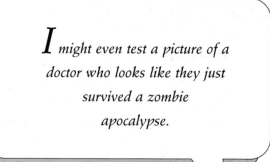

If you are selling to moms looking for a new dentist, a picture of a busty woman with a beautiful smile is almost guaranteed to work. Remember, women like to look at beautiful women, especially if they think the product may help them look beautiful, too.

Selling Dating Services?

Test pictures of the opposite sex within the same age range of your targeted prospects. This is specifically recommended by Facebook for dating ads. Teens want to see other teens. You can do this in Facebook by targeting different image ads based on the sex and age of your prospects.

Showing a picture of a 19-year-old girl to a single, 47-year-old man for your dating website is a little creepy, and it may not get you the response you are looking for. On the other hand, I bet it does interrupt.

Selling Vacations?

Show pictures of adventurous people doing something brave or seemingly dangerous!
If I were selling trips to New Zealand, I would definitely test images of bungee
jumpers, like the one in Figure 8.3.

Awesome Adventues

People on vacations like
to try new things.
Feature images of
awesome adventures.
Stand out from the
mundane.

FIGURE 8.3–Images of Adventure

WHERE ARE THEY LOOKING?

If you walk into a crowded room and look around at all the people, who do you
think you are more likely to notice?

· A person looking at her friend.
· A person looking directly at you.

Of course, you'll notice the person looking directly at you. It is a primal
response. Deep inside of your head your brain sees a person looking directly at you
as a possible threat or love interest—both get your attention.

All things being equal, images of people are more effective at interrupting when
they are looking directly at you, as is the image in Figure 8.4.

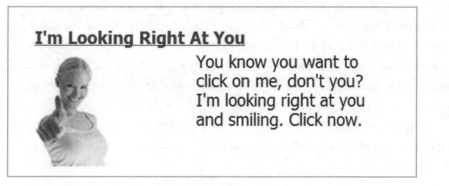

I'm Looking Right At You

You know you want to
click on me, don't you?
I'm looking right at you
and smiling. Click now.

FIGURE 8.4–People Looking at You Catch Your Attention

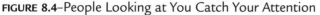

Figure 8.5 illustrates another automatic response we have, which is to look where other people are looking. On a landing page, have the image of a person looking directly at the action you desire. If you want them to press a button or fill out a form, post a picture of a person looking at the button or the form.

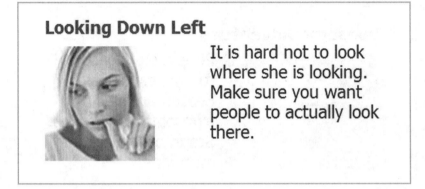

FIGURE 8.5–Have People Look at Action Items on Your Landing Page or in Your Ad

PICTURES OF THINGS

If about half of the ads in Facebook use pictures of people, the other half include pictures of things. If you have a picture of a thing, make it a good picture. If you are selling a digital camera and you include a poor quality picture of a digital camera, well, you get what you deserve.

Selling mortgages? Test a picture of a house.

Selling cameras? Test a picture of the camera.

Selling car insurance? Test a picture of a wrecked car. For male targets, use a picture of hot sports cars. For female targets, try pictures of a child safely buckled into a child car seat.

Selling pizza? Test a picture of a mouth-watering piece of pizza. For male customers, test a picture that combines pizza and football. For females, test pictures of children eating pizza. Does this sound too sexist? Then test the same picture for males and females and let the demographic reports sort them out for you. We bet, however, they sort the same way. But don't guess, test and see for yourself. Don't be afraid to harness stereotypes to your advantage. Many times, "stereotype" is just a not-so-sexy term for psychographics.

Selling tires locally? Test a picture of a tire, or a picture of a sexy girl who got dirty after changing a tire. Or a picture like the one in Figure 8.6 of a girl with a tire on her head.

FIGURE 8.6–Tires Are Not a Fashion Statement

Silly pictures can lead to interesting headlines and copy. The following ad copy jumps out of this ad:

Tires Are Not a Fashion Statement
The right tires will save your life.
Learn 5 essential questions to ask
when buying tires. Free video.

Selling jewelry? Sell romance; text that complements a close-up picture of a heart-shaped pendant draped over two lovely breasts.

Selling cat products? Test a picture of a cat. Or, better yet, test a picture of a kitten too. Or, better yet, test a picture of a cute, sexy girl holding and petting a kitten!

Just looking at the cute kitten in Figure 8.7 makes me want to click on the ad. In a situation like this one, the landing page should provide additional, immediate reward for the kitten lovers. How? More pictures of cute kittens!

FIGURE 8.7–People Who Love Kittens Are Triggered by Pictures of Kittens

We can think of 1,000,000 more ideas for images. TEST. Test lots and lots of different images.

The main thing to test: A picture of what you are selling!

This seems perhaps a bit too simple, but the reason it works is simple. If you are advertising tires for a local tire store, post a picture of a tire. In your community, somebody needs to buy tires for his or her car, right?

When this person sees the tire ad, he or she is actually interrupted by the image of a tire. Why? Because he or she is already spending some mental energy thinking about the need to buy tires soon. The tire image triggers these individuals. Now, do you have something interesting to say to this potential customer?

PICTURES WITH WORDS

Facebook lets you include text in the image, and it adds a new dimension to your ad. If you include a word or two in your picture, it is essential to include text that is readable in the very tiny image size available. Many images we have seen with text are truly awful, with text that is unreadable.

Done properly, text in the image box will be much more visually powerful than the headline—meaning it will be read first.

These images are really, really small, so pay attention to the text in the image and to the contrast between text color and background color. Contrast needs to be high, like that in Figure 8.8, for the text to be readable.

FIGURE 8.8–The Words Embedded in This Image Will Be More Powerful than the Headline

PICTURES OF WORDS

A powerful technique you should test is simply making the entire image a word that is a trigger word for your target audience. What are some examples of making your entire image a word?

A language tool has as its image the words, "LEARN FRENCH," as shown in Figure 8.9.

A movie theater has as its image the word, "CINEMA."

A local cupcake shop has as its image the words, "HEY Cupcake!"

Of course, these words can be really simple or very fancy. They can be all one color or every letter can be a different color from the rainbow. Images that include text may be endlessly creative with different fonts, styles, shapes and colors. And they may be framed in different colors, too, if you simply change the background color around the text in an image.

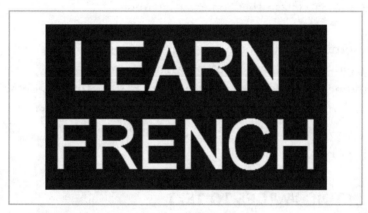

FIGURE 8.9–Everyone Will Read These Words

How many times have you driven by a highway billboard that interested you—but it was so crammed with text you couldn't read it? Facebook images are micro-billboards. So please, if you use text in your images, take a long, hard look at the image text and ask yourself "Is this easily readable?"

If it not easily readable, then go back to the drawing board and start again. If a word image works well for your business, continually changing its color, background, and framing helps prevent ad fatigue.

STRANGE OR SILLY IMAGES

The goal is attention. So don't be afraid to try strange or silly images like the one in Figure 8.10. Be the shiny new object—the most interesting thing on the page. Ads that fall into this category tend to fatigue more slowly.

The boy's eyes looking up and the slight smirk on his face tell an interesting story all on their own.

Groupon ran an ad recently with an image of a little baby pig in red rain boots standing in the mud. You cannot help but want to click on the little pig. It is

FIGURE 8.10–Silly Image That Somehow Interrupts

adorable. Unfortunately the landing page after you clicked on the little pig was the same boring, old Groupon sign-up offer—what a waste.

If the landing page had been a Facebook page full of more adorable baby pig pictures or videos, Groupon might have been able to get that page to go viral, and still include their discount offer on the page. Groupon, are you reading this? We want more baby pigs!

CONNECTING IMAGES TO TEXT

Finding new images can be fun. Thinking up new copy for your ad can be difficult. Use new images you discover to inspire new text—new headlines and body text. Use new images to start a new story. Make the story good enough, and you get the click.

A mother told me a story about her daughter so enjoying using HomeSchool Advantage that she asked for an alarm clock to wake her up in the morning. When I saw the image in Figure 8.11, it reminded me of the testimonial, and I decided to share the story in an ad. The ad performed very well.

FIGURE 8.11–Use a New Image to Inspire a New Story

ONCE YOU FIND SOME GOOD IMAGES, FIND SOME MORE

No matter how good your images are, your ads will fatigue with time. And your ad will fatigue even though there are still many new customers on Facebook who will want to purchase from you; they just don't want to click on your tired, old ad with that tired, old image.

Even before you first turn on a new ad, you should be planning for how to keep your ad going with new images after ad fatigue sets in. The first time you create an ad, go looking for at least three different images that can support the ad. Then plan from the very beginning to rotate multiple images through each and every ad—without necessarily even changing the text.

Some of your customers will be interrupted by people crying, some by people covered in finger paint, and some by people smiling; you need to plan to use all three. Other people will not be interrupted by a person at all but will pause for the picture of a delicious cupcake. We want them all, for with the same ad we can rotate in the picture of crying, painting, and smiling people, and cupcakes too.

The good news is that images are so powerful in Facebook that you do not need to struggle to create the perfect headline and body text for the ad anymore. Seriously, in search advertising you are frequently sweating every last hyphen to make an ad work. In Facebook, mediocre ad copy with a funny image may get a ton of reasonably priced clicks—it is great!

It is easy to change the image and get dramatically better CTR in Facebook. It is harder to see a dramatic improvement just by changing the text. This is great news for beginners, because it is a lot easier to find compelling images than to write compelling copy. Simply learn to take careful note of images that catch your attention and use those images.

IMAGE EXTREME MAKEOVERS

You can add a border to an older image or change an image's background color as a way to refresh the ad, enhance the image, and fight ad fatigue. Test different colors and styles, as shown in Figure 8.12. Have something that is boldly colored—a bright color such as yellow, hot pink, hot orange, hot green—something like that. That's a shiny new object. Liven things up a bit.

QUICK-DRAW ADS

Two gunslingers slowly enter into the dusty street of a frontier town, faces grim. It is a faceoff. They are about to shoot it out and settle their scores like men.

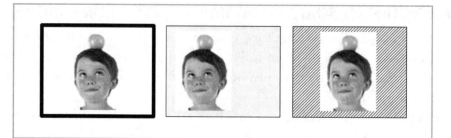

FIGURE 8.12–Try Different Colors and Textures Around Your Image

The shopkeepers, seeing men with cool determination in their eyes and guns on their hips, dive for cover. Mothers hustle children to safety.

A challenge of nerves, speed, and skills is about to occur. If you can draw fast and shoot true—victory is yours. Speed is essential, but so is accuracy.

Men already practiced in the fine art of quick draw show no fear. Their lives depend on the quality of their practice.

Your life does, too.

Not as dramatically, of course. But your life as a Facebook ad-slinger is totally dependent on your ability to produce and test new ads quickly.

How quickly can you go to your favorite image site, find a new image, duplicate a working existing ad, upload a new image, and launch the new ad?

How quickly can you do the same adjusting the title and copy, too?

See if you can do this in seven minutes or less. Practice the art of ad-slinging. It will still take some time for Facebook to approve your ad—but that is not the challenge. The challenge is: Can you get in the habit of creating new and exciting ads without making it a long and laborious process?

Your mission, should you choose to accept it, is to survive in the world of advertising by developing the skills to move fast and move true.

Draw!

HELP, MY BEST-PERFORMING IMAGE JUST GOT REJECTED

Facebook requires that your images be relevant to your product or service. Images of beach-bathing beauties in swimsuits are fine if you are selling swimsuits, but will likely be rejected by Facebook if you are selling tablet computers. If your ad was rejected but you think your image was relevant, create another ad and submit it again. Different reviewers will have different perspectives on images in ads.

Facebook is trying to be a family-friendly place. Although you are supposed to be at least 13 years old to create an account, it is almost certain that even younger children are present. Facebook immediately deletes those younger users when it finds them. Facebook seeks to balance freedom of expression with prudent censorship in a single site that crosses all traditional boundaries of cultures and state. It is almost a guarantee that Facebook will piss off everybody everywhere eventually.

Facebook reviewers will make mistakes.

If you think they have made a mistake with your ad, you do not have much recourse. Submit it again and fill out a contact form. If you spend enough money, send an email directly to your Facebook contact. Otherwise, crank out another ad.

Once I had my best-performing ad rejected when I changed a target. The reviewer claimed the ad was violating some sort of policy but was unspecific about how. This was an ad that had already been displayed millions of times to other targets.

So I waited a few days, created a new ad from the ground up that was exactly the same, and submitted it again. Accepted. Remember, there are humans in the chain, and different humans will have different opinions about what is acceptable.

By the way, my rejected ad was totally relevant and contained absolutely nothing remotely objectionable. Not even close. You could display the ad in church on Easter Sunday and nobody would take offense. Go figure.

FINDING IMAGES

You can find free images online in places like Wikimedia Commons (http://commons.wikimedia.org). Never use an image you find on the internet unless you know its license allows you to use it in an ad. The license terms for images in Wikimedia Commons are included with the images.

Such excellent, low-cost commercial images are available that it is easy to use an image with a clear knowledge of its license. Unless you purchased images 20 years ago for commercial use, you have no idea how amazingly reasonable and simple this is. It is the best money you will ever invest in your ad. Some places to look for images:

- *Fotolia* (http://us.fotolia.com/) offers high-quality, commercial images for low prices, often for $1 to $4. The site's smallest images are frequently sized 400 x 300 pixels at 72 dpi and can sometimes be loaded directly into Facebook without additional cropping.
- *iStockPhoto* (http://www.istockphoto.com/) carries excellent photos, although they can be a bit pricey.

In all cases, when using images you did not create, remember to confirm that the copyright holder will allow for the commercial use of the image on a site like Facebook.

Image Size

Your image should generally try to fill as much of the available space as possible. Use the space to actively try to interrupt the Facebook user. If you have white space in your image, it should be because you are trying to cleverly use the white space. Grab all the screen real estate you can to capture your user's attention. Facebook ads must carry the following:

- *Image dimensions*: 110 pixels wide x 80 pixels tall.
- *Size restriction*: No image may be larger than 5 MB.

Images that are not 110 pixels x 80 pixels will be resized by Facebook. If you do not know what an aspect ratio is and how images resize and rescale, now is the time to learn. Your best rule, if you want the user to truly see the image you want them to see, is to upload an image as close to 110 pixels x 80 pixels as possible.

The aspect ratio of an image is the ratio of the width of the image to its height. The ratio is usually expressed as two numbers separated by a colon, as x:y. Facebook suggests an aspect ratio 4:3 or 16:9 for uploaded images, so if you upload larger images without the appropriate ratio of horizontal to vertical pixels, your final image will not look right.

SOFTWARE TO EDIT IMAGES

If you are going to advertise on Facebook, you need to get some software that will let you do basic editing of images. Here are some different free packages you can consider:

- *PicNik* (www.picnikcom/). An image and photo editing site that lets you edit your pictures online. Nothing to install. For more advanced editing features, you can pay extra.
- *ShrinkPictures* (http://shrinkpicturescom/). An online service for resizing and publishing photos. Nothing to install. It integrates directly with Facebook for publishing photos to your user accounts.
- *Paint.net* (www.getpaint.net/). Image and photo editing software for Windows computers, meant to provide the features seen in Microsoft Paint. This software downloads and installs on your computer.
- *Dr.Pic* (http://drpic.com/). A primitive and simple tool to resize, crop, rotate, and perform other, basic operations online in a web browser. If you find a large image on Wikimedia Commons and you just want to crop it and get it down to 110 x 80 pixels, this free tool will do the job. Nothing to install.

The web is a dynamic place, but know this: there will always be some site offering this service for free. To find one, search for the phrase "free alternatives to Photoshop and other graphic editor software" and you will always find more tools you can use to edit images.

SORRY, ANIMATORS!

Facebook does not allow for animated or flash images in its standard ads. Seriously, think how obnoxious the site would become if they gave us a tool that powerful to visually interrupt its users. Even I might stop using Facebook.

Chapter Nine

Nobody Ever Regretted Mastering This $10,000 Per Hour Skill

YOUR NEW $10,000 PER HOUR CAREER

How would you like a job that paid up to $10,000 an hour? The good news is, you may already have that job. The bad news is, to have an hour's worth of effort return $10,000 you have to write an absolutely killer ad and sales copy. In the ad business, this is called copywriting, and great copywriting can make or break a business.

Give me a so-so product with the world's best copywriter, and I will sell millions of dollars worth of the product. Give me a great product and a bad copywriter, and the company may go bankrupt. This is not fair, but it is true. There is a reason top copywriters are among the best-paid professionals on the planet.

In advertising, copywriting is king. And if you can write an ad that gets the world to stop and take notice, you are worth your weight in gold. If you write a landing page that leads to a sale, then you have created an online money machine.

This is not necessarily easy. Getting John Q. Public to pry open his wallet and give you his credit card is challenging. It may well be the most difficult task you have ever

> "*I*f you don't like what's being said, change the conversation."
>
> —DON DRAPER

undertaken, especially if the transaction is online. Your customer is at home, sitting at his computer, bored, and probably lazy, and getting him to do anything is a chore. Getting him to pay you is a miracle.

By the time a Facebook user gets to your message, she has already been exposed to as many as 3,000 advertising messages that day! Advertising from radio, TV, newspapers, billboards, placards, store signs, and websites have all tried to catch her attention.

Logos on T-shirts, cups, and boxes; sexual images, sensual images, happy images, funny images, and cute images have already been used to try to attract the attention of your prospects. Each one of them has been assaulted by direct mail, telemarketers, network marketers, nonprofits, and more—3,000 have already been fended off.

There is a reason corporations spend more than half a trillion dollars (trillion with a "T") annually trying to make their products seem attractive, interesting, and worthy of buying. This is the fray you choose to enter when you run an ad: to get John Q.'s attention in a world saturated with advertising,

There is a reason that good copywriting is the hardest skill to hire out. There is so much work in copywriting that some people make a living writing ads without ever really getting very good at it. And, those who do get really good at it will eventually figure out they can make the most money selling something of their own. Some retire. And if they work, it is as much for the challenge as for the money.

In addition, copywriting, for those who are truly masters at it, is not always that much fun to do for other people. Even when the world's best copywriter writes the world's best ad, more than likely the client will want to change it. The world's best copywriters get tired of defending their ideas to people who do not, and cannot, recognize great copy. So, if they have already bagged their cash, they give up and go home. Too painful to try to consult.

This puts the typical entrepreneur in a bit of a pickle. You find you have to acquire another skill—you need to learn how to write your own ad copy. You need to learn how to write it, test it, and measure it.

Because copywriting is so essential, even if you choose to contract this work out, you still need to know how to objectively evaluate the results, at least. It is OK, even recommended, that you write bad ads at first. The key is, how fast can you recognize the ad is bad and replace it with one that works? I actually recommend that you write bad ads because if some of your ads are not bad, it means you are not trying enough different approaches.

Another reason you should at least try to write your own copy is because nobody else will ever be as insightful, passionate, or interested in all the fine nuances of the business as you, the entrepreneur. Your passion and insight lead to great copy.

Your job is tricky. It is to get Jane Q. Public so interested and engaged in your message that she ignores the 3,000 other messages coming at her this day. Instead, she focuses on yours. She gets so excited, engaged, and interested that she can't think about anything else. She has to have what you sell. She has to have it now!

DIFFERENT GOALS AT DIFFERENT TIMES

Different copy has different goals at different times. Do you know the goal of writing a resume? The goal of writing a resume is to get the interview. That is it. In most cases, the resume doesn't get you the job, the interview does. However, to get the interview you need the resume.

If you forget the goal, you make serious errors in writing the resume, like making it too long.

Your Facebook ad is like the resume. It is not trying to close the deal, it is just trying to get the click. What can you say in your ad to get the click?

CAPTAIN HOOK

Your ad may have all of a quarter of a half of a second to try to capture your prospect's attention—to hook the user. A half of a second is how long it takes for your prospect to see your image and read your headline.

Facebook describes your ad as a headline and body text. This is likely how the ad is read. If the image is interesting, they read the headline. If the headline speaks to them, they read the body text—all of this process is incredibly quick.

Your entire ad itself is also a headline. It is a headline to the experience readers will receive if they click! Your ad is a headline that makes a promise to the user. When they click on the ad, they get to experience the story told on your landing page.

Your ad needs to be so compelling that it draws those who read it to continue to experience your story on your landing page. If they don't click, they feel bad. They regret not clicking later. That is a true hook.

INSANELY GOOD TITLES

Insanely good titles have one thing in common—they all trigger emotions.

If the image is the lure drawing wandering eyes over to your ad, then your title is the hook. Give it a slight jerk and try to catch your prospects' thoughts. Connect a word or phrase in your title to the emotional trigger in your readers.

Something they love or hate. Something of deep interest or importance to them. The easiest way to do this is to have the title contain the psychographic target word. If that word is the name of someone famous they admire, it is really very easy.

Targeting members of the Jaycees service organization? "Jaycees" is probably a good word for the title.

Targeting Saint Bernard lovers? "St. Bernard" is a good candidate, too.

Targeting fans of Van Halen? Hard to go wrong with "Van Halen" somewhere in the title. In fact, for something with such strong affinity, it is hard to beat "Do You Love Van Halen Too?"

You get the idea. It is actually amazingly simple to create a great headline in Facebook once you know the psychographic target.

When I target "home-schooling" parents, the vast majority of my best-performing ads have the word "home school" in one form or another in the title. Why? Because it is a trigger word for that psychographic. The ad in Figure 9.1 performed amazingly well for months with a silly picture, a three-word headline for ADHD parents, and body text that made an interesting promise.

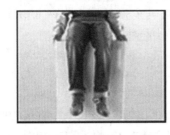

FIGURE 9.1–Psychographic Trigger in the Headline

COMPELLING BODY TEXT WITH A CALL TO ACTION

Make an offer in your ad that you deliver on your landing page. If you claim "Scientific research ends tooth decay," then make a call to action (read it now) and offer immediate access to a white paper, audio, or video on your landing page. A call to action is always best when it is explicitly stated.

Include the image from the ad on the landing page, and conversion rates will improve even more! The repeated image offers greater comfort and consistency to visitors and lets them know they are in the right spot to continue the story.

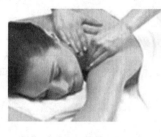

Best Present Ever

A soothing massage can relax you like a summer vacation. Makes a great gift! Click to save 50% on your next massage.

FIGURE 9.2–A Very Clear Call to Action

The body text in the ad is the start of the story you continue on your landing page. Make it as interesting a story as possible. Make a compelling offer—click to save 50%!

The massage seen in Figure 9.2 triggers pleasant memories in anyone who has ever enjoyed a massage. The headline implies a great present to give or receive. The body text begins the story, "a soothing massage can relax you like a summer vacation." It has a very clear call to action—"click" to save 50% on your next massage!

The body text makes a compelling offer with a call to action. The offer is why the user clicks. The call to action encourages "click."

If you are an auto mechanic, offer a coupon for a "Free Brake Inspection." Deliver the coupon on your landing page or immediately after a user clicks "like."

Immediately delivering on the offer builds credibility and begins the front porch relationship. No matter what you are selling, always find a way to make an attractive offer in the body text of your ad.

If You Are Selling	You May Offer
Cupcakes	A Free Cupcake
Training	A Free Lecture
Dental Services	A Free Teeth Whitening
Tires	A Free Tire Inspection
Restaurant Experience	A Free Birthday Meal
Marketing Services	Free Tips Video
Printer's Ink	A List of Seven Ways To Save Money on Printing
Software Development	A Free Guide on How To Stop Projects From Failing

Do you see a pattern here? Marketing on the front porch is about giving things away. Lemonade, snickerdoodles, or free advice. If you are a dentist trying to find a lifetime customer, you may want to give away something bigger.

The "free" word is a powerful word.

We frequently give away free information such as a "Free Guide" or "7 Secrets to _____" where you can fill in the blank based on your business. People like lists, people like secrets, and people like free.

POWER WORDS TO TRIGGER EMOTIONAL RESPONSE

Set your hook with powerful words. If you search for "words that sell," you will get hits on all sorts of different power words used in advertising. Take a look at these lists. Get your mind flowing with words that have the power to trigger emotional responses.

See what emotional response you have to the words. "Amazing" makes me want to smile. "Lifetime" make me feel more secure. How do these words affect you?

Words do not have to be positive to trigger emotional response and interest. "Defeat" is a powerful word that may be negative or positive depending on the phrase.

There is a reason you see certain words over and over again in ads—they work. SALE captures almost everybody's attention. A compelling ad appeals to the prospect's emotions, needs, desires, and dreams. A single word in your headline can dramatically improve your ad's effectiveness if it captures your prospect's attention, and excites, motivates, and compels the user to click.

Here are some words to get your juices flowing when writing headlines and copy. These are words that advertisers have had luck with in the past. Slowly read through the list. Say each word out loud. What—if any—emotions does each word trigger in you?

A—Absolutely, Achieve, Act, Amazing, Anybody, Astonishing, Automatically

B—Bargain, Believe, Benefit, Best, Bewitched, Big, Bigger, Biggest, Bonus

C—Creative, Clouds, Colorful, Colossal, Competitive, Confidential, Conquer

D—Dream, Defeat, Delivered, Demand, Desire, Direct, Discount, Dominate

E—Easy, Easily, Endorsed, Enchanted, Enormous, Excellent, Exciting, Expert, Explained

F—Famous, Forbidden, Forever, Fortune, Free, Full, Fundamentals

G—Guarantee, Guaranteed

H—Health, Healthy, Heart, Helpful, Hidden, Highest, How (How to), Huge

I—Immediate, Immediately, Improved, Informative, Inspire, Interesting

J—Join

K—King

L—Launching, Lifetime, Like, Limited, Love, Luxury

M—Magic, Mammoth, Money

N—New

O—Obsession, Outstanding

P—Passionate, Perspective, Pioneering, Popular, Powerful, Practical, Professional, Profitable, Proven

Q—Quick, Quickly

R—Rare, Reliable, Revealing, Remarkable, Revolution, Revolutionary, Reward

S—Safe, Safely, Sale, Save, Scarce, Secret, Secrets, Secure, Sensational, Simple, Sizable, Skilled, Special (Special Offer), Strong, Sturdy, Successful, Suddenly, Super, Superior, Surging, Surprise

T—Tasty, Temptation, Terrific, Tested, Tremendous, True

U—Ultimate, Unconditional, Unique, Unlimited, Unparalleled, Urgent, Useful

V—Valuable, Virgin

W—Wealth, Weird, Wild, Wonderful

Y—Yes, You, Your

As you work in your business, make your own list of words your audience is specifically attracted to. Keep both lists handy when writing new ads. If you are blocked, just pick a word from each list and see what happens when you put the words together. You are seeking to create powerful word combinations to trigger an emotional response.

How many power words can you spot in the ad in Figure 9.3?

A need is stated clearly in the headline. An attractive woman looks up toward the headline statement with a bit of whimsy and contemplation. The body text makes a simple promise with power words sprinkled liberally throughout the text.

Here is a quick test. So what is missing in the ad in Figure 9.3?

Did you say, "A clear call to action?"

It is implied in the text but could be made stronger. Test different calls to action with your ads to see what converts best: *Click now. Free guide. Click for free guide. Click for free video. Click for list. Like.* Test them all. See if one outperforms the others.

Need a Present for Him?

7 amazing gift ideas your man will absolutely love— guaranteed!

FIGURE 9.3–How Many Power Words Can You Spot in This Ad?

FACEBOOK LIKES AND INTERESTS

This is Facebook. We don't have to guess at the words our customers respond to. For those who "like" our pages and set their profiles to be public, we can see tens of thousands of fan pages they have already "liked"! We can review these page titles to discover words that our fans (our targeted psychographic) have already responded to! These words, commonly found on our "HomeSchool" fans lists of likes and interests, are golden:

> awesome, candid, chaos, clever, coupons, executive, exclusive, fun, games, home, imagination, natural, solution, freebies, fun, ministries, mom, natural, soothing.

How may these words work together as a headline if we combine the psychographic target with words that our audience already responds to? There are countless ways! Some examples:

- Clever HomeSchool Games
- HomeSchool Chaos Solutions
- Mom's HomeSchool Coupons

Words right out of our prospects' profiles. What words appear frequently on your fan's likes and interests? The more fans you collect, the more words you capture, the better you can find common words that naturally appeal to your fans.

PLAIN, CONQUERING, ENDEARING, HEROIC, SARCASTIC, HYPED, COMPASSIONATE, AND SENSUAL COPY

Men often do not discover until they are married that their voice has a tone. They need their wives to tell them—and they do. Everyone has a tone, and in ad copy you should actively choose to create a tone. Name your tones in terms like Romantic, Sensual, Endearing, Conquering, Heroic, Hyped, Compassionate, Sensual, Friendship, to help give them meaning and identity when you write.

When writing ad copy, select a tone you believe may be appropriate for your targeted demographic. Write an ad in that tone and write an ad in an opposite tone. See which ones your users like better. Or put multiple tones into rotation since a different tone may appeal to the same person on a different day.

Certain words lend themselves to different tones:

· *Sensual*: love, kiss, caress, magic, moon, heart, secret, forbidden, virgin, lover, lure, forever.
· *Conquering*: destroy, decimate, achieve, conquer, smash, crush, extract, overthrow, beat, skunk
· *Endearing*: cute, puppy, kitten, adorable, pretty, sweet, poignant, affection.

Other tones require more than one word to pull off:

· *Hyped*: world's lowest prices, make money now, crazy discounts, limited time offer.
· *Compassionate*: I feel your pain, find relief.

Here are some examples of writing a headline using different tones:

· *Boring*: Lose 10 Pounds
· *Conquering*: Destroy Fat Forever
· *Sensual*: Love Your Body Again

SELL A BENEFIT, NOT A PRODUCT

Write a headline that features your benefit, not your product. Feature what you plan to deliver to your customers to make their lives better and more exciting. If possible, be specific. "Flatten your belly" is a good headline. "Lose 10 Pounds in 5 Days" is a better headline. It tells the prospects exactly what you can do for them. If you could follow "Lose 10 Pounds in 5 Days" with the phrase "without ever being hungry," now you would really have people's attention.

Benefit-delivering headlines:

· Magical 6% Monthly Return
· Grow CTR 29% in 5 Minutes
· Sleep Like a Little Baby
· Land a $100,000 Dream Job

These headlines are not selling a system or a product; they are selling a dream. If you are selling a dream like a "Magical 6% Monthly Return," you can even feature the benefit of the benefit. What do you get if you make all that money?

· Retire Early with Millions
· Travel the World with No Worries
· Create a Financial Legacy

COMMIT TO STUDYING COPYWRITING

If you want your business to be a success, commit a few hours every month to studying copywriting. We can only scratch the surface of the subject of copywriting in a book on paid Facebook advertising. This topic can and does fill volumes. Some of the best copy on copywriting is actually quite old and can even be found for free online.

· *The Robert Collier Letter Book* by Robert Collier
· *Advertising Secrets of the Written Word* by Joe Sugarman
· *On Writing* by Stephen King
· *Outrageous Advertising That's Outrageously Successful* by Bill Glazer
· *Scientific Advertising* by Claude Hopkins

SUCCESSFUL ADS STILL FAIL

Successful ads must do more than deliver high CTR. That sounds a bit strange, but it's true. There are multiple measures of success. The one reported by Facebook is CTR, click-through rate. Unfortunately, CTR is a very poor measure of true success. To succeed, you need people to do a lot more than click. You need them to purchase. An ad that gets you a lot of clicks but no sales is a failure. It is that simple.

One of the hardest things to learn how to do is to turn off an ad that is driving you a lot of clicks. You turn it off because it isn't giving you any sales.

Always remember your ad is just the first step of a more complex ecosystem. A good ad complements the landing page and leads the prospect to an eventual sale. If no one ever buys from the ad then something is broken.

Your landing page is the story behind your ad. It is a mistake to create your ad without first building your landing page, because the ad is the headline to the compelling offer you deliver on your landing page.

The ad provides

· an image,
· a headline,

· a compelling offer.

The landing page provides

· a short description of what you provide (bullets are a good idea here if using text);
· an explanation of how you get it;
· a promise not to violate your trust (privacy policy, no spam);
· the opt-in form itself.

Although we will cover this concept in more detail in a chapter on landing pages, let's introduce the topic here. The goal of your landing page is not to make an immediate sale. It is to engage your prospects in "front porch" conversations by capturing their information and beginning the process.

What you are offering in your ad and on your landing page may not be your product at all!

Instead, your ad and your landing page are themselves simply hooks—hooks to entice your visitor to engage in further front porch communications. Hooks may be

· product samples;
· webinars or teleseminars;
· packets of valuable email information (seven secrets to health and happiness);
· packets of valuable mailed information;
· software to download;
· audios to listen to;
· videos to watch.

When you write your ad, you are writing to get a specific result on your landing page. That result is the beginning of a front porch conversation. Your ad sells your front porch!

If you do not get a real result from your ad, a measurable response that starts a front porch conversation, then the ad has failed. Even if the ad delivered a lot of clicks.

More accurately, if you do not get opt-ins for additional conversations, then the ad, the landing page, or both have failed you.

AUTOMATIC HEADLINES

If you set your ad's landing page as a Facebook page, event, group, or application, then the ad headline is selected for you automatically by Facebook. This makes selecting the name of a Facebook destination (which is difficult to change) extremely important because that name will be your ad headline unless you specifically target those destinations using the "external URL" selection.

Unfortunately, there is one problem with using the external URL to target pages within Facebook. You lose the social credibility indicators when targeting external URLs. Your prospects no longer see the total number of people who have already "liked" the destination, nor can they see which of their friends have already liked the destination. Your prospect is not provided with the opportunity to directly like the ad. All of these are big losses.

This is a tradeoff to be aware of if you use a custom headline to an internal Facebook target. If possible, test many headlines first and name your Facebook pages based on the best-testing headlines.

Chapter Ten

The Power of Hidden Psychological Triggers

WRITE IN THOUGHTS

Deciding to write ads puts you into a unique and new category—a thought writer. Your writing puts thoughts in other people's heads. You change what they think, what they believe, and what they do. If you do it correctly, they don't even notice that your thoughts have become their thoughts. They don't even notice as they bend to your will.

Do it well, and you join Don Draper and the other Mad Men—influencing for better or for worse the hearts and minds of the people of the world.

> "*Advertising is not a science, it is persuasion, and persuasion is an art, it is intuition that leads to discovery, to inspiration, it is the artist who is capable of making the consumer feel desire.*"
>
> —BILL BERNBACH

If you choose to take on this new role in the Matrix, you are choosing to take the red pill. Your eyes are about to be opened. You can no longer be blissfully unaware of the nature of the advertising around you. You can no longer be a passive consumer of advertising. You must now become its master.

Have you ever heard people say "Advertising doesn't affect me" as they drink a Coke and chomp on a Big Mac, their feet clad in Nikes?

Neo, if you take the blue pill, you wake up in your bed and believe whatever you want to believe. Go ahead, dear consumer, keep thinking that advertising doesn't affect you.

You can no longer afford to be so naive. Take off the blinders, open your eyes, and learn to take a deep look at the world of advertising.

Begin to look at the messages around you. Ask yourself: Where do they come from? Why are they placed here? How are they measured? Are they effective?

You are now asking yourself these questions. You are a marketing maniac.

Specifically examine direct response advertising where the customer has to complete an action "now" for the ad to be effective. Watch to see if those same ads continue to run over time. If they do, there is a good chance they are actually working. Time to understand why, so you can do it, too.

DIRECT ATTACK ADS

Type "weight loss" into a search engine and instantly see ads for weight loss products. In fact, you only see ads for weight loss products. Same with arthritis; type "arthritis" into a search and you see ads for pain medications and clinics.

When you do an internet search, you type in your immediate need and interest. You are looking for it "right now." Ads that speak directly to what you are searching for "right now" are direct attack ads. There is very little nuance to this. Search advertising comes at you head-on and at full speed. None of the ads catch you by surprise.

RIGHT ANGLE MARKETING

But here is a secret the masters of marketing understand. Ads do not have to come at you head-on. They can also approach from the side—from a right angle to your direct line of vision. Visible only out of the corner of your eye.

Right angle marketing, originally a concept for masters of search and print advertising, is especially powerful on Facebook. Right angle marketing is advertising a product or service not based on users' immediate needs, but on

· who they are,
· where they hang out,
· what they believe,

regardless of what they happen to be doing right this minute.

What makes the sale a right angle? Selling a product that is not "obvious" to sell to your target customers.

For example, a group of people love the tiny dog breed shih tzu. Advertising veterinary services to someone who likes shih tzus is direct attack marketing. A good direct attack at a shih tzu lover for a veterinarian in Facebook is an ad that says you "specialize" in the needs of this specific breed. Great ad. But not a right angle.

So, what might be a right angle ad to a shih tzu owner? That is the problem. You don't know. It isn't obvious.

It may be the case that shih tzu owners are five times more likely to purchase a Caribbean cruise than the average American. This would be a right angle. If it were true, you would run Caribbean cruise ads to people who own shih tzus—but how would you ever know that?

Maybe shih tzu owners are often Jewish women in New York City. If that's true, how would you figure that out?

Most people treat Facebook as another method of search advertising. They only come at their prospects head-on. Facebook demands a bit more finesse. Facebook requires more right angle marketing. A hidden power in Facebook is that it can help you discover these right angles.

Facebook will help you discover ways to connect to your prospects that you never imagined. Discovering ways to increase CTR and conversions that are only obvious in hindsight.

Does this really happen?

All the time.

CONNECTING PEOPLE TO MARITAL BLISS

Before the internet took off, people mainly dated and married people who lived in the same town. Only a few pioneers embraced the idea of dating and marrying strangers. Only a few hearty souls were relationship pioneers. One was my friend, who I'll call Bob. Bob ran a mail-order bride service for Christian, single men. He helped connect Christian, American men to Christian, Filipino women.

Bob ran advertisements, did lead generation, and sent letters to guys talking about how it was hard to find a woman who shared their values. "Wouldn't it be nice to find a woman with character who wasn't just after your money and wouldn't leave you when the going got tough? Are you sick and tired of our decadent society where people are so disloyal and divorce is so common?" This message resonated with his audience.

Bob advertised in all of the easy-to-spot locations. Specifically, in magazines read by Christian men. The business was a success. Connections were made,

CONNECTING PEOPLE TO MARITAL BLISS, continued

and marriages resulted. Bob, of course, wanted to figure out how to grow the business even more.

We were in a group with Dan Kennedy, and Dan asked the right angle question, "Are there any idiosyncrasies that your customers have in common? Where they hang out? Hobbies? The type of work they do? Something other than just being Christian men?"

Bob said "Well, I don't know." Dan said, "Why don't you find out?"

So he did.

When we got together again Bob had discovered something significant. Over half of his customers had the same job: 50% of them were truckers!

Bob had never noticed this before. In hindsight it made sense. Driving over the road is a hard and lonely job. Lots of time away from home, making it hard on existing relationships and even harder to start new ones. Truck drivers, as an occupation, needed relationship help. The need was so acute that these men were willing to try brides from overseas.

Advertising to truckers was a right angle approach to reach potential customers. A right angle totally changes your approach to a market.

Bob could now put ads in trucking magazines and fliers and signs at truck stops.

Bob could write new ads in the language of trucking, making his prospects feel immediately at home. His business skyrocketed.

Most customer bases have something in common that is not initially obvious, just like Bob's. Once you learn this new connection, a whole set of new opportunities emerges. Not only can you place new ads in new locations, but you can write ad copy to appeal to the specific psychographic. You, just like Bob, can leverage right angle knowledge everywhere in your business.

RIGHT ANGLE IMMERSION ASSIGNMENT

Today I am going to give you a right angle advertising immersion assignment. Make a trip to your local library, newsstand, or bookstore where you find many different magazines. There are thousands of magazines available on specialty interests: knitting, horses, history, cars, guns, cooking, etc., and a selection of the more popular ones should be easy to get your hands on.

Grab a stack of these magazines and head to a location where you can sit down and study them.

Take a magazine like *American Civil War History* and flip through it a page at a time. Look at each advertisement in the magazine. Ask yourself one question: Is this advertisement obvious or a surprise?

An obvious advertisement in an American Civil War history magazine is an ad for Abraham Lincoln DVDs, because the ad is "on topic." If the ad comes straight-on at the interest being represented by the magazine, it is obvious. In our *Civil War History* magazine, obvious advertisements would include

- Civil War re-enactor gear,
- Civil War history books and videos,
- Any history books and videos,
- Tours of Gettysburg.

It does not take marketing insight or genius to target selling Civil War costumes to people who buy an *American Civil War History* magazine. This is obvious.

So what is a surprise? A surprise is: "Why are they advertising a manure vacuum in *Civil War History*?"

Now that you know a manure vacuum exists, would you be surprised to see it advertised in a horse racing magazine?

When you review *Civil War History*, you might be surprised to see ads for

- Watches,
- Men's jewelry.

It was a surprise. I would not have guessed in advance that a direct-marketing ad for a watch or a pendant was a good fit for *Civil War History* magazine. The watches were tied into the theme as historic "re-creations" but the jewelry was, well, jewelry.

This is right angle marketing.

The jewelry advertiser discovered that the demographics and psychographics of *Civil War* magazine readers made them more inclined than the average man to purchase jewelry. Jewelry has a permanence appreciated by people who study history.

DO YOU SELL CHECKS, MUGS, PENS, AND T-SHIRTS?

If you sell commodity items, you can still market at right angles. In fact, it is probably easier to market at right angles. While reviewing a magazine on dogs I was surprised to find an ad for checks. Printed checks, with pictures of dogs. A commodity item in a dog magazine targeted, of course, to dog owners.

If you sell commodities, one solution is to target a niche; a niche that is technically at a right angle to your commodity but easily accessible. It is hard to get people to switch from their normal check printing service to your discount check printing service. Even if you save them money, it is probably not enough money for anyone to care about.

But imagine if you find somebody who totally loves their Saint Bernard and you offer them beautifully printed checks featuring world-famous prints of Saint Bernards. Now you have targeted their love. You have connected emotionally. Tell a good-enough story, and they will purchase your checks even if it costs them more.

Don't focus on the low price, look for right angles. There's a million of 'em!

Right angles can be inexpensive to target on Facebook. It costs a lot to put a full-color check printing ad in a dog magazine. You can add free tabs to your Facebook page and test ads selling to Saint Bernard owners, and 20 other specific breeds, all for $400.

SEARCHING FOR RIGHT ANGLES

Not all right angle opportunities show up automatically in your Facebook reports. In fact, if you are selling a commodity item, you will have to do the homework yourself to find right angle or niche opportunities.

Search on "magazine categories" and look at all of the various categories of published magazines. One website sells more than 1,500 magazines across 75 categories. Magazines are a great overview of people's likes and interests. Think about what it means for a magazine to be written, published, and delivered to your local newsstand. There must be enough interest in these categories to support an entire publishing industry. Here is just a tiny sample of magazines in the "A" category.

- Animals and Pets
  - Birds
  - Cats
  - Dogs
  - Fish and aquariums
  - Horses
- Art and Antiques

- – Antiques
- – Art
- – Dance
- – Painting
- Auto
  - – Auto news
  - – Auto repair
  - – Classic cars
  - – Hot rods
  - – Motocross
  - – Motorcycles
  - – Off-road vehicles
  - – Trailers and motor homes
  - – Trucks

Remember: your product doesn't have to automatically intersect with these likes and interests to target them. You can craft a message to relate any like or interest back to your core product.

What is more interesting to discover is whether your customers already disproportionately relate to one of these topics, like "hot rods." If they do, you can emotionally appeal to and target them based on a "seemingly unrelated" interest.

I was surprised to find checks advertised in a dog magazine. But after getting over that initial surprise, I would not be surprised to find them advertised in a cat, horse, fish, or bird magazine too. Why? Because I now see the natural connection between the product and enthusiasts wanting customized checks. They use checks to emotionally connect to a pet or companion.

I found a couple of Alaskan cruise ads in an arthritis magazine. What do Alaskan cruises have to do with arthritis? Nothing—except that many older people are highly interested in both curing arthritis and going on cruises. Right angle marketing.

Here's another example: if you pick up a magazine like *Black Belt*, in the back you will frequently find ads for make money at home opportunities, real estate, etc.

What does martial arts have to do with real estate investing? Obviously there is no direct connection. But martial arts enthusiasts are ambitious and competitive. They also relate to authority in a certain kind of way. So an ad for a real estate investment course that talks to them in alpha male language stands an excellent chance of doing well.

At my Maui Elite Master's Summit, a $5,000-per-person marketing seminar, I asked for a show of hands: "How many people in this room are brown belt or above in martial arts?" Out of 100 people, 8 raised their hands; 8% of my high-end customers are accomplished in Karate, Tae Kwon Do, or some other similar sport.

That's probably five times the percentage of accomplished martial artists in the general population. Right angle marketing once again. My best are highly competitive, achievement-oriented people. They also know that winning is a *mental* game.

THE RIGHT ANGLE REPORT

There was a report that Facebook used to produce for advertisers automatically called the "Responder Profiles" report. Facebook turned it off because advertisers didn't know how to use the data it generated. This is not a surprise, because it generated data about right angles. We called it the "Right Angle" report. We are going to describe what it was and why you should care, in the hopes that Facebook may again, someday in the future, make this type of data available again. In the right hands the report helped you do the following two things:

1. Increase conversion rates;
2. Find totally new sources of prospects.

The report is simple. It lists the most commonly liked interests, books, movies, music, and TV shows of people who have clicked on your ads—ranked by CTR. Previously, you may have found this information interesting, but you would not have known what to do with it. Now you know. This is a right angle report. Use this information to relate better to your leads and prospects.

In the responder profile report in Figure 10.1, compiled over just a few days, the fans had the following interests, in order of importance:

1. Reading
2. Sewing
3. Cooking
4. Gardening
5. Music
6. Photography
7. Quilting
8. Scrapbooking

You have a solid lead from this report to target for right angles based on these words. You can test ads that incorporate these themes, add references to them to landing pages, incorporate them in status messages, and on and on. The same report may say your fans' favorite book is the bible and their favorite TV show is *House*.

The report is telling you what your fans like, and they like Dr. House. Perhaps mentioning Dr. House on the landing page may increase conversions. Certainly worth testing.

Interest	Rank by Estimated CTR (Interests)	Book	Rank by Estimated CTR (Books)	Movie	Rank by Estimated CTR (Movies)	Music	Rank by Estimated CTR (Music)	TV Show	Rank by Estimated CTR (TV Shows)
reading	1	bible	1	fireproof	1	country	1	house	1
sewing	2	facing giants	2	christian	2	bones	2		
cooking	3	princess bride	3	contemporary christian	3	criminal minds	3		
gardening	4	lost	4						
music	5	greys anatomy	5						
photography	6								
homeschooling	7								
quilting	8								
scrapbooking	9								

FIGURE 10.1–Responder Profile Report

Right angle thinking.

This right angle report was so powerful, we used to recommend everyone do at least some advertising on Facebook just to read the report and discover new right angles—even if most of their advertising remained outside of Facebook.

Some entries in the responder profile report are so commonly popular (like the bible) that they do not provide actionable information—they are not surprising. However, if *The Purpose-Driven Life* by Rick Warren showed up in a report, that would be significant. The book is popular, but it's not that popular.

In music, U2 and the Rolling Stones doesn't tell you nearly as much about your audience as the Jonas Brothers or Talking Heads. In movies, *Cool Hand Luke* is much more telling than *Star Wars*.

Other data in the report should surprise you. And just like a surprise in our magazine exercise, a surprise here should trigger you to think more deeply about what that entry on the report might mean about your customers. Ask yourself a specific question. Ask yourself, "How might I use the most popular books, music, or TV shows to increase my conversion rates?"

Keys Not Keywords

Do not think of the likes and interests listed in the responder profile report as keywords. If you think of them as keywords, then you miss the real opportunity. They are not keywords to improve a search. They are keys to unlocking your prospect's mind.

The real opportunity in the likes and interests common to your prospects is improving how you target and talk to those prospects. It is to incorporate the most common likes and interests of people who click on your ads directly into your ads, your landing pages, and your follow-up copy.

The more you know about your prospects, the more you can speak to them in words they understand. You can reference books they like to read, TV shows they like to watch, movies they love, and celebrities they like to follow. If you are having front porch conversations, is it better to talk about Dan Brown's *The Da Vinci Code* or Aldous Huxley's *Brave New World*?

It will make a difference.

The more you reflect and connect to your prospects' personal interests, the more comfortable they feel standing on your front porch. They respond more frequently to your status messages, they read your copy with more passion, they purchase your products with more confidence. Why? Because you connected with them.

If you find someone who loves the same books you love, doesn't that person become more interesting to you?

Of course. It works for you, and it works for your prospects.

ONE RIGHT ANGLE SENTENCE GROWS THE CONVERSION RATE 11%

You get the idea that "likes and interest" may uncover a key concept you hadn't thought of, like, "I should advertise directly to truckers." But you are not convinced that mentioning the right novel on a landing page will improve conversion. You are pragmatic. "Does this stuff really make a difference?" you ask.

Bryan Todd was driving traffic to the website www.CosmicFingerPrints.com. This site discusses the intersection between science, astronomy, and religion. Bryan was running ads on Facebook driving traffic to the page and seeking an opt-in to "Learn the Secrets of the Universe."

After a while, Bryan noticed that his responders had an interest in science fiction, history, and really liked the books *Brave New World* and *1984*. So, he split-test two landing pages, which were identical except that one page inserted the following two lines:

ONE RIGHT ANGLE SENTENCE, continued

This ultimate question touches the distant past, and—with the fore-warnings in Orwell's *1984* and Huxley's *Brave New World*—it touches the distant future as well.

Bryan recognized that people who like science fiction think about the distant future and the distant past, and he already knew specifically that his prospects liked these two books.

In hindsight, like most right angle marketing connections, they all go together. If you're inclined to click on an ad that says "Where Did the Universe Come From? Did it come from God?" you probably do all of these things. Bryan added the sentence to the page.

It's hard to anticipate the effect on your landing page, but we know it has some value.

The conversion rate for the page increased 24% immediately with the addition of the two lines. Over time, that conversation improvement settled down to a steady 11%.

Do you want an 11% improvement in your landing page?

Relate better to your readers.

Reach inside their heads and reflect their secret thoughts back to them.

It really is a brave new world.

Of course, unearthing this level of detailed information about your customers is nothing special. It's not like you couldn't do this before. You would build a survey, hire the Gallup organization, and call two or three thousand customers on the phone and see what they told you.

You'd ask them about their education, family, and job. Ask them their hobbies and interests. Ask them what they are watching, reading, doing in their spare time. And who they hang out with. You'd ask them what organizations they belong to and what they believe. You'd ask them hundreds of prying questions and hunt for patterns. Not hard at all.

Perhaps now you see why Facebook is so special. Advertise on Facebook—and collect this information automatically, for no extra charge.

THE AD IS FATIGUED, IT MAY NOT BE DEAD

A successful ad is a success. Celebrate it—it cannot run forever. If everyone in your target has seen your ad 20 to 30 times and you received a great CTR, then give yourself an advertising award. The ad was great. Ad fatigue is a signal to try a new right angle. It is the clue to change the subject in your front porch conversation.

Facebook says its most successful advertisers change their ads about every 12 days. Here is an amazing secret. You can also change them back.

If an ad fatigues after 12 days, it will probably come to life again in another 90 to 120 days—sometimes even faster. As you create more and more successful ads, finding more and more right angles, put them into new campaigns. Eventually, you have more and more campaigns to put into rotation. Ad fatigue will have helped you test and build hundreds of tiny conversations. Keep the ones that work and use them over and over again. You will be so intimately connected to your target audience that you will have customers for life.

Chapter Eleven

The Well-Paid Facebook Anthropologist

FACEBOOK IS A STUDY IN HUMANITY

Facebook is perhaps the most profound anthropological experiment ever conducted. And you are about to become a Facebook "likes and interests" anthropologist. Put on your lab coat, bring your magnifying glass and lab journal, and start observing. Anthropology is the study of humanity, and humanity is on Facebook. Anthropology asks simple yet profound questions, such as:

> "*Anthropology demands the open-mindedness with which one must look and listen, record in astonishment and wonder that which one would not have been able to guess.*"
>
> —MARGARET MEAD

- What defines us as human?
- How do humans behave?
- Why do different groups behave differently?

Facebook is an anthropologist's dream. Untold gigabytes of human thought and activity laid bare for analysis. In the process of building the world's most amazing social connection tool, Facebook has built the world's most amazing anthropological tool. Especially for marketers. Facebook is an absolutely amazing source of psychographic anthropology.

As an advertiser you are also trying to better understand your slice of humanity, including:

· What makes them tick?
· What grabs their attention?
· What motivates them to purchase my product?

Do you wish to understand your prospects better? Then understand Facebook likes and interests better. These really are likes and interests, not keywords, not concepts.

Facebook is not a general search tool, and Facebook does not give any indication that it is inclined to ever become a general search tool. Search has been left to the capable hands of Google and Microsoft. Facebook is a social graph tool, an anthropological tool that Facebook users wield themselves to understand and organize their world, to describe who they are, what they like, what they are interested in, and how they connect socially to other people.

SEARCHING ON FACEBOOK

Facebook connecting people to others, and to their interests, has practical applications for you. It helps you find right angle marketing opportunities. You can begin your anthropology studies simply by typing in a psychographic target word or phrase into Facebook's search bar and seeing what Facebook finds.

You may notice as you type a word into the Facebook search box that Facebook gives you "real-time" search results in a pop-up menu below the search box. You see different results as you type in each letter of your search. Facebook only shows you a few search results at a time; to see a full page of results, press "see more results" at the bottom of the pop-up.

Facebook shows people, pages, groups, apps, and events that match your search. When doing Facebook anthropology, press "see more results" dozens of times to get a good look at the results available. When you see a good potential psychographic target (one with lots of fans or members), you should

· write down the name;
· visit the page, group, and app;
· like the page or join the group;
· see if it is possible to directly enter the name in your ad interface as an interest.

Write down unique potential targets and test them in your ad interface as you build your advertising campaign. Just because a page has a lot of likes doesn't mean the page name will necessarily be available to be directly targeted as an interest.

It can be helpful to use a new user's account when doing Facebook search anthropology, one that does not have any initial friends, likes, or interests. Facebook search results are customized to the individual user. If you want to see more natural search results, not results based on the likes and interests of the one account holder, use a new account.

THERE IS GOLD IN FACEBOOK SEARCH

Searching on a like or interest using Facebook search can turn up targeting gold. However, a good psychographic target word or phrase may not at first appear available for interest targeting in Facebook ads.

Keep trying. It may be available in the ad interface under a different spelling. I searched Facebook and discovered "The Old Schoolhouse Magazine" as a new potential psychographic phrase to target. The page has more than 18,000 fans.

Back in interests, I tried to enter *"The Old Schoolhouse Magazine."* Rejected. It did not match directly on the page name. Not wanting to give up, I looked for another way the magazine may have been a legitimate psychographic target. I tried adding a space between school and house. No help. Next, I tried dropping "The," Facebook immediately listed *"Old Schoolhouse* magazine" as a choice.

Perfect.

Remember, Facebook does not allow you to directly target another user's group, event, app, or page. However, its psychographic lexicon may closely or even exactly match existing names of groups, events, apps, or pages.

When you find a group, event, app, or page that looks like it might be a good psychographic target, you need to explore your ad interface to see if there is a Facebook match. If Facebook says "no," keep looking a little while longer. The match may still be there with a slightly different spelling or phrasing.

In this case, I found more than 15,000 highly profiled, new targets with just a few minutes of searching.

FAN ANTHROPOLOGY

In Facebook, people voluntarily profile themselves. Every time users add a friend, click "like" on a page, enter an interest, feature a book they enjoyed reading, or mention music they enjoyed listening to, they are profiling themselves.

Many Facebook users allow their detailed activities and interests to be visible to the public. This allows for detailed fan anthropology where you can study fans of your pages and even fans of other pages that match your psychographic target.

Public profiles contain detailed psychographic information neatly arranged into categories, including

- music,
- books,
- movies,
- television,
- activities,
- interests,
- basic information.

If you are an administrator of a page someone "liked," you can click on that person's name and see if you have access to this detailed profile information. If you are on another user's page, you can click on users who have made a public comment on that page to see the poster's profile, if it has been left open for view. If you click through to a few dozen fans, you will likely find that most of their profiles are visible.

These are amazing profiles.

"Activities and interests" is the ultimate gold mine in these profiles. There is so much information there that most of it is hidden and you have to look for buttons that are labeled "show other pages" or "more." Behind these headings may be a list of literally hundreds to thousands of likes and interests for each individual.

The interests list appears to record every page this user has liked. What an amazing source for discovering hidden, related psychographics and right angles! Somewhere in Figure 11.1 are targets perfect for you.

To make it even nicer for the Facebook anthropologist, these titles have hover displays. Hover over the links, and you can see how many people have liked the page, indicating how useful that word or phrase may be as a psychographic target in Facebook.

People may like dozens of books, movies, actors, athletes, movie stars, musicians, TV shows, music groups, schools, universities, teams, and more. These likes are available in their profile. As users browse Facebook, they may like hundreds to thousands of additional community pages, private pages, events, and groups. All

Other	A2 Breaking News, Realize Your Business - Finding Your True Fans, ~The Knights of Ni~ Fraternity, Fidelity, Shrubbery, Robert Pasick's LeadersConnect, Better Homeschools, Ann Arbor SPARK, Workantile Exchange, Homeschool Advantage, New Missions (official page), Pure Visibility, 1960s Pop and Rock Music Trivia™, Homeschool, OnStartups, Get Your Church Fan Page, Double Your Likes, Kirtan Central, DoubleYourLikes.com, ASAP Checks, Joplin, MO Tornado Recovery, Zingermans, In Loving Memory of Sharon Tate, IFrame Apps, Welcome Applet, North Social, Pepsi, Victoria's Secret, RedBalloon, BRUT, GNOME ENTERPRISES, Zingerman's Delicatessen, Zingerman's Roadhouse, Support Japan, Sizzle Bop, Adrenalin Experiences Melbourne, Steve Spangler, Red Bull, Adrenalin Experiences Sydney, Like Button, Click "like" if you love reading to your kids, I love someone in the military, Geekbox Computers, Personalized Children's Books, ABtests.com, Over The Top Marketing, Sunny Hills "The Affirmations Genius", Tom's Golden Cafe, Social Graph, Where 2.0 Conference, Working Michigan, The Ark - Ann Arbor, The Cupcake Station, You: "I'd like a Coke." Waiter:"Is Pepsi ok?" You: "Is Monopoly money ok?", AnnArbor.com Photo, Charcot-Marie-Tooth Association: The Time is Now, Schoolhouse Expo, MountainOcarinas, Puppies, U.S. Naval Forces Central Command / U.S. 5th Fleet, FamilyMint, MamasHealth.com: easy, simple to understand information about health, SOAR Study Skills, Allstate Insurance, Kristi and Jason Adopt, Local Marketing Tactics, Get 10,000 Fans, Static FBML, Branding Personality, KOHLER, Camp Woodhaven in West Boylston, Facebook

FIGURE 11.1–Everything This Facebook User Has Liked

of these form parts of a user's complex, psychographic profile. People are complex, with many diverse and eclectic likes and interests. This becomes quite evident when reading their profiles in Facebook.

We are always looking for patterns. Among all of this complexity we ask a simple question, "Which likes and interests appear again and again in the profiles of our customers?"

More "Likes and Interests" Anthropology

- *Search for acronyms.* Create a list of acronyms that are used by your target psychographic group. Search for the acronyms in both Facebook search and in the Facebook ad interests field. See if they are available as a target.
- *A great psychographic target* for Tom was not available under the organization's name but was under the organization's acronym, HSLDA. Needless to say, watch acronyms carefully in case you accidentally match the wrong target.
- *Follow the chain of page likes.* Pages that you have found when searching your likes and interests also like other pages, and those pages also like other pages, creating a chain of pages that like each other. Once you have found pages with large numbers of likes themselves, see what pages they like, and visit those liked pages, too. There is a good chance the immediately liked pages represent an interest you may also want to target.

· *Watch your Facebook page's right-hand column.* Sometimes Facebook displays other pages popular with your fans in the right-hand column of your page. As an administrator, take a look and see if suggestions for you are placed there by Facebook.

ANTHROPOLOGY AT THE "INTERESTS" AD INTERFACE

Facebook serves up anthropology opportunities even as you are creating your ads. As you enter an interest into the ad interface, Facebook provides anthropological clues—some actively, in the form of additional suggestions, and some passively, if it doesn't match your selection.

Previously, I described a trick for finding additional interests. You enter the basic interest you are targeting in the ad interface, followed by a space, followed by a letter from the alphabet. This is a way to get Facebook to volunteer additional, possible categories. I called this an alphabet search.

If you are targeting "hot rods" enter:

· hot rods a,
· hot rods b,
· hot rods c,

In the above example, I call the word "hot rods" a base word. It is the base of the expanded psychographic phrase I am looking for. As Facebook anthropologists, we also want to look for additional base words. After you do the alphabet search on your first base word ("hot rods" in this example), go back and read some of the longer interests that Facebook suggested, and that you added to your list.

Do you see any other base words in these phrases? If you see a single word in the longer phrase that you believe may be a good root for another interest, then enter that word into interests all by itself, to see what Facebook recommends.

For example, for hot rods, Facebook suggested I add "hot rod circuit," but it did not suggest the base word "hot rod." If you notice that "hot rod" is singular in Facebook's suggestion,, you greatly expand the Estimated Reach.

I don't know why Facebook didn't suggest hot rod, but it didn't. So you need to go looking for it. All new base words you find this way can be separately entered into an new alphabet search:

· hot rod a
· hot rod b . . .

· hot rod z

It is simple, but it works.

For a live demonstration video of this technique visit www.perrymarshall.com/ fbtoolbox/ and watch the demonstration tutorials.

Keep alphabet searching around your base words until you don't find any more interests. Then look for the next base word. Of course, over time you find fewer and fewer variants on the base word.

By now, if you are really doing this work, you are getting a little bored. But don't stop. There are even more people to add to estimated reach. You want to find everyone who should see your ad.

There are several reasons this process is so difficult. One is that people can create a page with almost any name they want, and Facebook doesn't protect any given page name. There are many, many pages and groups named variations of "hot rod." These pages are created by many different people and contain many varieties of the term, including different spellings. Perhaps somebody spelled "hot rod" without a space between hot and rod. If you think of a spelling variation, test it, and see if Facebook considers it a legitimate interest. If it is legitimate, then alphabet search it to look for additional phrases.

Save all of the interests you find in a dummy ad, an ad you create but never run. I fill up lots of dummy ads with target psychographics and use the "Create a Similar Ad" button to later create ads from the dummy. It saves a lot of time.

Do not run every interest you find in one ad. Break them into different ads when they are really targeting different things.

Broad Interest Category Anthropology

The broad categories that Facebook makes available for targeting as interests are also anthropological clues worth investigating. The Family Status category especially offers some new ways to divide up and study demographics that are not available in any other way (see Figure 11.2). You can target people in a geographic target area who specifically identify themselves as being engaged, newlywed, parents, or even parents of children of a specific age.

Simply reviewing the broad category interests that Facebook has identified is an intresting anthropological overview of the data in Facebook. The categories visible under activities (see Figure 11.3) represent activity interests of the Facebook community. Seeing the lists may inspire you to create new ads targeted to these broad category interests.

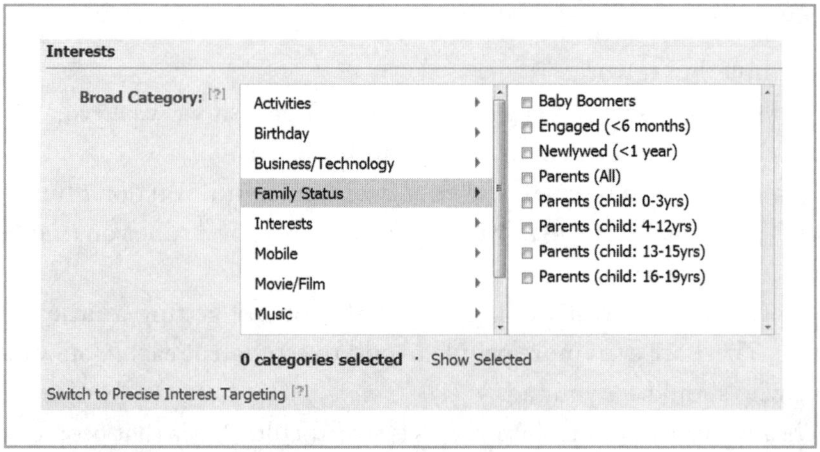

FIGURE 11.2–Broad Category Family Status

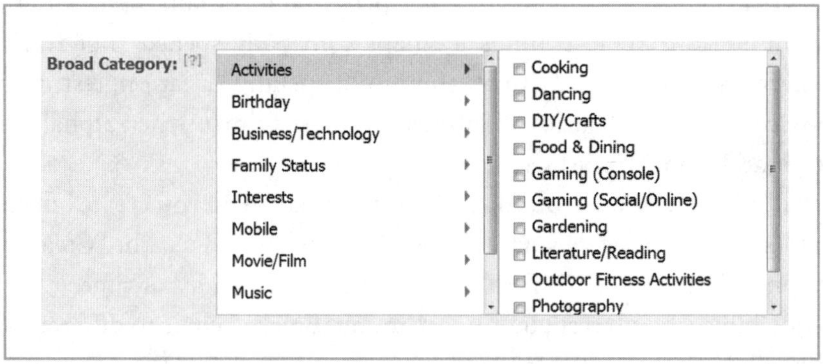

FIGURE 11.3–Broad Category Activities

ANTHROPOLOGY OUTSIDE OF FACEBOOK

You can do interest anthropology outside of Facebook. Look at these outside sources for additional right angle and direct-marketing targets. Three quick tools to use without leaving your desk are

· Google search tools,

· Amazon.com,

· eBay.

Google Search Anthropology

Enter your base interest word into Google search. Visit the first 20 or 30 recommended links. Look for and record names, products, destinations, websites, and other interesting bits of data that Google relates to your target.

While using Google search, always look for web pages linking to Facebook pages. Visit any Facebook pages you see and write them down.

After you visit the websites displayed as Google search results, look at the rest of the incredible results screen Google has displayed for you. It is chock-full of direct marketing and right angle marketing ideas. Did you notice all of the menu items Google has on the far left of the screen? Here are just a few you may discover:

· Images
· Videos
· News
· Shopping
· Blogs
· Books
· Discussions

And further below:

· Related searches
· Timeline

These links all contain related information Google has discovered for the search term you entered. I want you to click on all of these at least once for your most important interests.

RELATED SEARCHES. Shows you in one location a large list of terms related to your original search term. These related searches provide great hints for other potential interests to try to target in Facebook. If you search on the term "Hot Rods" in Google, you may see the following related searches.

This list (Figure 11.4) contains new terms you may be able to target in Facebook in addition to "hot rods." "Hot Rods" and the singular form "Hot Rod" together in Facebook have an estimated reach in the United States of 171,000 people.

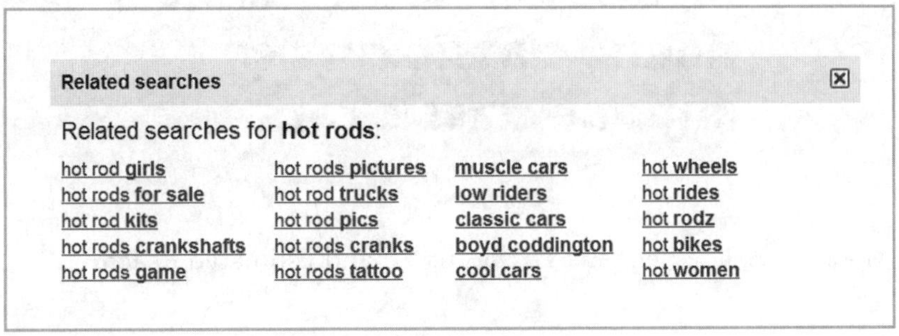

Related searches			☒
Related searches for **hot rods**:			
hot rod **girls**	hot rods **pictures**	**muscle cars**	hot **wheels**
hot rods **for sale**	hot rod **trucks**	**low riders**	hot **rides**
hot rod **kits**	hot rod **pics**	**classic cars**	hot **rodz**
hot rods **crankshafts**	hot rods **cranks**	**boyd coddington**	hot **bikes**
hot rods **game**	hot rods **tattoo**	**cool cars**	hot **women**

FIGURE 11.4–Related Searches for Hot Rods

If all you add is the term "muscle cars" displayed in Related Searches, you can now target 274,000 people. If you actually enter the word "Hot Rod" into Facebook as a precise interest, it will not automatically suggest or recommend muscle cars. You need to come up with that term on your own. Fortunately, Google related searches makes finding related terms easy.

In order to understand which of these terms bring you more clicks, you may wish to break different sets of terms into different ads and not lump them all together. Have one ad for hot rods, another ad for muscle cars, and yet another ad for classic cars. They are demonstrated together here simply to display the expanded estimated reach.

Some terms, like hot wheels, may be avoided because too many people may be thinking of the toy and not the hot rod car.

Add more related terms as precise interests and you will add tens of thousands of additional people to your estimated reach. With just a few additional terms, you are suddenly targeting 332,000 people in Facebook, almost twice as many as you were with just "Hot Rods" alone, as seen in Figure 11.5.

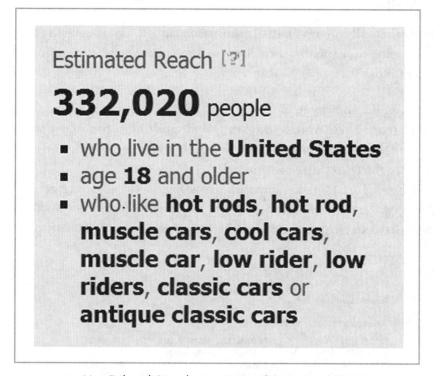

FIGURE 11.5–Use Related Searches to Expand Estimated Reach

If you click any of the terms displayed in related searches and select "More like this," then Google will display to you a whole new set of related search terms to consider. You can find hundreds of potential interests by clicking on related search terms and seeing where they take you. However, it is important to note that many of the specific keyword phrases that Google displays as related searches will not be directly targetable in Facebook as a precise interest. Fortunately, enough will be targetable and the time you spend in Google related searches looking for new terms will pay off in expanded estimated reach making the exercises worthwhile.

Search Amazon for Interests

Use Amazon.com to identify products, authors, and books for direct attack and right angle marketing. Search on your interests terms in Amazon to discover the names of authors, books, products, music, and artists that relate to your terms. If one of these items is popular enough, it may have a lot of "likes" in Facebook and may be a good item to add to interests.

Sometimes this is easy. If you are promoting a book that is in the same genre as another popular book, you could use the popular book as a precise interest target in Facebook. If you guess that people who like *The Da Vinci Code* might be a good target audience for you, then test it.

In Facebook, *The Da Vinci Code* as a target has an estimate reach of 744,080 people in the United States alone. Add in the author, Dan Brown, as a target and reach another 24,000 people.

Facebook itself also suggests adding Dan Brown's other titles, *Angels and Demons, Deception Point,* and *Digital Fortress*—the same books you discover on Amazon.

If you were targeting *The Da Vinci Code* and decided to also target *Angels and Demons*, add the *Angels and Demons* target into a separate ad and track that ad independently.

Amazon also lists titles by other authors. These are authors of books also purchased by people who purchase *The Da Vinci Code*. These authors may be additional right angle targets to try. Test these authors also in independent ads.

Hit eBay to Research Interests

Another great place to search for direct and right angle marketing ideas is eBay. Search for a target term in eBay and it will automatically display to you hundreds of related names, categories, and products. Specifically look for the following:

- Search suggestions from eBay that appear as you enter a term into eBay search. These search suggestions represent other terms you should test in Facebook.
- Categories displayed by eBay after you search on a term. The category names themselves are potential interests you can target in Facebook.
- Product suggestions from eBay inside the suggested categories are also potential direct and right angle interests you can target in Facebook.

Chapter Twelve

We Who Are About to Die Salute You

YOUR ADS FIGHT TO THE DEATH, LIKE GLADIATORS IN THE FACEBOOK COLOSSEUM

Writing great ad copy is tricky. It takes time to learn and years to master. How do you cope with this unbearable burden? How do you master the fine art of writing great ads? The answer is simple, and it is the secret to great wealth.

Ready?

Make your ads fight to the death. Ads that amuse and delight the bloodthirsty crowd are allowed to live. The others are destroyed.

Show no mercy.

Be brutal to your ads. Don't become emotionally attached to them. They must fight, win, or die.

They are your gladiators in the Roman Colosseum of Facebook.

If it's difficult to write a great ad, don't try to write great ads. Instead create multiple ads, as many as five at a time. Submit them to the Facebook Colosseum. Let the crowds decide the winner. All ads must be tested in combat. There is only one way

> "*A*ve, Caesar,
> *morituri te salutant.*"
>
> —SUETONIUS, DE VITA CAESARUM

to know that an ad is truly great—a high click-through and/or conversion rate. The other ads lay bleeding at its feet.

If your gladiator delights the crowd, they vote to keep him alive for another day. They vote by clicking on it. Some votes—your ad lives. A lot of votes—your ad is a champ. A flood of votes, and they'll write poems about your ad for years to come.

If your ad is good enough—if it delights, amuses, and engages—then it gets to entertain an even larger crowd. For your ad, to live is to fight, and to fight is to live.

There is no other way.

You ads must compete not only with each other, but also with every other ad on Facebook. Not enough votes? Your ad dies for the glory of Rome.

Always write at least two ads for any targeted profile. Display both ads at the same time. Whichever performs best is victorious—use it more. The loser is killed with the sword—deleted! In our world, competition never ends, and survival of the fittest rules the day.

You do not pick the best ad in this scenario—your customers do. Your job is to create and train a whole field of gladiators. See what delights the people in the bleachers. See what inspires them to click. Then give the crowd more of what it demands.

Be warned, your crowd is fickle. What amuses Rome this week may bore it next month. You have to anticipate this change, always be designing new ads, always be competing for the attention of the crowd.

A/B AND SPLIT TESTING

The idea of letting your ads compete is called A/B or split testing.

You are always running at least two ads, "ad A" and "ad B." In a pure split test, you show half of your customers ad A and the other half ad B. The winner keeps running; the loser gets deleted and replaced.

The idea of split testing is central to direct marketing. Companies that advertise in newspapers, magazines, radio, and television have done split tests for years. Have you ever noticed a line in a newspaper ad that says, "Ask for department 1215" when calling?" We will tell you a secret. There is no department 1215! That number on the print ad was the ID number used in the advertiser's split test. Half of the print ads said department 1215, and the other half said department 714. Based on which department you asked for when you called, the company tracks the success of one print ad over another print ad.

In online marketing, we track ads automatically. Everything in an ad can be separately tracked, tested, and measured. You can split test small changes and large changes, looking for the best-performing ads.

Not a Real Split Test

To do a proper split test in Facebook your two groups should only see one of the ads, A or B.

They should not be shown ads in random order: A, B, A, B, A, A, B, A, B, A.

Instead one group should see all As: A, A, A, A, A, A, A, A, A, A, A.

The other group should see all Bs: B, B, B, B, B, B, B, B, B, B.

Facebook could do this for us, but currently they do not. So you never really have a proper, scientific split test. Facebook may be showing ALL of your ads to the same person for all advertisers know. Or switching between showing ad A and ad B and ad C.

Eventually a user clicks on an ad. In our case, the user may have clicked on a particular ad because it was the most effective one, or it could have been the combination of ads he saw that inspired him to click. We don't know! We could know, but Facebook doesn't tell us.

Oh well, we work with what we have. But unlike Google search, where you generally try to optimize for the absolutely best ad, in Facebook you frequently allow multiple ads with a reasonable click-through rate (CTR) to keep running. Even with multiple conversion rates, as long as the conversion is still profitable, you'll usually keep the ad.

Part of the reason for this decision is that the split tests aren't as "scientific" on Facebook as in other advertising campaigns. The other part of the reason is that ad fatigue is always messing with the certainty of your results. What matters on Facebook is what's working today.

Duplicate Ad Test

The simplest test is the duplicate ad test. You create an ad and then copy it in its entirety using the Facebook "Create A Similar Ad" button. This button creates a new ad with the same targeting and copy. It is a great way to start a split test.

You now have two copies of the exact same ad. In the second ad, make one thing different from the first ad. You could change the headline, the image, the capitalization, the punctuation, the body text, or even the destination URL. We suggest you change the image first.

This process is as close as you can get in Facebook to a formal split test.

Facebook does not currently support automatic, formal split tests, which would allow you to select two ads and show each 50% of the time. So you have to do your split tests by hand. To run a split test by hand, simply let each ad run for a predetermined number of impressions.

If you are not there to watch the ads closely, you can place them into two separate campaigns with a fixed daily budget and an identical cost-per-impressions (CPM) bid calculated to give you a reasonable number of impressions. When each campaign ends, your test is over.

Choose in advance a test of at least 4,000 impressions per ad to see if you get any clicks (you may need to use CPM bidding to get this number of impressions if the ads have low CTR). Pick the number in advance and stick with it, letting the test run to completion before making adjustments.

A key to running a split test is to not stop before reaching the predetermined number of impressions. Otherwise, the random chance of a few extra people clicking on one ad over another may lead you erroneously to believe that one ad is performing dramatically better than another. This may not be true. Sometimes an ad just gets lucky. As each ad reaches the target number of impressions, temporarily turn off the ad and look at your data, as in the example in Table 12.1.

Ad Name	Impressions	Clicks	CTR
Test 1	4,057	3	0.074%
Test 2	4,351	6	0.138%
Test 3	4,912	4	0.081%
Test 4	4,810	2	0.052%

TABLE 12.1–Split Ad Data

In the above example, the target number of impressions per test was 4,000. They all went a little over to ensure the target was hit.

Which ad performed best? Test 2.

Was there a clear winner? Test 2.

Or so you might think.

Brian Teasley and Perry Marshall offer an online split-test algorithm that tells you how confident you can be that one ad is actually a winner. The test is available at http://splittester.com/. You enter the number of clicks and the CTR for two tests, and the tool will tell you how confident you can be in the results.

If we compare Test 2 to Test 4, SplitTester.com tells us: "You are approximately 85% confident that the ads will have different long term response rates." So there is a high probability that Test 2 is really beating Test 4. Still, we may want to run another 4,000 impressions on both to be sure.

If we compare Test 2 to Test 3, SplitTester.com tells us: "You are not very confident that the ads will have different long term response rates." We cannot be confident at all that Test 2 is really beating Test 3 or Test 1.

We need to run more impressions on Test 1, Test 2, and Test 3 to get more clicks, to be confident enough that one ad is really outperforming the other. Run another 4,000 impressions for these three tests and get some more clicks.

Once SplitTester.com says you have a clear winner, pause the underperforming ads and try again with new ads. Perhaps test a new image, a new headline, or a new offer in the body text. Always look for a better-performing ad.

In many cases in Facebook, a reliable 0.138% CTR is great. In other cases, you might even be happy with a 0.052% CTR. It all depends on your targeting. No matter what CTR you are happy to achieve, always keep looking for better-performing ads.

If your estimated reach is large—a few hundred thousand people or more—then it really pays off to split test 10 to 20 ads or more as you look for the most effective ad before opening up the advertising budget and purchasing tens or hundreds of millions of impressions.

Make a list of things you are going to change for your split tests and work your way through the list, doing one at a time. We will order these changes in their likelihood of having the greatest impact. Change the following during split tests:

- Image
- Headline text
- Headline word order
- Headline punctuation
- Body text (offer)
- Body text call to action
- Body text sentence order
- Body text punctuation

Split Testing in a Highly Profiled World

For years in other systems, all you had to do was select your keywords, run your split test, and throw out the loser with the worst average CTR. Don't do this in Facebook. In the highly profiled world of Facebook there is a another step you need to complete before you declare one ad the winner and the other ad the loser. You may still learn some interesting things from your loser ad before you toss it into the ash heap of history.

In a Facebook split test, don't look just at the total CTR and throw away the underperforming ad. That ad may have been highly effective for a targeted subset of your users. In Facebook, when judging an ad's effectiveness, look at the total CTR and the CTR for different responder demographics and geographics.

Look at the detailed, Facebook responder demographics report summarized by ad before you dismiss any ad as underperforming. You may have accidentally discovered a highly effective ad which works only for certain demographic, geographic, or psychographic targets.

Remember our previous test illustrated in Table 12.1?

I said Test 2 performed better than Test 4, and was the clear winner.

I lied.

We don't know yet.

It is an important lesson to learn in Facebook. If your ad is getting any clicks at all, you do not know how good your ad really is until you look at another Facebook report, the responder demographics report summarized by ad, which will give you different information than you found in the responder profile report.

The responder demographics report summarized by ad displays the specific demographics of those who clicked on your ads. You see, Facebook has multiple CTRs to report. The first CTR reported is how well the ad does with EVERYONE to whom it was displayed.

The responder demographics report shows how well your ad does with specific demographic and geographic groups. Your ad may do very well when it is displayed to a specific, narrower demographic.

For example, Test 4 may have received all of its clicks from men in California. Test 4 may be the perfect ad for that target group, getting a CTR of 0.265% (Figure 12.1).

Ad Name	Demographic	Bucket 1	Bucket 2	% of Impressions	% of Clickers	CTR ↑
Test 4	gender_age	M	California	0.154%	0.363%	0.265%

FIGURE 12.1–Responder Demographic Report

Test 4 was potentially the best performing ad! But only for a very specific target group. If that group is a good target for your ad, and it is large enough, you will need to run more tests to see if it continues to do well. It may well turn out that Test 4 was our best ad when properly targeted only to men in California.

If a specific target like men in California is important enough for you, create a whole new split test, testing two ads against the specific target and improving your ads even further.

Remember, if your ad is getting clicks, you must also check the responder demographic report before declaring it a loser.

Testing Multiple Variables

In the first split test we described, we changed only one thing at a time. We changed the image or the headline but not both at the same time. This type of testing is called single variable testing. We varied only one thing, the image, so that when we compared the two ads we were absolutely sure it was the image that made the difference, not the headline.

Single variable testing is why we are so sure that your image is 70% of the effectiveness of your ad. When you are first doing split testing, it is nice to change only one thing at a time to try to understand exactly what your market is responding to.

However, it is also essential to test changing multiple variables all at once. The advice given to you in the last section assumes you're trying to figure out what parts of the ad are working and what parts are not. You do that when you're trying to optimize and fine tune something that is already working.

But initially you should probably try a spectrum of completely different ideas, just to get yourself in the ballpark. Let's say you're advertising gift packages for Mother's Day. You can approach this from many angles:

- "Hey Dad: Don't screw up her special day." (Focus on his fear of not coming through.)
- "Her face will glow with delight." (Focus on how she looks when she's happy.)
- "Make her feel so incredibly special." (Focus on how she feels when she's happy.)
- "A gift from you AND the kids." (Focus on the younger family members.)

In a brand new Facebook campaign it's best to test all four of these at first. If you find that the third one works best—"Make her feel so incredibly special"—then you can optimize that headline. You can test the following:

- Make her feel cherished.
- Make her feel valued.
- Make her feel like your #1.

If you change multiple variables at once you may not know which change caused the improvement, but you will not care as long as you get a significant improvement.

Sometimes you need to try a totally new ad with everything different from your best-performing ad: a different headline, a different image, and a different body text.

Test a totally different ad at least every fifth test.

Sometimes you need to change everything to discover something new to appeal dramatically better to your target audience. So break out of the rut and try a totally different ad. If some of your new ads do not fail miserably, it simply means you are not trying. If you do this right, you should have some wonderful failures! If you don't take some risks, you may never find just how high your CTR could have been.

Fatigue and Split Testing

On Facebook, where ad fatigue is so common, split testing begins to merge with other techniques of continually rotating images, changing headlines, and changing copy just to try to engage the potential customer in new and unique ways.

Because the environment is so dynamic, we frequently have four or five different ads competing with each other in the same campaign at the same time because we are running split tests to improve a single ad, fighting ad fatigue, or just trying something crazy and new.

In Facebook, we are no longer really trying just to find the best ad that works. In Google, we obsessed about that. We don't here. On Facebook, we're trying to keep the user community engaged and entertained. So we provide and test a lot of different ads, and we have many ads available for the user community to view at any given time.

Split Testing More Than Ads

It may already be apparent to you that you can apply split testing to more than just your ads. Any step in your entire sales funnel may be tested, including messages, product offerings, opt-in bonuses, landing page designs, videos, audio, fonts, colors, text size, copy length, prices, button designs, button names, images, page layout, and calls to action.

(Perry had one guy who wrote him to announce he'd started split testing girlfriends. Perry does not advocate that practice.)

If you can change it, you can test it. After you get in the habit of split testing ads, get in the habit of split testing each step and element in your sales process.

Tons of marketing books and articles have been written about split testing and—hopefully—most of the readers of this book do not find this a brand new concept. If it is a new concept to you, then it is especially important that you continue to investigate the entire topic of continually testing and refining your sales funnel. You must continue to study and learn about split testing after you complete this book. We have links to a series of excellent articles on split testing at perrymarshall.com/ fbtoolbox.

Amazing tools are available to help you split test and develop your website. Google's Website Optimizer is one such tool. It helps you split test and optimize the sales paths on your website. It is free!

By using this tool, you can track and improve the performance of hundreds of different things on your existing website in order to create the world's most effective sales funnel. You do not have to be a marketing expert to gain profound insights into how changes to your website may affect the behaviors of your visitors.

Will a call to action button that says ORDER NOW perform better than an call to action button that says ORDER HERE? Don't guess. Split test. Website Optimizer will tell you which performs better and by how much.

Google provides you these tools for free because it believes that helping you get better at converting traffic you drive to your website will make you want to buy more ads to drive more traffic. Google is right.

A MARKETING MACHINE

Almost everyone who comes to me starts by asking me to increase their traffic.

They ask me to do this because they assume something I do not assume. They assume they are already getting optimal performance out of their landing pages. They assume they just need to get more people to see them.

Years of experience has taught me that this is a dangerous assumption. There are always low-hanging fruit opportunities to address on your website or fan page before you focus on increasing traffic. Low-hanging fruit represents small improvements to existing sites delivering disproportionate results, like changing an offer page and watching conversions go from 17% to 41%. These tiny tweaks have an amazing compounding effect. Small hinges swing big doors.

For example, if you triple the effectiveness of your conversion page, and then halve the cost of an ad leading to the conversion page, your net result is six times the number of total conversions for the same amount of money.

For many Facebook pages and websites, every step of the path leading to a conversion has low-hanging fruit. Best of all, the results are multiplied!

The multiplication effect is extremely powerful.

Is it really possible to have that level of end effect? Absolutely.

Let me tell you about a student I had, Christopher Snow, who was mostly using Google traffic to sell nutritional products online. He employed the multiplication

A MARKETING MACHINE, continued

concept to improve the segments of his sales funnel. He experienced 156% growth in four months. He wrote:

"Every week I am making it better. I'm tracking, I'm testing. I'm split testing. I'm peeling and sticking. I'm testing landing pages. I'm killing ads that don't perform well and testing them with new ones. Doing this process alone puts me way ahead of the competition. Here are some of my latest stats:

Month	Sales	Orders
Jan	£8,347.40 or $16,400 USD	91
Feb sales	£12,539.05 or $24,650 USD this is about 50% in sales from Jan pre -run.	166 82% increase in orders from Jan
March sales	£ 30,792.45 or $61,647USD This is about 368% increase in sales from Jan sales.	396 435% increase in orders from pre-run
April sales—up to April 24	£ 24,001.45 or $42,048.00 USD That is with 7 days of being out of the office on holidays.	288 People are spending more per order than March.

6X The Traffic

Number of Clicks	Ad Spend	CTR	Average CPC
January 3: 144	$2020.00 USD	1.78%	$0.67 USD
February 12: 196	$4607.00 USD	3.73%	$0.38 USD
March 20: 179	$8,057.00 USD	3.88%	$0.40 USD
April 1–24: 22,077	$7,765.00 USD	4.36%	$0.36 USD

I have told Perry that to me a successful business follows processes and is not some kind of magic like so many "gurus" want you to believe. I have looked at my time studying in the course as a process of learn, implement, tweak. Learn, implement, tweak. Learn, implement, tweak. It is working."

—Christopher Snow, Ottawa, ON

Chapter Thirteen

Facebook Secret X: Superior Bidding Strategy

FINDING SIGNALS WHERE OTHERS HEAR NOISE

I have a friend named Brad who used to work at the rail yards in western Nebraska. He would watch huge trains pass through on their way from one coast to another, full of commodities like corn and soybeans and coal.

One day he realized that just by watching the flow of commodities through the rail yard from day to day, he could figure out what the fat cats were doing on the futures markets. He used this "insider information" to buy futures and make money.

> *"No method of advertising is too expensive if it brings proper results."*
>
> —S. ROLAND HALL

Most people saw trains. Brad saw money changing hands. That's the difference between a clock puncher and a businessman.

Every successful trader of commodities, futures, and stocks will tell you, the secrets to success are:

· Recognizing priceless information where other people only see noise, and
· Applying strategies other people ignore.

Every Facebook ad you see potentially offers you valuable insights that "normal" people merely shrug off as "advertising" or "spam."

And many times, just changing your bidding strategy gives you a distinct advantage over others. Facebook gives you several choices, each of which can be implemented in several ways.

CPC VS. CPM BIDDING

When you choose to bid on your ad using Facebook's "Pay for Clicks (CPC)" bidding option, you pay if and only if someone clicks on your ad. This is also referred to as pay per click (PPC).

Another type of bidding available in Facebook is "Pay for Impressions (CPM)." If you select to bid on your ad using CPM, you pay for every 1,000 times the ad is displayed, whether or not anybody clicks on the ad. Paying for impressions is also referred to as pay per view (PPV).

Many people think CPC is safe and CPM is risky, and believe you should always do CPC.

They are wrong.

CPC cuts risk, but at a price. CPC bidding is almost always the more expensive way to advertise. Still, I frequently use CPC bidding, especially when I am first testing ads. I frequently move ads and whole campaigns back and forth between CPC bidding and CPM bidding. I recommend CPC bidding if

· you are testing new ads,
· you are not confident in the ability of your ads to get and maintain a high click-through rate (CTR),
· you need to start fast,
· you know your ad may soon be fatiguing,
· you cannot or will not regularly check up on your ads, and
· if the cost of maintaining a CPM campaign does not justify the money saved.

Use CPC Bidding When You Test New Ads

It's hard to write ads with high click-through rates (CTR) at first. My first suggestion for good ads is go ahead and write bad ads. Then let the users tell you which ones are good by clicking on them. This can be expensive if you bid CPM because you pay for the good ads and the bad.

However, if you bid CPC, Facebook will display both good and bad at least a thousand times to see if anyone will click on them. You do not have to pay for the thousand impressions on your bad ads because nobody clicked on them!

It's difficult to impossible for you to guess in advance which of your 10 ads will perform best. So test a bunch of different ads with CPC. If you need to test beyond 2,000 impressions because of low CTR, then switch to a CPM bid.

Watch how your ads perform. Look for emotional triggers that drive users to click and so produce high CTR. Write more ads and activate those same triggers. You can improve your best-performing ad. If you change your image, tweak a word in your ad, or narrow your target group, you may be able to get another .1% or higher increase in CTR.

Once you have identified your best-performing ad, you might want to rebid the ad as CPM, slashing your cost.

Use CPC When You Need to Start Fast

Many people who are new to digital advertising are intimidated by the risks of CPM bidding. Most of us are more comfortable beginning a new ad campaign with CPC bidding. We feel more in control.

That control is mostly an illusion, but it's a helpful illusion if it gets you going. If you're brand new to Facebook ads and want to get your toes wet, feel free to start your first campaign using CPC bidding. Once you understand Facebook ads better and feel ready to raise your game, try CPM.

Use CPC if You Can't or Won't Regularly Check Your Ads

CPC bidding has the wonderful quality of automatically shutting off when ads stop working. Facebook turns it off if you are not generating enough clicks to pay a reasonable price from the impressions you're consuming.

You only have so many hours in the day. If your business can afford higher-cost ads and you don't want to think about the more detailed nuances of running a CPM campaign, then run CPC and focus your energy on more important things.

When you're starting out, you may want to focus on the quality of your landing page, sales funnel, and marketing machine. You can start with CPC campaigns to get the rest of your sales funnel working and spend more time on CPM campaigns later, when you are trying to reduce costs.

If you leave your ads running unattended for more than a day or two, or if you're forgetful or busy and know you will not check in on your ads on a regular basis, then bid CPC.

Ads fatigue. If you bid CPM, you might accidentally pay for hundreds of thousands, or even millions, of impressions when people are no longer interested in clicking on the ad. Very bad. To avoid blowing cash on ads that no longer perform, bid CPC. Facebook will stop running the ad automatically if nobody clicks.

Use CPC Bidding if You Calculate Your Ad May Soon be Fatiguing

If a formerly high-performing ad is beginning to tire (people grow tired of it and stop clicking on it), you should bid CPC or stop it altogether. This is really just a slight mod of the first rule. Ads can fatigue fast, sometimes very fast. You may also just want to switch out your ads.

It's not unusual for an ad to be successful in Facebook even if the CTR is as low as .05% to .07%. People in Facebook are not actively shopping, and so they do not click as frequently on ads. Facebook is willing to serve your ads millions of times, even if your CTR is low, because they have a lot of ad space to fill. They still make good money because they force you to bid higher on CPC ads.

If your ad has low CTR, then CPC bidding is better. If your reach is large, you may be able to run the ad for weeks, even months, until the ad finally dies. You pay at most your maximum bid per click, and you are not too heavily penalized because of the low CTR.

Consider just how poorly an ad with a CTR of .05% is performing. If the ad has a CTR of .05%, the ad has to be displayed 2,000 times to generate one click. Seriously, write a better ad!

Use CPC if CPM Maintenance Cost Is Too High

The time you spend optimizing a CPM campaign costs money. It's easy to forget because the CPM game is fun. But time is money. It is almost always possible to spend dramatically less per click by running aggressive CPM campaigns. If they're simple to set up and maintain, CPM is an easy choice.

But if you're wasting a lot of time struggling to make CPM pay, devoting time and energy to high-performing ads, keeping them fresh and up-to-date, and fighting ad fatigue, you may be better off with higher cost but lower labor CPC campaigns.

The campaign that runs slow and steady for months on end with a lower CTR without much maintenance or attention has a big advantage. If you do not have the time, or your time is highly valuable elsewhere, then a simple CPC ad releases you from worry.

If a cosmetic dentist can make $1,000 an hour doing full mouth reconstructions, then it doesn't pay for him to spend three hours a month shaving $200 off his ads.

Like everything in your business, time optimizing ads is an investment. Be sure the investment is sound.

THE CRAZY WORLD OF CPC BIDDING

Technically, you are bidding on the ad space when you bid on Facebook ads. You enter the maximum you are willing to pay for the click in a field labeled "Max Bid." You're up against other advertisers unseen and unknown, and you don't know what they're bidding. From your perspective, the "bid" word is a bit of a sham. Initially, the higher your bid the more likely your ad will be displayed.

After a few thousand impressions, additional factors weigh in to affect the cost of your ad if you are bidding CPC; these include the CTR, the location of the ad (you pay more for prime locations), and whether users "like" or complain about your ad.

The good news? Facebook reserves the right to "lower the price" you pay per click. You almost never pay what you bid, at least at first. You read that right! They will actually charge you less than you bid, and lucky for you, they do this quite frequently.

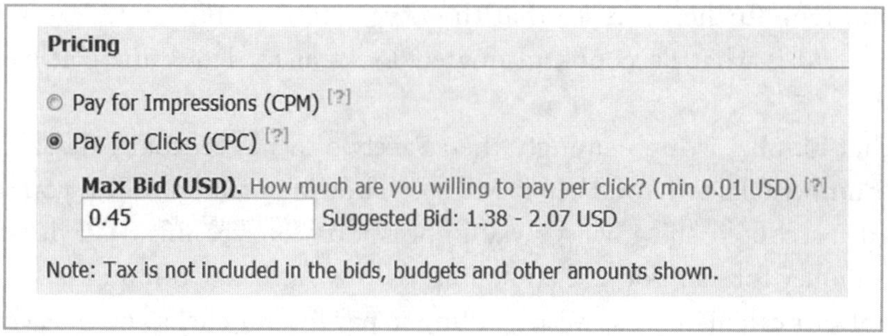

Pricing

○ Pay for Impressions (CPM) [?]
● Pay for Clicks (CPC) [?]

Max Bid (USD). How much are you willing to pay per click? (min 0.01 USD) [?]

| 0.45 | Suggested Bid: 1.38 - 2.07 USD |

Note: Tax is not included in the bids, budgets and other amounts shown.

FIGURE 13.1–Pay for Clicks Bid of 45 Cents

In Figure 13.1, you can see we entered a "Max Bid" of 45 cents for this specific ad. This is a real ad with real data.

Facebook proposed a "Suggested Bid" of $1.38–$2.07.

You would think that the ad would not even be displayed once, since it is bid dramatically lower than the suggested bid. However, so far today Facebook has shown the ad more than 20,000 times and charged only .38 cents for each click. This is reported by the system as "Avg. CPC" (Average Cost Per Click) as you see here in Figure 13.2.

What exactly is Facebook doing? Why do its ad guidelines suggest bidding higher when it is actually charging less than the bid—an entire U.S. dollar less than

Bid	Type	Impressions	Social % [?]	Clicks	CTR (%)	Avg. CPC	Avg. CPM
$0.45	CPC	20,066	0.0%	15	0.075%	$0.38	$0.28

FIGURE 13.2–Clicks, Average CPC 38 Cents

the minimum suggested bid? Five times less than the maximum suggested bid? Why is Facebook doing this? For the love of advertising, why?

Google AdWords works the same way, and this lowers advertiser anxiety considerably. Built into Google's pricing is this formula:

Ad Score = Bid Price x Click-Through Rate.

This formula shifts the emphasis from bid price to ad quality and automatically rewards you for writing better ads. Facebook works much the same way.

If we raised our bid, we might see even more impressions in the same period of time. Facebook doesn't want to bore its users, so its pages may occasionally show other ads with lower bids just to keep it interesting. (It makes more money this way.) We would do this, too, if we were Facebook gurus.

If you look further, you see that the "Avg. CPM" in Figure 13.2 was 28 cents. Average CPM is what Facebook ultimately looks at to determine if it will display your ad.

If that number is high enough, then Facebook will eventually display your ad. If that number falls too low, then it will stop showing your ad unless you raise your CPC bid. Facebook isn't giving away impressions for free. If an ad doesn't make enough money for Facebook, then it simply stops showing your ad.

We always calculate what we are willing to pay for our clicks and bid accordingly. I've learned not to blindly follow Facebook's bidding suggestions.

At any given moment, Facebook selects ads to display based on what each advertiser is bidding, the performance of all the advertisers' various ads, the space Facebook has available, the number of minutes left in the day, and the limitations of each advertiser's budget. Facebook ad folks even rotate in some ads just to shake things up a bit.

Dynamic behaviors mean we should explore multiple different bidding strategies. Some will be successful; some will not. The success or failure of any strategy may change over time as Facebook continues to evolve. Your strategy is a function of what you want to achieve and how much time you have to achieve it.

Here are a few different CPC strategies I've succeeded with. Test them and devise your own. Which works best will vary based on your goals, markets, competition, and how Facebook has groomed its bidding system on any given day.

Strategy 1: CPC Recommended Bid (Fast Start)

Here, you aggressively follow Facebook's suggested bid. It is good for getting your ad to display fast and keeping it visible. You try to ensure you are not perpetually overbidding by following these five steps:

1. Start by bidding two cents higher than the minimum suggested bid.
2. Check your ad every two to three hours each day. If the suggested bid has decreased, then lower your bid to two cents higher than the new minimum suggested bid.
3. Continue step 2 until the ad fatigues.
4. If the suggested bid is increased rather than lowered, ignore the increase.
5. Only raise your suggested bid if Facebook stops displaying your ads for 24 hours.

Strategy 2: CPC Bid Down (Fast Start)

This strategy seeks to aggressively follow the suggested bid at launch and then dramatically reduce bids near to what is actually being paid for clicks. In this way, you keep yourself from overpaying for clicks when the ads start to fatigue. It also keeps the bid near what Facebook has been willing to accept for a click.

1. Start by bidding two cents higher than the minimum suggested bid.
2. Check your ad every two to three hours each day. If the suggested bid has decreased, then lower your bid.
3. Once you have reached the lowest suggested bid, keep reducing your bid 10 cents an hour.
4. Continue step 3 until you approach within 10 cents of the average CPC you are actually paying for your ad.
5. Keep your bid at this lower level until Facebook stops displaying your ad for at least 24 hours.
6. If Facebook stops displaying your ad and the ad has not fatigued, begin again at step 1.
7. If Facebooks stops displaying your ad and the ad was fatigued, then turn the ad off. Turn the ad back on without changing the bid if you use it again in a future rotation, perhaps waiting as long as 30 to 90 days before using the ad again.

The bid down strategy is the one I've used most.

Strategy 3: CPC Bid Up (Slow Start)

This strategy has only been used for testing purposes. The goal of including it is to encourage you to think of different ways you may choose to bid campaigns. Do not get set in any one pattern.

This seeks to discover the lowest CPC bid price Facebook will accept to display your ad while never overpaying. I also used it to test how Facebook would display low-bid ads and discovered that it might display these ads at the end of the day and off hours. Your ad may show at off hours or at the end of the day, but if those clicks work for you, then this strategy is worth trying. Don't use this if you're in a hurry.

1. Start your CPC bid at five cents a click (in the United States; less elsewhere).
2. Wait 24 hours. If your ad has not been displayed, then raise your bid another five cents.
3. Repeat step 2 until your ad begins to display.
4. Once the ad is displaying, decrease your bid by a penny an hour while the ad keeps displaying. If the ad turns off, change the bid back to the last working bid. Go to step 2.

Depending on your expected actual CPC, your starting suggested minimum bid, and your patience, you may make these changes in increments of 10 or 20 cents, instead of five cents.

LONGER CAMPAIGNS

It is possible to run long-term, profitable Facebook campaigns with relatively little oversight and affordable prices for nine months. I had a high score on the "Is Facebook for Me" test and set a low daily budget, keeping impressions down to an average of about one impression a day per four estimated reach users.

The demographic and psychographic profiles, and the current competition, led Facebook to suggest a minimum bid of $1.35 on average across the ad series.

I created eight different ads in the original set and implemented bidding strategy 2. I used CPC because I did not want to spend a lot of time managing the ads. As long as the campaign delivered clicks at 50 cents each or less, I was comfortable leaving the campaign running.

Strategy 2 ultimately led to bids on the various eight ads ranging between 41 and 65 cents.

LONGER CAMPAIGNS, continued

Over nine months, 20 million impressions were served with CPC bidding, resulting in 15,000 clicks and an average CPC of 36 cents.

The total: just over $5,000.

After nine months the ads fatigued, and the CPC rose above 50 cents. I replaced the ads and the campaign.

There were multiple reasons why the campaign lasted so long, including:

- High score on "Is Facebook for Me" test
- Low daily budget
- Totally new product
- Multiple different display ads with new ads occasionally added
- User growth in Facebook
- Additional users occasionally targeted by expanding the psychographic targets.

It is interesting to note that using multiple ads may have had a bigger impact than you would originally suspect. No new ads for that product, produced since the original campaign, have lasted much longer than 30 days without showing significant fatigue, most likely because the frequency cap I use now is closer to four impressions a day, not one every four days.

Chapter Fourteen

CPM Bidding Strategies That Get You Even More Clicks for Less Money

CPM BIDDING CAN BE MAGICAL

Mastermind Club is my advanced private forum for pay-per-click marketers. Club member Francesco Tinti from Tuscany, Italy, wrote me with this fabulous Facebook ad success story:

> Here you have a picture of a successful FB campaign with less than $210 investment.
>
> A very small investment with great results!
>
> In Verona (Italy) each year we have the Vinitaly fair, an event dedicated to wines. A company asked me, 6 weeks before the fair, to promote a private club for wine amateurs and connoisseurs. In other words a tasting list.
>
> With a small investment or nothing more $200, a Facebook campaign, and a soft email marketing strategy we got about 1,600 fans in a Facebook fan page and over 250 people to the fair!
>
> In the fan page we integrate posts from a blog . . . and a email registration form on the left. To our fans we launch only a private message and a public message to subscribe here. . . .

> "*The whole interest of reason, speculative as well as practical, is centered in the three following questions:*
> 1. *What can I know?*
> 2. *What ought I to do?*
> 3. *What may I hope?*"
> —IMMANUEL KANT

Subscribers received in email a coupon for a free wine tasting to the fair and at their home a physical wine tasting card. Of course now subscriptions are closed and the page works as a waiting list.

Results ? Over 300 real interested people to the fair.

Ciao, Francesco

You can listen to my seven-minute interview with Francesco at perrymarshall. com/fbtoolbox/. CPM bidding was a key to the success of Francesco's campaign.

WHEN TO USE CPM BIDDING

The CPM ad report seen in Figure 14.1 describes an ad we just ran in the United States for a very targeted audience (we used only one word in the psychographic profile and restricted age and sex). It delivered 527 clicks for a lifetime average CPC of seven cents.

Bid ?	Type ?	Impressions ?	Social % ?	Clicks ?	CTR ?	CPC ?	CPM ?	Spent ?
$0.78	CPM	235,331	2.5%	527	0.224%	$0.07	$0.15	$35.73

FIGURE 14.1–CPM Ad Report Showing Seven-Cent CPC

It is possible to get very affordable clicks in Facebook. During the early days of this ad, it was delivering clicks for five cents. The bidding type used for this ad is displayed under "Type," and it was CPM. The bid was 78 cents, but the CPM paid was only 15 cents.

So what is CPM advertising? It is a second bidding method that Facebook offers. CPM stands for "Cost Per Thousand impressions" (M = 1,000). You can tell Facebook that you are willing to pay to simply have it display your ad 1,000 times whether or not anyone clicks on the ad. Facebook's Help Center recommends using CPM if you are doing brand advertising. However, CPM is also a perfectly reasonable way to bid on direct response ads where the goal is clicks.

Would you like to create fans for your Facebook page for five to seven cents a piece? It can be done, even if your target location is in the United States. The best way to achieve inexpensive clicks? CPM bidding.

Outside of the United States it is still possible to get clicks very inexpensively, for less than a tenth of a penny. How? CPM bidding coupled with a very high CTR.

A key difference between CPC and CPM is who becomes the gambler, who takes the risk. In CPC bidding, Facebook is the gambler; it displays your ads for free; payment comes only if someone clicks on the ad, and Facebook has no guarantee that will happen. You will usually get at least 1,000 free impressions on each new CPC ad. In CPM bidding, you are the gambler. You pay for Facebook to run the ads, and you will pay even if no one clicks on them.

Not surprisingly, the savvy gambler earns the bigger reward. And if you are the gambler, that reward can be lots and lots of clicks at deep-discount prices.

CPC and CPM are, in many ways, two sides of the same coin. It is really important to understand that you can calculate the CPM on an ad even if it was bid as CPC, and you can calculate the CPC on an ad even if it was bid as CPM. Facebook reports average CPC ($) and average CPM ($) for all ads no matter what big method was selected.

For those who write compelling ad copy, want to actively manage their ads, don't mind spending the time, and like the challenge of trying to squeeze every last penny out of their advertising expenses, CPM bidding is the best game in town.

Selecting CPM does increase both risk and reward for you the advertiser and is almost always the least expensive method to advertise on Facebook. I (Tom) frequently use CPM bidding and, as stated previously, I sometimes move ads and whole campaigns back and forth between CPC bidding and CPM bidding.

Consider using CPM bidding if

- having a low cost per click is essential to the success of your campaign;
- you are spending a lot of money on Facebook clicks;
- you are highly confident in the ability of your ads to get a high CTR;
- you believe your ad will continue to perform strongly during the CPM campaign duration;
- you have the ability to regularly check up on your ads' performances;
- you are running a more formal split test.

Use CPM Bidding if Low-Cost Ads Are Essential for Success

Certain business models are supported only if clicks are obtained inexpensively; for example, businesses that advertise to get users to visit a web page and then immediately sell those visitors to other advertisers.

If you are undertaking an initiative that requires inexpensive clicks to survive, then likely the only way you will achieve it on Facebook is by bidding CPM.

I strongly encourage most entrepreneurs to avoid business models that rely entirely on inexpensive, paid clicks, unless you want your business to be short lived.

It is hard to keep inexpensive, paid clicks coming in reliably year after year after year. Still, they are fun to capture when they are available.

CPM is the only bidding method on Facebook that can deliver to you clicks for less than a penny a piece.

Use CPM Bidding If You Are Spending a Lot of Money on Facebook Clicks

A well-managed CPM campaign can easily save you at least 20%. If you are spending a lot of money on Facebook paid advertising, the savings of bidding CPM become too compelling to ignore.

The extra work involved in monitoring CPM campaigns and keeping them successful quickly pays for itself when you are spending thousands of dollars a month on paid clicks. If you are spending several thousand dollars a day on paid clicks, you should talk with a Facebook representative directly.

Use CPM Bidding If You Are Highly Confident in the Ability of Your Ads to Get a High CTR

If you have tested and proven that an ad reliably delivers a CTR near or above 1%, then that ad is a great candidate for CPM pricing. The secret to a good CPM campaign is using well-targeted psychographics, demographics, and geography to capture a highly responsive user group. A highly responsive user group increases CTR, but since you are not paying for clicks but for impressions, your cost per click falls dramatically.

Say I was willing to pay on average as much as 50 cents a click. What might 1,000 clicks cost me if my ad has a CTR of 1%? Well, if I am bidding CPC, I just buy the clicks at 50 cents a click. It costs $500 to buy 1,000 clicks.

The CTR doesn't matter; it always costs $500. However, if I buy 1,000 impressions for 75 cents (a reasonable bid), and I have a 1% CTR, then I get 10 clicks for 75 cents. I am buying clicks at 7.5 cents each. Now 1,000 clicks costs me only $75.

Experts love CPM bidding for good reasons. There is a bit to learn to make CPM highly effective, but once you do, it can be a lot of fun. And the secrets to making CPM highly effective are actually just good general advertising and marketing skills. This is a reason we have spent so much time on general advertising skills in this book.

Facebook has a lot of ad space to sell, and we calculate they may add as much as two trillion new "inches" of advertising space in 2011. Think about it. Two trillion inches! What does this mean to you? To us, it means Facebook has a lot of advertising space to sell. A CTR rate as low as 0.2% or 0.3% may still be good enough to bid campaigns as CPM. Let's look at the math again.

Say I was buying 1,000 clicks at 50 cents a click, and my CTR is 0.07%. What will it cost me to buy 1,000 clicks paying 50 cents CPC? $500.

- What will it cost me to buy 1,000 clicks paying 50 cents CPM? $714.
- What if my CTR is 0.08%? I can buy 1,000 clicks paying 50 cents CPM for $625.
- What if my CTR is 0.09%? I can buy 1,000 clicks paying 50 cents CPM for $555.
- What if my CTR is 0.1%? I can buy 1,000 clicks paying 50 cents CPM for $500, breaking even with CPC bids.
- What if my CTR is 0.2%? I can buy 1,000 clicks paying 50 cents CPM for $250.
- What if my CTR is 0.3%? I can buy 1,000 clicks paying 50 cents CPM for $167.
- What if my CTR is 0.4%? I can buy 1,000 clicks paying 50 cents CPM for $125.

Do the calculations on your ads. Determine how high your CTR needs to be to make CPM bidding dramatically less expensive than CPC bidding. It may, with a CTR as low as 0.2%.

Use CPM Bidding If You Believe Your Ad Will Continue to Perform Strongly During the CPM Campaign Duration

CPM is about getting a CTR high enough to be less expensive than CPC, and keeping it high enough long enough so that you save money over bidding CPC. If you fear your ad may soon fatigue, or that it cannot maintain a high CTR long enough, then you may not want to use CPM bidding.

Alternatively, you may want to set shorter durations and lower daily limits and run CPM anyway until it clearly starts costing more than your original test CPC campaign.

Use CPM Bidding If You Have the Ability to Regularly Check Up on Your Ads' Performance

Because CPM ads are so negatively affected by ad fatigue, it is best to choose CPM campaigns only if it is possible to frequently check in on the campaigns and turn them off if the ad stops delivering enough clicks.

Use CPM Bidding If You Scored an 8 or Higher on the Test

To score an 8 or higher on "Is Facebook for Me?" means you have a great target product for Facebook, which means you should be able to get high CTRs. You should work hard to get CPM working because you will likely save a lot of money over time.

Use CPM Bidding If You Are Running a More Formal Split Test

If you are split testing several ads across more than 1,000 impressions, then use CPM bidding. As each ad hits the targeted number of test impressions, simply pause the ad. This will get all of the ads displayed and the test completed quickly. Purchasing 1,000 impressions is very affordable, and this bidding method gets them displayed relatively evenly, even if some of the ads are not getting clicks.

YOU CAN PREDICT AD FATIGUE USING FREQUENCY

Ads can fatigue at any time, but if your ad is already working, frequency can clue you into how quickly it may stop working. A frequency of:

0 to 3:	Very Low Risk
3 to 6:	Low Risk
6 to 9:	Moderate Risk
9 to 12:	High Risk
12+:	Very High Risk

An ad with a frequency of 9 is at a high risk for fatigue and should be watched closely. Still, there is probably some life left in this ad, especially if estimated reach is not too close to reach. We've seen ads run into the 30s successfully and into the 50s not so successfully.

THE ROLLER COASTER RIDE OF CPM BIDDING

Here are a few different CPM strategies we suggest trying. Test our strategies and then come up with your own. Facebook continually changes, so there is no guarantee which is the best strategy on any given day.

Strategy 1: CPM Recommended Bid (Fast Start)

This strategy seeks to aggressively follow the suggested bid. It is a good strategy for getting your ad to display fast and for keeping it displayed. It uses one tactic to try to ensure you are not perpetually overbidding.

1. Start by bidding two cents higher than the minimum suggested CPM bid.
2. Check your ad every two to three hours each day. If the suggested bid has decreased, then lower your bid to two cents higher than the new minimum

suggested CPM bid. If the suggested CPM bid has been increased, rather than lowered, ignore the rise.

3. Continue doing step 2 until Facebooks stops displaying your ad or the ad has fatigued. Only raise your suggested CPM bid if Facebook stops displaying your ad for 24 hours and the ad is not too greatly fatigued.

Strategy 2: CPM Bid Down (Fast Start)

This strategy seeks to aggressively follow the suggested bid at launch and then to dramatically reduce bids near to what is actually being paid for clicks. This strategy seeks to prevent overpaying for clicks when the ads start to fatigue. It also keeps the CPM bid near what Facebook has been willing to accept for 1,000 ad displays. Facebook may be quicker to stop displaying your ad using this strategy.

1. Start by bidding two cents higher than the minimum suggested bid.
2. Check your ad every two to three hours each day. If the suggested bid has decreased, then lower your bid.
3. Once you have reached the lowest suggested bid, keep reducing your bid five cents after every few thousand impressions.
4. Continue step 3 until you approach within five cents of the average CPM you are actually paying for your ad.
5. Keep your bid at this lower level until Facebook stops displaying your ad for at least 24 hours.
6. If Facebook stops displaying your ad and the ad has not fatigued, begin again at step 1.
7. If Facebook stopped displaying your ad and it was fatigued, then turn the ad off.

Strategy 3: CPM Bid Up (Slow Start)

This strategy seeks the lowest CPM bid price Facebook will accept to display your ad without ever overpaying. Your ad may be displayed at off hours or at the end of the day, but if those clicks work for you, then this strategy may be worth trying. You should not be in a hurry if you want to use this strategy.

1. Start your CPM bid at five cents per 1,000 impressions (inside the United States).
2. Wait 24 hours. If your ad has not been displayed, then raise your bid another five cents.
3. Repeat step 2 until your ad begins to display.

4. Once the ad is being displayed, you may try decreasing your bid by a penny an hour until the ad stops displaying. Then raise the bid back to the last level where it was displayed.

Depending on your expected actual CPM, your starting minimum suggested bid, and your patience, you may make these increments at 10 cents or 20 cents, instead of five cents.

CPM CLICKS FOR 0.1 CENT?

Fans of 1980s hard rock feel a little like a persecuted minority in the music community. Most people like to diss 1980s hard rock, and if you are a fan of that music, it is truly a delight to find another true fan who will understand your passion and not ridicule it.

Josh Barsch, who loved 1980s hard rock, noticed that when conventions and concerts featuring the music were always packed. The fans may have been in hiding, but they came out to meet each other. So Josh created a fan site years ago called MamasFallenAngels to talk about and feature the music he loved, 1980s hard rock. The fan site has existed for many years—first as a blog and later as a social networking site.

Josh did some advertising on content networks to find his fellow fans; Myspace was a great place to find like-minded fans for a while. He found fans all around the globe, paying only pennies a click on Google and other content networks to find them.

"MamasFallenAngels" has members from all over the world. They are loyal to the music and to each other. The fans created subgroups in multiple foreign languages where members themselves translate messages and music news to other languages.

The fans even wrote and translated the content network ads into other languages, to help find more fans worldwide.

Josh started running his ads on Facebook. He simply copied his Myspace ads to Facebook ads. Of course, on Facebook, the targeting is amazing for psychographics, language, and country. It is possible to specifically advertise to people who like Mötley Crüe in Hungary. It turns out this is a great thing to do.

CPM CLICKS FOR 0.1 CENT?, continued

Josh's Mötley Crüe ad on Facebook drew a 3% CTR in Hungary. Simply bidding the suggested CPM rate (a rate lower in Hungary than in the United States) captured so many clicks that MamasFallenAngels got the report seen in the figure below.

Date	Imp.	Social %	Clicks	CTR (%)	Avg. CPC ($)	Avg. CPM ($)	Spent ($)
02/16/2011	8,498	0.0%	72	0.847%	0.00	0.01	0.12
02/15/2011	17,966	0.0%	251	1.397%	0.00	0.01	0.26
02/14/2011	4,855	0.0%	105	2.163%	0.00	0.04	0.18
Lifetime	**31,319**	**0.0%**	**428**	**1.367%**	**0.00**	**0.02**	**0.56**

CPM Costs So Low They Do Not Display in the Report

You are seeing that correctly. The cost was a little more than a tenth of a cent per click. Josh had to do the division himself to determine what he was spending. He actually got used to seeing CPC being reported for less than a penny a click. If he saw a higher CPC, he would simply go to another band, another language, or another country.

Internationally, in just a few months, MamasFallenAngels purchased 68,000,000 impressions and 101,000 clicks for about $1,000.

When Josh first saw 43 clicks come in for only 6 cents, he knew it was going to be fun. And because he had an international audience, his fans volunteered to translate the ads into even more languages. They are fans! And they want to talk with other fans. They like Mötley Crüe and want to talk with other fans around the world who share that passion.

MamasFallenAngels is a labor of love. But it does display some ads to keep the server running. It is hard to imagine, but technically MamasFallenAngels found a way to arbitrage CPM bid clicks for a profit on a global scale.

Josh has tried CPM for other Facebook business and freely admits it can be hard. However, if you can target a narrow niche of true fans, well, it is pure joy

CPM CLICKS FOR 0.1 CENT?, continued

to purchase 105 clicks for 18 cents. His biggest hint for the rest of us: the more obscure the country, the longer you can expect amazing results. Some of his ads ran for as long as two weeks at these amazing rates before the ads began to fatigue.

Josh runs StraightForward Interactive in Rapid City, South Dakota.

PERRY'S ADVICE FOR JOSH. There's not a lot of money to be made selling CDs or sending people to iTunes. But there's a lot of money in tickets. I went to a Rush concert just a few weeks ago, and front-section tickets were going for $600 apiece. That inspired me to write a series of articles called "Marketing Secrets of RUSH." You can get that at www.perrymarshall.com/rush/.

I once had a client who sold $2,000+ VIP entertainment packages for couples which included things like front-row seats, limousine rides, dinner, drinks for VIPs during intermission, and backstage passes to meet the band.

Is there money in music? You bet. If you're willing to cater to all those kinds of needs, you can build a business that goes far beyond brokering clicks for pennies.

Chapter Fifteen

Landing Pages

SET SPECIFIC GOALS FOR LANDING PAGES

Aristotle understood landing pages probably better than anyone, even though he lived more than 2,000 years before landing pages were invented. Technically, of course, he wasn't talking about successful landing pages—but why split hairs over amazingly good, landing page advice?

A well-executed landing page is the difference between a successful Facebook ad campaign and a miserable failure. Getting a prospect to successfully click on an ad is only the first step of a relationship that can continue for days, months, or even decades. If you are going to establish a long relationship with a customer, you must first survive the first 15 seconds of his visit to your landing page.

Within 15 seconds your prospect is deciding whether to stay with you or press the back button and abandon your presence forever. If you paid a dollar for a click and you lose your prospects in the first 15 seconds, you just paid $240 per hour to fail to engage the people who clicked on your ads.

> "*First*, have a definite, clear practical ideal; a goal, an objective. Second, have the necessary means to achieve your ends; wisdom, money, materials, and methods. Third, adjust all your means to that end."
>
> —ARISTOTLE

You cannot afford to spend that much money on lost leads. Once prospects click on your ad, you have to capture their attention, trigger their interests, and not let them go. Your very livelihood depends on it.

This chapter is your crash course on landing pages. You will learn to build and execute a successful landing page on Facebook and on your website. You have no choice in the matter. Learn to do this well or go down in flames.

When you apply the technique of split testing to your landing page, you will—eventually—develop a stunningly effective page. It is hard work—but it is work that pays.

THE PAGE MUST HAVE A GOAL AND AN OFFER

First and foremost, you must establish a clear goal for your landing page. The goal must be measurable. In some cases, that goal will be to actually have the prospect complete an order. However, we always recommend an intermediate goal to capture prospects' information so you have more than one chance to connect with them and complete a sale. Landing pages are often called "lead capture pages." Remember that name because it implies the real goal of the landing page is to capture contact information.

The goal—to capture a prospect's contact information—is one we recommend for almost every landing page. On a Facebook landing page, this goal has the following two parts:

1. Get the prospect to "like" the page.
2. Get the prospect to provide you with additional contact information, usually an email address, so you can deliver to their email something of value.

It all begins with a compelling offer presented in your original ad. A quick way to establish credibility and build a relationship is to offer something in your original ad that you instantly deliver in your landing page. In a digital world, the offer and the delivery is frequently some form of information. You may deliver the information in videos, in papers, or on web pages. The benefit of delivering information is that it is easy to provide without incurring additional costs.

If your offer is to provide free information, it should be information that somebody who would buy your products would likely find interesting.

Are you a dentist? Offer tips on ways to "Avoid These 5 Foods That Will Stain Your Teeth." Or "Three Simple Ways to Remove Tooth Stains You Can Do at Home."

Are you a bookstore? Offer "Five Life-Changing Books Every Child Should Read," or "Four Secrets to Improving Your Grades Without Doing More Studying."

You get the idea. In figure 15.1 you can see some free information Perry offers, a series of letters about the "Nine Great Lies of Sales and Marketing." This is just one of dozens of offers Perry has created on different landing pages for his business alone!

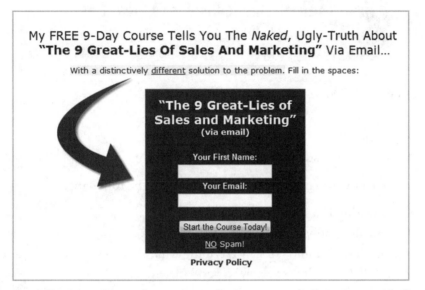

FIGURE 15.1–Offer Something of Interest to the Prospect—Collect Contact Information

There is something else you should include on the form collecting contact information. It is a privacy policy and a "NO Spam!" message. When you are collecting information, you should make a commitment to your visitors that you will not violate their trust. And, of course, you should live up to that commitment.

The landing page has a real and a strong goal, to capture the prospect's contact information. Try to do that as soon as possible.

On a Facebook landing page, immediately ask for a "like," in order for prospects to receive access to free information, as seen in Figure 15.2.

After prospective customers like the page, we then request their names and email addresses in order to send them the free information.

In our experience, it is best to minimize the information and the steps you put in front of the users before you collect their contact information. Focus your message and focus your prospect on providing you with contact information. Look at your Facebook ad and ask yourself if it has all the necessary elements. You ad should have the following elements:

· An eye-catching image
· A compelling headline

FIGURE 15.2–Request a "Like" First in Facebook

- A specific offer
- A call to action, such as "click now" or "like this page."

Next, look at your landing page; it should have the following:

- A captivating headline
- A compelling offer
- A short description or video describing what it is you are offering and what's in it. Bullets are almost always a good idea here.
- An explanation of how to get what you are offering. Do prospects fill in a form, make a phone call, or do something else?
- A promise not to violate trust. At minimum, include a link to your privacy policy. You may want to openly state that you do not spam.
- The opt-in form itself.

Don't stop thinking about your prospects' experience after they opt in. After the landing page, arrange for the following steps:

- Take them to another interesting page with an additional offer
- Automatically follow up with interesting and engaging information
- Make a specific request for a deeper connection.

To achieve the maximum results from your ad, you design the entire user experience from ad to final purchase.

VISUALLY PLEASING LANDING PAGES

If you send Facebook prospects to a landing page that is just a few text boxes and fields to fill in, they are likely to simply leave the page. Give the page some color. A little life. On Facebook—where people go specifically to connect to people—a landing page with a picture of people looking right at you is highly appropriate. It is called Facebook, after all, and it is hard to go wrong with faces. You don't always need pictures of people on landing pages, but the pages should always be visually compelling.

Facebook users come to the site to be entertained and amused. Tom's best landing page sequence contained an animated video. Animation is fun. Your presentation can be fun even when the topic is serious.

If your opt-in page is off of Facebook, this is even more important. Leaving the Facebook environment is especially jarring so don't send your guests out into a dark alley, alone, to sit by the dumpsters. Facebook Connect, a Facebook programming interface, even makes it possible to extend the Facebook environment directly to your landing page on your website.

MAKE A COMPELLING OFFER

A lot of people want to offer a raffle or a contest to capture initial contact information. Although this technique works, I do not think it is generally as compelling as providing prospects with free information that complements your business.

Why? Because a raffle or contest is a short conversation. "Here. Enter my contest. Done." Not much else to talk about. But a well-written piece of information, in print or video, draws the prospect onto the front porch and into a conversation. It is the beginning of a relationship. In most contests most people lose. Not really the best way to start a relationship. More like not showing up to the first date.

So what is your compelling offer? Well, it will be unique to you. Describe your customers, who they are, and why they would buy from you. Then ask yourself this question: Is there something these customers would like to know that I could tell them? If there is, then make that your offer. By the way, there is always something your customers would like to know that your can tell them. If you can't think of it, then simply ask your customers. They will let you know!

DOUBLE YOUR OPT-IN RATE

Are you currently advertising on Facebook and driving clicks to your website? You have the potential to double your opt-in rate with one simple change.

Direct traffic to a Facebook landing page instead of to your website.

This strategy repeatedly delivers double-digit improvements in opt-ins and has doubled them in many, many cases. The Facebook ecosystem has an inherent trust factor that is almost unique on the web. A Facebook page has known rules and behaviors. Fans of the page are visible. Users leave comments and report abuse to

Facebook. All of these interaction points make Facebook more trustworthy. Users know it. And users respond better to content delivered on Facebook.

APPROACHES TO LANDING PAGE COPY

Different people will provide dramatically different suggestions on what constitutes a good landing page. We will review several different approaches you can test, including:

- Minimal
- Long Copy
- Squeeze

Minimal

A minimal landing page may not have much more on it than a restatement of the original promise in the advertisement, an opt-in form, and a request for a "like." Our favorite description of a minimal page is "a message in a vacuum." The prospect is not distracted by other offers or lots of text. Just a simple call to action.

The thinking behind this is straightforward. If someone clicks on an ad that makes a specific offer, then he or she has already expressed his or her interest in that offer. Don't keep selling after the prospect is ready to buy. Instead, provide the simplest opt-in form imaginable to complete your delivery.

If you enticed your prospect with an ad that promises, "Avoid embarrassment. A simple test to discover if you secretly have bad breath," then, on the landing page, you may not need to do much more than say, "Enter you name and email address and we will send you the simple test!" Perhaps add some bullet points for just a little emphasis.

Or if your landing page is on Facebook, you may say, "Like this page to get access to our free video: 'How to know if you secretly have bad breath!'"

It is highly likely that anything more than a minimal opt-in page will decrease your subscriber opt-in rates, not increase them. Of course, this claim should be split tested by you.

Long Copy

There is another approach to landing-page writing. That approach asks, "Why stop writing if the prospect is willing to keep reading?" Some marketers have a great deal of success spinning a story and drawing the reader into very long copy with multiple headlines, bullets, teasers, testimonials, and multiple calls to action. Some successful long copy pages I've written didn't even offer an opt-in opportunity until after the prospect had scrolled a page or two!

Now you might ask, "Why would you ever write an opt-in page with the first opt-in scrolled off the page?" Our answer was simple: we didn't want a long list of prospects; we wanted only prospects who were clearly emotionally attached to the message. We wanted prospects that read to the end of a long page of copy and finished by saying, "I want to learn more."

What type of business might want to do this? A high-end consulting business with limited delivery capability would. If your delivery system doesn't scale, then you really do want to focus on finding the best customers—best for them and best for you. Prospects who read your long copy and then request a white paper are really interested in what you are saying.

They are investing their time and their energy into reading your messages. They are much more likely to be better consulting clients than those who refuse to read more than 25 words.

If you are selling a complex product that requires deep understanding from your customer to make a purchase decision, test long-copy messages. Even if the long copy is not in your original landing page, it may be appropriate in your emails, videos, articles, white papers, and blog posts.

In long-copy landing pages, the prospect may be given multiple opportunities

> "*The* fundamental metric in retail sales is dollars per square foot. The fundamental metric in online marketing is cost per thousand impressions. Both measure the economic power of space."
>
> —PERRY MARSHALL

to respond. The page may tell a bit of a story, provide some testimonials, and then provide an opt-in. If the user doesn't opt-in, then the copy continues offering more stories, more testimonials, and more opt-in opportunities. This could go on forever.

There is another benefit to long copy for some customers. Some customers, especially corporate customers, are looking for a specific solution to a specific problem. They may be wary of providing their contact information unless they are convinced you have something they want. Long copy can convince them you have the answer they are looking for.

Long copy provides prospects with an opportunity to stand on your front porch and find out what you have to offer. They need to read and think about your long copy in order to become comfortable enough to trust you with their name and email address. These customers would likely never be captured with a short-copy landing page, and they can be some of the most lucrative customers because they control multimillion-dollar budgets.

Although short copy may convert to more opt-in leads than long copy, it may not convert some of your best leads. Therefore, it may be wise to test both short copy and long copy landing pages to catch both ends of the spectrum.

THE LONG AND THE SHORT OF IT

Long copy and short copy are not an "either or" proposition. Selling on the front porch offers an infinite number of landing page opportunities. Your original Facebook ad may lead to a short landing page with an opt-in offer. In your follow-up emails, you may send messages that link back to long page sales copy. It is perfectly OK to have both.

I suspect that it is much harder to do a successful long-copy landing page in Facebook. There are multiple reasons for this, including:

· The user gets distracted by Facebook ads and navigation
· You have limited width for your long copy text
· Facebook users are relaxing and may have a mental predisposition away from long copy
· Facebook users are not searching for answers and don't really want to read yours

My suggestion: if taking a long-copy approach on a Facebook page, replace text with a longer video. Even then, display the video only after getting at least a "like."

Squeeze Pages

You may have read or heard the term "squeeze page" in your study of online marketing. Squeeze pages are single web pages designed only to capture an opt-in response. Frequently, a squeeze page is the only web page clearly visible on an entire URL, and it has very long copy. I've seen single squeeze pages that were actually 36 pages long.

The squeeze page typically has no additional navigation and no external links. The goal is to focus the attention of the user on the opt-in offer only. It makes the user feel like the easiest way to leave the page is to provide an email address. The page squeezed visitors until they finally relented and gave up their email.

Highly aggressive squeeze pages display pop-ups asking for an opt-in, even if the user tries to leave the page without opting in by using a back navigation button.

Google considers "hard" squeeze pages (opt-in pages with no links) to be counter to good user experience. It no longer gives them good ranking in Google search and may even refuse to run your ads if you direct your customers only to a hard squeeze page.

EXAMPLE LANDING PAGE RULES

Facebook has a series of reasonable requirements around landing pages and destination URLs. Many of these requirements were specifically created to prohibit advertising to hard squeeze pages.

If you include a URL in the ad text or image, then the landing page must be at that URL. Landing pages cannot generate a pop-up, pop-over, or pop-under when a user enters or leaves the page.

Landing pages cannot disable the browser back button or in any way try to trap the user on the page, aka "mouse trapping." Landing pages cannot use "fake" browser behaviors like offering a close button that should close a window but instead opens another window.

Facebook was clever. By allowing for the "like" relationship between your visitor and your Facebook page, Facebook provides a friendly method for you to capture some of your visitors' information in a friendly way so you do not need to squeeze them nearly so hard.

Facebook does have rules about what can occur on a landing page pointed to by a Facebook ad. Make sure your landing page is following these rules or risk having your account banned.

Chained Landing Pages

One way to think about the experience you are crafting for your visitors is to realize that you are creating for them a series of linked-together landing pages—a chain of landing pages. An example chain is shown in Figure 15.3.

The first link on the chain is the "like." In order to provide free information and services to your user, they must first "like" your Facebook page. Only after they like the page are they even offered the second link in the chain, the opt-in form. Many sellers think that once the user has opted-in and provided their email, the job is done. Wrong. This is actually the best place to now close a sale.

Your customer has committed to two actions. They liked your page, and they submitted their email to you. They are in the habit of saying yes so don't stop asking now. After they have completed your opt-in form, they should be taken to another

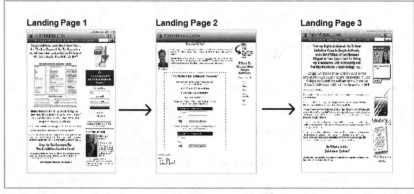

FIGURE 15.3–A Chain of Landing Pages and Offers

landing page that contains a video further describing your products and services. They are likely amenable to watching a three- or four-minute video at this point.

If they like the video, it is perfectly reasonable for them to make an even bigger commitment in the relationship, like buying now! If they buy, you can take them to yet another page with yet another offer. Perhaps on this page there is a request for them to contact their friends in Facebook to tell them about this great new product they just purchased. This chain of pages and offers, as seen in Figure 15.3, can continue on and on. If they want to keep the conversation going, then there is no reason for you to stop.

This is just one example of a chain of events around your landing page. It may not be appropriate for all businesses and offers; still, if your potential customers are willing to keep reading or watching, then you should keep writing and showing. As long as the visitor is on your front porch, offer them more ways to amuse themselves, more ways to learn about your products and services, and more opportunities to interact and buy.

Dynamic Landing Pages

Facebook allows you to build dynamic landing pages on your Facebook page. By dynamic, we mean that the content of the page can change as the user interacts with the page. So the same page in Facebook can look different to the user based on how he responds to prompts on the page. You can even detect if the user has "liked" your Facebook page and change the contents of the page based on that like.

First your landing page encourages liking the page, then it requests contact information, then it seeks to get a sale, and then it shares the news with your customer's friends. It is possible for all of this to happen within a single "tab" of a Facebook page. You will need a web page developer to make this work.

Dynamic landing pages that require a like before the visitor is offered access to free information outperform static landing pages 300% at acquiring likes. Moral of the story: if you have a good, free information offer, request a like before giving away the information.

Autoresponders

The vast majority of successful Facebook marketing campaigns we have seen include an autoresponder. I (Perry) think it's a big mistake not to use email marketing in conjunction with Facebook.

Think about it: Facebook was actually built through viral email marketing. When you signed up, Facebook invited you to supply your Gmail or Yahoo! login so it could "spam" all your friends and invite them to join you on Facebook. Many, if not most, people get email notifications every time something happens in their Facebook account.

Email is still the chassis that online marketing is built on.

An autoresponder is a program that automatically sends emails in sequence. These emails are almost always written and scheduled in advance. The forms on your landing page should lead directly to an autoresponder that sends the initial package of free information and also a series of well-written follow-up messages. All of these messages should be packed full of value, great conversation, and great ideas so they are not perceived as spam.

Simple autoresponders you can use:

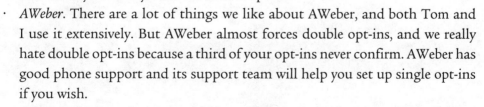

The vast majority of successful Facebook marketing campaigns we have seen include an autoresponder. I think it's a big mistake not to use email marketing in conjunction with Facebook.

· *iContact.* If you are looking for an inexpensive autoresponder that's basic and easy to use, consider iContact. It does not try to force you to use double opt-ins.

· *AWeber.* There are a lot of things we like about AWeber, and both Tom and I use it extensively. But AWeber almost forces double opt-ins, and we really hate double opt-ins because a third of your opt-ins never confirm. AWeber has good phone support and its support team will help you set up single opt-ins if you wish.

· *Infusionsoft.* If you have a sophisticated business, or if you're going to have a sophisticated business, I recommend that you just go to Infusionsoft. You can go to www.ManageProSoftware.com and sign up. I have a video that outlines my own autoresponder strategy at http://www.perrymarshall.com/buildingthemaze/.

One of the keys to effective Facebook marketing for a lot of people is not going for the jugular right out of the gate.

I learned from Alex Mandossian 10 years ago: If you sell an e-commerce product, or virtually any kind of product on the web, you're likely going to find more success by targeting people, connecting with them, starting a conversation, and building a relationship with them first, before you try to monetize your clicks.

InfusionSoft founder and CEO Clate Mask tells me that only about 10% of marketers have more than the most rudimentary autoresponder sequence. This is an easy opportunity to separate yourself from the competition. Just 10 well-timed messages can substantially improve your traction.

Chapter Sixteen

Who Cares If the Ad Is Cheap? Are You Making Money?

ADS IN CONTEXT

When I (Perry) was brand new to search marketing, one of my fellow marketing maniacs, Yanik Silver, told about a fascinating case study. The keyword "typing lessons" was getting more than 100,000 searches per month, and the cost per click was under 10 cents. It looked like a golden opportunity: you could get lots of traffic for cheap.

> *"Being good in business is the most fascinating kind of art. Making money is art and working is art and good business is the best art."*
>
> —ANDY WARHOL

But there was a problem: there were so many free, online typing courses, hardly anyone was willing to pay for products. So even though the clicks were cheap, getting a good return on investment for that traffic was tricky.

The principle applies to any kind of advertising, online or off. Just because it's economical doesn't mean it pays.

Your success in Facebook advertising is not measured by your click-through rate or cost per click. You must understand how the ad campaigns impact the bottom line of your business.

You have to be able to describe clearly each step in your sales process. What you can't describe, you will not measure. What you do not measure, you cannot manage.

A potential customer clicking on an ad is the first step in a chain of events that hopefully ends with money in your pocket. Are your current ads making you money?

To answer this question, start by putting labels on the people in your sales funnel based on where they are in the sales process. This allows you to describe the funnel more effectively and to measure and report on each stage of the sales process. Any labels will do, provided you have a clear definition for them. In this chapter, we use the following labels:

- *A lead*: someone who clicks on a URL you have provided them. The click may be from an ad, organic search, affiliates, purchased email list, silly videos, or any other source. The key to being a lead is a person has specifically clicked on your link. She is now in your hands, and you are guiding her on a journey.
- *A prospect*: a person who opts into at least one offer you make and provides you with additional contact information. A prospect is followed up with additional marketing and sales materials. If the prospect has not yet paid us, then he is counted as a prospect and not as a customer. "Likes" in Facebook are a form of a prospect. So are people who opt in to email lists. These are referred to respectively as "like prospects" and "list prospects." We want both. (By the way, an email address is about 10 times more valuable than a "like." Never forget that.)
- *A customer*: a prospect who has purchased a product from you or otherwise generated revenue.

For your ad campaign to succeed

- leads must become prospects;
- prospects must become customers.

This is hard to learn, but traffic is not necessarily your friend. Having millions of leads that never produce customers is not a win. It is a wasted expense. It can destroy your business.

The goal of your campaign is not to increase traffic; it is to increase sales. And everything prospects do after they click on the ad is part of a choreographed dance from first click to closed deal. All of this must occur at a cost that is reasonable enough so that profit is generated.

There are many parts of the dance, and each part should be tracked. You are seeking to drive the prospect to measurable actions you can use to judge the effectiveness of your marketing decisions, from initial ad to final call to action. Measurable actions include the following:

- Clicks
- Likes
- Visits
- Opt-ins
- Purchases
- Refunds
- Complaints
- Referrals
- Repeat business.

If you track and measure only CTR, you are getting only a tiny part of the story.

A BASIC TRACKING SPREADSHEET

The most basic tracking spreadsheet you should create for your Facebook advertising campaign should follow

- leads,
- cost per lead (CPL),
- prospects (list),
- cost per prospect (list),
- customers,
- cost per customer.

Facebook ads automatically provides you with

- leads, reported as clicks,
- cost per lead (CPL), reported as cost per click or CPC in the Facebook report.

Tracking the remaining values requires more effort on your part. If you have multiple traffic sources, you also need to separately track which prospects on your mailing list come from which lead source. And, you also need to track how many prospects become customers.

Action	Facebook Ad Lead Source
Leads (May 1 to May 31)	1,547
Cost per lead (CPL)	$0.38
Prospects (May 1 to May 31)	129
Cost per prospect (CPP)	$4.56
Customers (May 1 to May 31)	13
Cost Per Customer (1 month)	$45.22

In the table on page 183, the price data at each point is important to understand. A click may cost only 38 cents, but we do not really understand the situation until we calculate that a customer costs $45.22. Depending on what you are selling your customers, $45.22 as a cost per customer may put you into a mansion or the poor house.

If you are doing a good job following up your prospects, you may, over time, convert more of them to customers and further reduce the cost of a customer. The cost per customer field has a lag to calculate it with complete assurance since you may try to sell that lead forever (or at least until they opt out of your list), but a week-to-week and month-to-month calculation provides you with actionable insights for your business, especially if the cost of conversion is obviously too high!

Notice the actions we choose to track are:

- *Specific*: everyone on your team can unambiguously describe the action.
- *Measurable*: everyone on your team can tell you with the exact same words the amount of the action that was performed.
- *Time Bound*: everyone on your team can tell you the time that passed to reach the reported measure.

TRACKING THE DESTINATION URL

Facebook allows you to select the destination URL for your ad. You can use a special tracking URL as the destination URL. A tracking URL tracks a click to a conversion and helps you later calculate the cost per conversion. The special tracking URL is created by a third party, which records clicks and help calculate conversion costs.

This is very powerful and is easy to do and makes calculating conversion rates and costs relatively simple.

All of your ads from all of your various traffic sources should use tracking URLs.

Google Analytics provides powerful and free tools you can use to track and tag destination URLs which make tracking URLs. You can track where a lead comes from and what percentage of those leads reach a conversion event (opt-in list or sale).

The URL builder in Google Analytics allows you to specify your original destination URL, and it creates a new destination URL to insert into the ad. You can provide tags for

- campaign source (referrer: Facebook);
- campaign medium (marketing medium: banner ad);
- campaign term (targeting used: U.S. males 18–24);
- campaign content (describe the ad itself: post sponsored story); and

· campaign name (name used in Facebook).

Later, Google Analytics provides reports to track clicks all the way from an original ad to a final conversion event, even if the conversion event occurred days later. You can even enter the cost per lead into Google Analytics, and it will calculate for you the cost per conversion.

Another ad tracking resource is HyperTracker. Many people are nervous about using Google Analytics because Google also sells ads to you and your competitors. If you are spending a lot of money and don't want the ad salesman also running your analytics, you may use an independent party tool like HyperTracker to track URLs and conversions. You can watch a video at www.video.hypertracker.net, or go to www.hypertracker.com.

A SLIGHT BUG IN THE SYSTEM

In theory, all of this automated tracking should be easy. We connect our original Facebook ad to a tracking URL and, to get the best conversion rate, we send our leads to a Facebook page.

Unfortunately, if you are sending your leads to a Facebook page, you have a slight problem.

To use a tracking URL in Facebook ads, we have to tell Facebook that the destination URL is an external URL. If we tell Facebook the destination URL is an external URL, we lose the Facebook social credibility features when the ad displays as shown in Figure 16.1 (e.g. "likes" on the ad, and friends who like the page).

👍 Like · 524 people like this.

FIGURE 16.1–Social Credibility Displays Below Some Ads

Currently, you are stuck. If you want to target Facebook pages directly to get the social credibility features, you need to use the pure Facebook URL and not your tracking URL. You can add additional tracking URLs on your Facebook landing page, and you can change those URLs when you change your ads, but you will not get a seamless report from original click to converting action.

Eventually, this will get better.

Chapter Seventeen

Bolt a Jet Engine to Your Business: Facebook Pages and Getting Liked

YOU LIKE ME, YOU REALLY LIKE ME

At first, the idea of putting up a Facebook page and asking people to "like" it might seem lame. Maybe you already put up a page or group a year or two ago, posted some status messages, and got a few hundred or even a few thousand likes. "Now what?" you ask. "I don't seem to be getting much out of having these fans."

Don't fret. Facebook has been working like Santa's elves to make your "likes" more valuable. In fact, *"Do I need to be liked? Absolutely not. I like to be liked. I enjoy being liked. I have to be liked. But it's not like this compulsive need to be liked. Like my need to be praised."*

—MICHAEL SCOTT, THE OFFICE

for almost every business getting likes (which translates into getting "fans") is one of the simplest and most powerful methods ever devised to gently nudge your customers toward additional sales.

Facebook has become one of the world's most powerful tools to announce special offers and events. You can remind your customers of your brand, presence, and offerings without offending or spamming them.

If you visit a web page for a new product, do you think it helps if you notice that five of your friends also visited that page and "liked" that product? You bet it does. Do you think it helps if you visit a web page and see the names and pictures of 10,000 other people who like that product? Right on. It's called social credibility, and it's the new order of marketing on the web.

"Wow, 10,183 fans. At the very least, I am not the first sucker to ever buy from this vendor. Perhaps this is even a legitimate product. Hey look, Diane likes this product. Diane is smart. Hey, Linda and Harold also like it. OK, I guess I'll give 'em a shot."

People look to outside sources to validate their purchase decisions. Facebook gives you social validation in the form of likes. Every legit product should have a Facebook page for visible street cred. I'll go one step further: every product should have a page so you can know precisely who likes or recommends that product.

Being "liked" is central to a well-executed Facebook advertising strategy. It provides social credibility, validation, and very reasonably priced follow-up advertising opportunities.

SEND TRAFFIC TO A FACEBOOK PAGE

You can send Facebook ads to any landing page that meets Facebook's guidelines. But may we gently suggest, strongly encourage, and forcefully demand that you send your leads to a Facebook page and not your own website?

If you send your clicks to a Facebook page, then the visitors remain in known and comfortable surroundings. Their defenses are much lower than when they are taken to a foreign website for the first time.

If you send your clicks to a Facebook page, visitors don't have to worry that you're about to install a virus on their computer, post offensive material, or assault them with pop-ups and ads. So they relax. Maybe even enough to look at your landing page, see your offer, and like your page.

Facebook provides the ultimate "soft opt-in"—the "like." Facebook users are very comfortable with, and have very little resistance to, the thought of liking your page. If you simply get the visitor to like your page, Facebook provides you with stunningly powerful methods to reach out to these fans again—both free and paid.

In test after test, driving a Facebook click to a Facebook page converts better than driving the click to a landing page on your website. Users know they can easily navigate away from a Facebook page, and they don't fear spending more time on your page reading, listening to, and watching your offers.

FIGURE 17.1–The Like Button

Of course you should try this for yourself, but do not be surprised if you see your opt-in rates jump 20% or more if you move your landing page to Facebook, especially after you've acquired a few thousand fans and built up some street cred.

A typical Facebook opt-in scenario may have the following steps:

- Users click on your ad and go to a Facebook page landing page, usually a welcome tab.
- You make an offer on this page that entices readers to "like" the page to receive more free content.
- After users like the page, you present them with an opportunity to opt in to an email list that will provide them with a free product or service or enter them into a competition or drawing.
- After they opt in to your email list, they see a different landing page with additional information, resources, and offers. This is the first step where they might be taken to a page that is no longer on Facebook.

The first three steps all occur within the warm, fuzzy cocoon of Facebook. Test this against another approach, and it is highly unlikely you'll do it the other way, especially after you discover what to do with the likes after you receive them.

ADVERTISING TO YOUR FANS

For more than a decade, I've (Perry) urged advertisers to capture email addresses to continue front porch conversations after the first visit. It takes bucks to get anybody's eyes on your landing page, so you should never let those eyes leave without first trying to capture a name and email.

Although well-crafted emails are frequently appreciated by opt-in customers, even the best-written emails sometimes feel like a pesky nuisance. Facebook provides another channel, a totally unique and friendly means of getting your brand message in front of your existing prospects and loyal customers. It can give them a nudge to provide a special offer, invite them to an event, or simply share timely news.

Facebook has created an entire new class of advertising: a "targeted opt-in banner ad" only for those who have declared a relationship with you by "liking" your page. Better yet, only you, the creator of the page, can specifically target as a group those who have "liked" your page. You have the exclusive ability to directly target the fans of your page.

THE POWER OF ADVERTISING TO EXISTING FANS

Zingerman's Delicatessen is an Ann Arbor, Michigan, institution. I mention it not because it is a client, but because I love Zingerman's food. I am a true fan. The deli owners and staff produce exceptional food, provide world-class service, and receive international press because of their dedication to these goals. It is a truly unique dining experience.

When someone visits me in Ann Arbor, I always take them to Zingerman's.

Zingerman's Facebook page has more than 28,000 fans. At any time, Zingerman's can now target these fans with a campaign. Forty-five days before the winter holiday season the deli can display to fans a fun reminder of its great holiday treats and mail-order gift packages.

Please note: I'm not talking about posting a status message. I'm talking about buying an ad that is only seen by fans—an ad that costs a few dollars.

It is highly unlikely 1,000 impressions of a sponsored story or ad will cost Zingerman's more than $1. Zingerman's can now get a "Remember Me" Christmas brand message in front of 28,000 fans—ten times for each fan—for about $280. It may only cost $70! The ad can take the fans to a dedicated landing page in one click where the customer can immediately place an order!

Stop and think about this for a minute. Sending a post card once to each fan would probably cost 30 cents each—$8,400! Snail mail is 30 times more expensive than Facebook and likely not nearly as effective.

Because, the annoyance factor on Facebook ads is zero, this is the world's least expensive spam-proof advertising.

Zingerman's has created in its fan page an amazingly affordable way to reach customers without spamming email, simply by having a liked page. Every small business needs a page to collect likes.

This technique is so simple and so powerful, so unprecedented in terms of marketing and advertising, I suspect it will be years before most businesses even begin to appreciate what Facebook has built for them.

If you are fortunate enough to be reading this now, you are at a distinct advantage. Pay close attention.

If you own a local coffee shop and you get 3,500 regular customers to like your Facebook page, you can place an ad in front of those customers on Facebook at will, at any time, for a few pennies per customer. You can offer specials, invite them to events, remind them of your brand in just a few minutes of time and for a few bucks. Got a special event this weekend? Most of them will know.

Facebook's new advertising modality is unprecedented in the history of advertising. It redefines the field of advertising for small and big companies alike. It means that EVERY business should create a Facebook page, even businesses who scored lower then 3 on the "Is Facebook for Me" test.

Your first goal is simply getting your leads and customers to like your Facebook page. Once your customers have liked you, Facebook makes it simple to reach them again quickly, inoffensively, and affordably.

TARGETING FANS

You can target Facebook fans, event and group members, and app users in the following three ways. Target:

1. only people who are not fans of your pages, events, groups, or apps;
2. only people who are fans of your pages, events, groups, or apps;
3. only friends of the fans of your pages, events, groups, or apps.

Use option 1 to reach people who are not already your fans. If you are just trying to add a fan or find a new lead, there is no need to advertise to people who already like you. When searching for new leads, use option 1 to exclude your fans.

Use option 2 to notify existing fans of something new. It is very inexpensive to get this message in front of them. If you have 10,000 fans of your local store's Facebook page, you can likely get your ad displayed 10 times to each of your existing customers for less than $100. Cheap—take advantage of it.

Use option 3 to reach out to friends of your fans. Use your existing social credibility to grow your customer base. Targeting tip: always split into a separate ad campaign when you use option 3. These campaigns will be more expensive, so you should advertise and track them separately.

"LIKE INFLATION" AND THE NEWS FEED

Many people caught on to the idea that they could post status updates to their Facebook page and have those status updates sent to the news feeds of their fans. Yes, this is an amazing, free, advertising opportunity. You may post any status updates you want, and you get free impressions with your fans.

A good status message should deliver at least as many free impressions as you have fans.

However, you should not rely on the free feed to get your messages to all your fans.

Why? Because eventually you will be only one of 1,000 or more pages your fans have liked. Your message may not make it into their feed at all. If they don't frequently "like" your status messages and comment on your page, then Facebook by default stops sending them your status updates.

I call this "like inflation."

Just like monetary inflation, over time, like inflation degrades the value of past likes. Unless a specific customer has been interacting and expressing ongoing interest in you on an ongoing basis, every three weeks, your status messages will start to get filtered out and not displayed. It simply won't appear in their news feed anymore.

To reach your fans, you need to specifically target them with additional ads.

SPONSORED STORIES

Facebook understands the power of reaching out to fans and to friends of fans with targeted advertising. To assist you, they have created and continually refine a whole new category of advertising called "sponsored stories."

If you select sponsored stories (see Figure 17.2), Facebook helps craft a special-looking ad with specific connection targeting. Facebook continues to add new types of sponsored stories based on the destination selected. To understand the types

FIGURE 17.2–Sponsored Stories Selection

of special ads available to you, select your destination, and then make the ad type "sponsored story." Here are a few sponsored stories you should consider running as part of your regular Facebook advertising.

"Page Like Story"–Sponsored Story

A "page like story" targets friends of fans with a special message. The message tells a user a friend has "liked" the page.

A page like story" is a very simple ad.

FIGURE 17.3–Page Like Story

For the example in Figure 17.3, I created a "page like story" for the Perry Marshall page. When somebody likes the Perry Marshall page, their friends see the ad. The ad displays a picture of the friend who liked the page. It says the friend "liked" the page. And it displays the page profile picture, name, and a like link.

The hope is that a person will click the like link for the page simply to join friends who have liked the page. A herd-friending response.

"Page Post Story"–Sponsored Story

A "page post story" targets fans of a page with a special message. The message features a new status message (a post) that has just been made to your Facebook page. In Figure 17.4, we see a page post story by Perry Marshall. This ad will be displayed prominently on the pages visited by Perry Marshall fans.

If you have a good status message that you want your fans to have a better chance of seeing, then feature the post in a page post story. You are paying to have your fans see your status message featured prominently on the pages they visit.

This type of ad may be used to feature specials, contests, or interesting news. It is also a way to reconnect some of your fans to your news feed. If your fans like or

FIGURE 17.4–Page Post Story

comment on your sponsored story, it increases the likelihood of future free messages getting to their feed.

You should display a page post message to your fans at least once every three weeks. For small businesses with 10,000 fans, bid the ad CPM, and set a lifetime budget to an amount where the ad will display 10 times to each fan. In my test case, this was a budget of only $40.

ADVERTISE TO YOUR CUSTOMERS' FRIENDS

Advertising directly to your customers' friends can be done outside of sponsored stories. In both cases, you are seeking to leverage social credibility to find new leads. Targeting friends of fans is tailor-made for a local store. Once you get somebody to like your Facebook page, you can get your ad in front of friends who also live nearby. Like all Facebook ads, when you specifically target friends, you can filter them further on geographics, psychographics, and demographics.

Anyone who sees this new ad will have, by the very nature of the ad type, at least one friend who likes your business. You get instant social credibility. If multiple friends like your business, they see multiple names. Again, even more instant social credibility.

Advertising to friends may also be a way discover people who have not liked enough Facebook pages to match your psychographic profile but still meet your psychographic profile. Real-life friends and family members frequently have a fair bit in common in terms of thinking patterns—things that would not be immediately obvious for you to target in another way.

You attract like-minded thinkers by advertising to friends of fans. In my experience, these are rather expensive clicks. I suggest you employ this strategy after exhausting most of the other strategies already mentioned in this book.

Facebook's strangely named "like story" is a way to advertise to friends of your page. Because it is a sponsored story," this type of ad is more prominently featured on the friends' home page. Facebook restricts editing the ad's creative and other targeting options. Facebook says that if your page has more than 3,500 fans, those fans may have more than half a million friends.

A like story is a new way Facebook offers to reach those friends of fans so you can try to get a click and a like. It is another way you can advertise to friends of fans.

LIKE WHAT YOU LIKE

A favorite techniques for getting likes is what I call, "Like what you like." It's dirt simple but delightfully effective. You just ask users to like things they have already declared that they like. They've already liked a particular book, author, actor, movie, place, person, food, restaurant, or thing. So you simply ask them to like that thing again in your ad.

Of course, whatever you are asking them to like should be somehow connected to your business. For example, if you are a motorcycle repair and customization shop, it's perfectly reasonable to run an ad with a picture of a beautiful Harley (I know, they're all beautiful!) and ask readers to like your page if they love their Harley.

5-CENT LIKES WITH CPM—YES, EVEN IN THE UNITED STATES

You might not be surprised to find out you can get extremely cheap likes in foreign countries. But you can even get five-cent likes in the U.S. Here's how one of my clients did it.

Renee wanted at least 1,000 fans for her "Heroes for Young Readers" Facebook page. Renee is an author of this successful children's series with hundreds of thousands of books sold. She speaks frequently at schools, churches, and parenting groups on heroic characters, building character in children, and writing.

She created a Facebook page to feature her events, sharing pictures, videos, and inspirational messages. She wanted more fans for her page to establish social credibility and to generate referrals and references for speaking engagements.

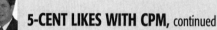

5-CENT LIKES WITH CPM, continued

Because Renee had written so many books on true heroic figures, she could find plenty of highly relevant topics to target when advertising. So she made a list of her personal top 10 heroes. She targeted people who like those same historical figures, authors, and celebrities. The fact that a Facebook user had liked a particular figure in the past triggered Renee's ad to display. Her ads had a picture and proclaimed, "If you like _____, then like my page." Her hero was a famous author.

Initially she tested all her ads using a $10 daily budget and CPC bidding (using CPC Strategy 1). Her goal was simply to identify which of the 10 heroic figures would provide the best CTR. Out of the 10 tested, two dramatically outperformed the others. The number 1 hero outperformed number 2 by a factor of 3:1.

She paused the nine underperforming ads and rebid the one high performing ad as CPM (using CPM Strategy 1). After she rebid the high CTR ad (around 1% CTR) as CPM, it delivered clicks as likes for less than 5 cents each. By the time the ad had entirely fatigued in the first cycle, the average cost per like was 9 cents.

The end result: a Facebook page with 1,047 likes, providing social credibility in less than one week, for only $91.

Any business can do this. Every business should do this.

On your landing page, talk about how you love your Harley, too, and you treat every Harley as if it is your own. Harley fans are maniacs. They tattoo the Harley brand name on their arms, legs and, uh, other parts. Die-hard fans. They'll like your ad, too.

An ordinary motorcycle mechanic can target lots of specific brands looking for fans. You can run an ad that says, "Press 'Like' if You Love Your Motorcycle."

These are simple, fun ways to get your page in front of your local audience. When you have 4,000 local fans who love motorcycles, you can very affordably advertise just to those local fans your events, specials, sales, and repair advice.

Chapter Eighteen

Free Traffic, Free Impressions, and Paid Advertising

FREE CLICKS CAN BE DEADLY

Bill McClure, founder of www.Coffee. org is a serial online entrepreneur, going all the way back to eFlowers.com and FlowersDirect.com, which he sold in 2002. He also did a stint as a member of my elite Roundtable group.

When Bill investigated the coffee market, he considered several existing websites that were available for sale.

One of them was doing $3 million per year in sales with a tiny staff and strong profitability. On paper, it was a superb business.

Only two problems.

> "*The small businessman is smart; he realizes there's no free lunch. On the other hand, he knows where to go to get a good inexpensive sandwich.*"
>
> —ADAM OSBORNE

1. Almost all the traffic was from free, organic "search engine optimization" (SEO) traffic. The left side of the search results.

   Now that SOUNDS really great. Free search traffic? Great SEO? What's not to like about that?

   The problem with it is this: what happens when the free traffic goes away?

Notice that I said "when" it goes away not "if" it goes away. It's an eventuality that there will be some Google dance, and one sad morning, the guy will be showing up on page 6 of Google search results instead of page 1.

The traffic dries up, and suddenly a $3 million business becomes a $300,000 business.

2. There was no benchmark of being able to buy traffic AT WILL (i.e. with paid advertising) and convert that traffic to sales profitably.

Which is to say: that business, even though on paper it was worth several million dollars, was not even a real business. It was built on the availability of free customers—which is a foundation of sand. Temporary success at best.

(As a matter of fact, the business owner was afraid to even TOUCH the website, which was clearly out of date, because he was afraid changing something might ruin his great SEO rankings.)

Instead of that business, Bill bought the domain Coffee.org and is building it into a traffic conversion machine and an established brand, Miss Ellie's coffee—a southern twist on America's favorite, morning beverage.

If your business is dependent on free customers, you do not have a business. You do not have any kind of "real" business until you have the ability to buy advertising from a variety of available sources and transform that traffic into sales and profits.

The kicker is, once you have solved the conversion puzzle, ALL forms of qualified traffic convert. You dominate your market in multiple dimensions, and you become nearly impossible to displace by other competitors. You are feared in your market. A force to reckon with.

Bill is feared in several markets, not just coffee. Once you've mastered this concept in one market, you can take it to others.

I am always and forever, totally wary of free advertising because eventually too many people try to join in, and your message risks getting diluted and lost in a flood of poorly conceived spam.

Make no mistake about it. The primary reason to create Facebook pages that get "likes" by your visitors is to have the opportunity to hit your "likes" with paid advertising.

It is always better to learn how to make a paid ad work and then, while the opportunity is available, apply those skills to make a free ad work, too.

This chapter, however, is about free impressions in Facebook. I would be remiss, in a book on Facebook advertising, not to provide additional suggestions on how to take advantage of those amazing, free Facebook ads: status updates.

STATUS UPDATES AS FREE ADS

When you post a status update on your Facebook page, everybody who liked the page may potentially receive a copy of that message in their news feed along with a thumbnail image. Your brand is instantly in front of hundreds to thousands of customers' free of charge.

Let's do the math. If you work hard and get people to like your Facebook page for your business, you can probably get up to 5,000 fans just from your existing customers walking in your Facebook front door. If you craft a status update for your customers 200 days a year, you may well receive—over the course of a year—500,000 impressions free of charge.

Improve your front porch experience just a little and you will receive at least one million free impressions a year. Post 365 days a year, and you are approaching two million free impressions.

Do you find this interesting yet?

These are one million free impressions reminding your existing customers you are in business and providing them with a reason to return.

If, just once a year, each of your customers repost just one of your status messages to their own Facebook walls, you will be introduced to as many as 250,000 new customers—free of charge.

(By the way, www.Coffee.org has 45,000 Facebook fans. It gets traffic from a dozen different places. It is not dangerously dependent on any one traffic source.)

Unfortunately, if you have 5,000 fans, very few of them may ever receive your status updates. Why? Because you write crappy status updates! Facebook does not want to feed uninteresting status messages to their users. They don't want to overwhelm users with too many status updates.

Facebook will not automatically feed every status update to every eligible user because it would be way too many messages—a mighty Niagara River of messages. Facebook doesn't want its users drinking directly from the Niagara River and risking going over the falls. So they dam the river of messages, filter the water, and route it to a tap where it can be dribbled out safely. If you want your updates routed to your users for free, you need to learn to write good messages.

ENSURING YOUR STATUS UPDATES REACH YOUR USERS

So what status updates get displayed to a user? Facebook hopes it is the status messages the user wants to actually see. How does it calculate this? Well, it is a secret. But if we ask ourselves "How would we calculate this?" we may be able to glean some insight on how to write better messages so that Facebook will forward them to more users.

If you were Facebook, filtering the news feed, you would be inclined to forward messages to users from pages where they

- regularly like status updates,
- answer questions,
- regularly comment on status messages,
- sometimes repost the status updates to their walls.

There are probably more ways for Facebook to determine if users like a page, such as watching how many times your fans actually visit your page, how much time they spend on the page, whether they respond to multiple messages at one time, and on and on.

But for the moment, we will suggest it is those actions listed above that primarily reflect a user's interest in your status updates. If you write status messages that entice fans to engage in one or more of these four activities, then Facebook will be dramatically more likely to send them your status updates.

We also surmise that the more the fan interacts with a response the more Facebook values that response. Reposting a status update to a fan's own status indicates higher interest in a status message than simply liking the message. However, any of these activities provide positive feedback to Facebook of a fan's enjoyment of your page and your status updates.

Facebook recently started displaying to page administrators how many impressions your status update has received and how many people responded to the message with a comment or a like. This information is in the form "X Impressions Y% Feedback."

3,048 Impressions • 1.54% Feedback

Facebook does not tell us how they compute X and Y, but clearly, the higher both numbers are, the better, and the feedback number is the most important because "liking, commenting, or forwarding the post" are clear examples of feedback. Make a game for yourself of writing status updates. To score your message, you need at least one impression for every two fans. If you have 1,000 fans, you need at least 500 impressions to keep score in the following way:

- Less than 0.5% feedback is a strike
- 1% feedback puts you on first base
- 1.5% feedback is a double

- · 2% feedback is a triple
- · 2.5% feedback or more is a home run
- · 5% or more is a grand slam

Our goal is to get on base as much as possible and to avoid striking out. You really do need to get on base fairly frequently or Facebook will stop showing your status updates to your fans. If users do not respond to your status messages at least once every three weeks, then new messages will likely not make their feeds.

DON'T SPAM—NEGATIVE FEEDBACK

If you keep striking out sending status updates, then take the hint. Your status messages are likely being considered spam by many of your fans. Watch your fan count to see how many people "unlike" your page. If the number is high, you may have problems.

Facebook provides its users with the ability to actively provide negative feedback on your messages as well as positive feedback. We suspect the feedback number it reports is only positive feedback.

At the upper right corner of your posts, when they appear in your news feed, you may click on an X. This X is for negative feedback. Clicking on the X pops up a menu (see Figure 18.1) with multiple, negative feedback choices: hide some or all posts, unlike a page, or mark the post as spam.

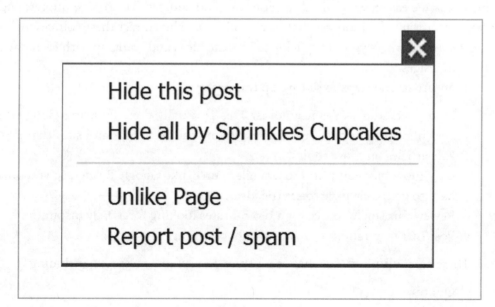

FIGURE 18.1–Types of Negative Feedback

One last thought about negative feedback: I (Perry) believe that the surest way to be loved by some is to be willing to be hated by others. This is true not just in marketing but in all spheres of life.

Take a look at any influential, famous, or successful person you care to name. Bill Clinton. Mick Jagger. Gandhi. Britney Spears. Nelson Mandela. Christopher Columbus. Lady Gaga. Gloria Steinem. Steve Jobs. Mother Teresa. Ralph Nader.

Every one of these people has (or had) a polarizing effect on the world around them. People either love 'em or hate 'em. These are people who have boldly presented themselves, their ideas, and accomplishments to the world and ignored the naysayers.

My question for you: What bold, controversial, and decisive stand can you take that will polarize people—that will repel some and attract others?

Success lies on the other side of your answer to that question.

That said, from the standpoint of Facebook's system, it does you no good to make people mad after they've become your fans. Of course, there are always going to be some disgruntled folks in every crowd. But the more precisely you target your traffic to begin with, the less mismatch there's going to be.

A WHEELBARROW OF CREATIVE IDEAS FOR DAILY STATUS MESSAGES

It can be a challenge to come up with great status updates to keep the front porch conversations going, especially if you are doing this 200 or more days a year. To make this challenge easier, get yourself a series of good sources for articles, quotes, and ideas. Specifically, find sources that offer RSS feeds. Then direct these sources into a single location where you can quickly review the ideas and come up with each day's status messages.

There are several steps to setting up this process.

· Find good sources for new ideas. This is usually done by using Google to search for your keywords and then finding the best blogs and sites that provide articles on those topics.
· Link those blogs and sites to a single source, like Google Reader, so you only have to go to one page to see the ideas.
· Review this single source for a few minutes looking for a daily inspiration.
· Post that inspiration into your Facebook status.

There are multiple things that can inspire good status messages, including:

· Quotes
· Articles

- Funny and educational videos
- Blog posts
- Websites
- Events that happened on this day in history
- News

In many of these cases, you post links to these ideas with just a brief introduction by you. In other cases, use these sources to spark a conversation on your page.

It is more important to spark conversation than to just repost interesting stories. It is really important to share front porch conversations and not to continually be selling. Unless you sell fun adventures or events, only the rare post should be directly about your product or service—as rare as 1 in 20 posts.

In addition, automatically reposting from your own blog or your Twitter account is not really a good idea. Sure it's quick, but reposting directly from a blog or a Twitter account feels like a repost. It doesn't feel like a warm and friendly, front porch conversation.

Also, Facebook knows they are reposted. If you were Facebook, would you treat a repost differently from original content? We would. And we bet Facebook folks do, too. Facebook status updates are a fundamentally different form than a tweet or a blog post. Take the time to reformat your message specifically for the Facebook environment. It is worth the extra minute or two of effort.

Turn Articles into Trivia Games

Frequently when we are looking for status messages to post to our pages, we read a really interesting article on a topic relevant to the page. At first we can be tempted to simply repost a link to that article or to rewrite a long summary. But remember, people are on Facebook mainly to have fun. Most of the time, they do not want to be linked to a multipage article, and they don't want to read a long summary.

Instead, we use the article to inspire a trivia question that the page users can quickly answer in a few seconds and then move on. Almost everyone likes trivia questions. And if they respond to the trivia question, we get credit from Facebook for getting the user to comment on our post.

It would not be surprising if getting a user to actually comment on a status post is one of the highest possible responses in Facebook's eyes since it reflects sincere interest.

So instead of getting credit for providing a link that somebody clicks on (a link that leaves Facebook may even be treated a little negatively in Facebook's rating system), you provide a simple trivia question that invites fast, short, and fun front porch conversation.

You discover an amazing article on the polio vaccine that your fans might enjoy. Instead of posting the article, write the following status message:

Jonas Salk was famous for inventing the _____ vaccine.

If the first person gets the correct answer right away, it doesn't matter. When the question shows up in a fan's news feed, someone else's answer will most likely not be included. And even if the answers do appear, people will not necessarily know whether that answer is correct and will keep posting guesses and comments on your page.

Note, we did not even write this as a question. We did not write, "Jonas Salk was famous for inventing what vaccine?" Although you can test it both ways, we've frequently gotten better responses if we just put in a blank.

Ask Them to "Like" Your Status Updates

Don't stop at just asking questions. Yes, it is great to get the user to answer a question, but we also want the "like" too. How do you do this? Specifically invite users to like your status post. It is a great way for them to interact with the page and participate in the conversation. Write the vaccine message as:

Jonas Salk was famous for inventing the _____ vaccine.
Press "Like" if you know the answer.

Now you will have some people who press "Like," some who provide a guess, and some who do both! And you get credit from Facebook for posting a good status update with a lot of positive feedback.

At least 30% of the time, ask the reader to specifically like your status message.

Almost Always End With a Question

Of course, we could still do even more. Our fill-in-the-blank question invites a short-term response, but we could also ask another open-ended question. To invite front porch conversation, you can add the following to your post:

Jonas Salk was famous for inventing the _____ vaccine.
Press "Like" if you know the answer.
Did you vaccinate your kids? Why or why not?

You are aware that there is some controversy around this subject, so you invite your fans to speak to the controversy; however, you take no position. Now you have a combination trivia question, like request, and front porch conversation starter, all in one status update. I bet this gets you at least a 1% response rate.

In some way or form, almost all of your Facebook status messages should end with a question. Ending with a question invites conversation from your fans, and conversation is positive feedback.

If you are running a Facebook page that features children's books and you run across a great list of 100 books every child should read, you may be tempted to just post a link to that list as a status update. The problem is, posting a link to a list of books doesn't really invite feedback. This list could be used instead to inspire a Facebook message that invites feedback.

> My favorite book when I was growing up was _____.

And now, instead of posting a link to a long list, you have posted a simple question that invites immediate feedback. Users can quickly respond, have a bit of fun, and go on their way.

If you really like the book list and really want to post it, then you can always add the list as a link in a comment after several people have replied with a comment. Another approach is to attach and post the list to your status update but to also write a message that invites participation.

> Here is a list of 100 amazing children's books!
> Press "Like" if your favorite book is on the list.
> What was the book and why was it your favorite?

This message provides the list, encourages a "like," and invites a comment. You could also invite your fans to share the list with their friends.

> Here is a list of 100 amazing children's books! Press "Like" if you think reading to children is a great way to promote literacy. Please support literacy and share this list with your friends.

Questions and Polls

Even Facebook has recognized that questions and polls are enjoyed by their users. So Facebook created a special interface called "questions." Questions supports asking questions, taking polls, and tracking responses—a great way to interact and engage fans.

Questions auotmatically records a fan's vote, shows how the fan's friends voted, and displays the total votes in numbers and a bar graph. Questions even allow fans to specifically follow and comment on a question or poll. To create a Facebook question or poll select "Question" instead of "Status" from the share interface.

Questions has a powerful viral feature where fans can specifically ask thier friends to answer a question. This feature has the potential to give your Facebook questions much more direct interaction than typical status updates.

Make People Feel Good About Themselves

The world has got enough bad news already. Right? People go to Facebook for some form of escape. It you want people to like a message, then send a message that makes them feel good about themselves. We call these types of status updates "Love Your Mother" messages. Basically, the post is some version of "press 'Like' if you love your mother."

On a page dedicated to home-schooling parents, I (Tom) posted the following status update:

> Did you know that on this day in 1887, Anne Sullivan began teaching
> six-year-old Helen Keller?
> Press "Like" if you think everyone who teaches
> six-year-olds is a "Miracle Worker" in their own way. :-)

It is not a surprise that this status update received a home run, with a response rate over 2.5%. It is positive, affirming, informative, and makes people feel good about themselves and what they have accomplished.

In Facebook, it is fun to help people feel good about themselves. And when they feel good, they press "Like."

No, I Do Not Like the Lincoln Assassination

People do not want to press like if you post a message about a tragic event. If you want to post a status update on the date Lincoln was assassinated you could write:

> On this date in history, President Lincoln was shot in Ford's Theatre.

But who wants to "like" the fact that President Lincoln was shot. Don't ask your fans to like the fact that Lincoln was assassinated. They won't do it, for one. And, if they did, wouldn't it be a little creepy? What might you post instead?

I wanted to honor President Lincoln by posting a message on April 14th to mark the tragic event that ended his life. I also wanted to post something that people could like and comment on. So, I asked a question that was highly likely to result in a positive response:

Press "Like" if you have ever been to the Lincoln Memorial in Washington, DC!

And then, to encourage comments, I asked my fans a question, too. The final status update was:

> Teaching History?
> Press "Like" if you have ever been to the Lincoln Memorial
> in Washington, DC! Do you know why I am thinking
> of President Lincoln today?

Notice I am not asking anyone to accidentally "like" the fact that President Lincoln was shot on this day. They have to come up with that information themselves. In addition, the question invites open-ended commentary. One person replied:

> My daughter shares his birthday—so he's become our most studied pres in
> this house! She actually cried when she first learned how
> he was assassinated. :/

I can think of no more fitting tribute.

Free Cupcakes

There is another type of status update that several small businesses have built entire marketing business models around. We call these "free cupcake" messages, inspired by Sprinkles Cupcakes. Sprinkles, which had surpassed 250,000 fans the last time I checked, frequently posts this style of status message:

> The first 25 people to whisper "make my day" at Sprinkles
> of Palo Alto will receive a free special cupcake.

Might we suggest you go one step further than Sprinkles? Occasionally offer someone who posts a funny comment a free coupon as well. It is a subtle way to encourage likes without violating Facebook's terms of service, which forbid using "likes" to officially enter contests.

Remember, Facebook needs to see responses to keep sending your feed to your fans, so you need to get responses on your post. Our recommendation for anyone using a free cupcake strategy is to write a status post like:

> The first 25 people to whisper "make my day" at Our Store will receive a free
> special cupcake. Press "Like" if you love our cupcakes, and tell us why!

Now you have the people coming to the store for free cupcakes and everyone encouraged to press "Like" and add a comment. Give someone who makes a funny

> *E*very business should give away cupcakes. Cupcakes are awesome! If you are a storefront, what is your cupcake? If you, as a coffee store, give away 15 free lattes a day but in return collect 250,000 fans, those fans will become the least expensive marketing operation you have ever done.

comment a free cupcake at the local store and post that person's picture back on the page to demonstrate you sometimes give free cupcakes just for funny comments.

If you have a local store, you should have some sort of free cupcake offer connected to Facebook status messages.

Pictures, Videos, and Links

Messages that contain funny pictures, emotionally moving videos, or really valuable links are great status updates for your page. However, they frequently do not get as many responses as simple fill-in-the-blank trivia question posts.

Why does this happen? The first and most obvious reason is that people are sharing your media content on their profiles and you are getting credit for posting the content.

Clearly, there is another measure of a successful message we may want to create. We offer you the following:

If you get 50% more impressions than you have fans when you post media, then you have hit a single. If you get 100% more impressions than you have fans when you post media, then you have hit a home run.

The best way to score these points with your status updates is to post items that get reposted. In our experience, funny or emotionally moving videos top that list. (Especially stuff that's drippy, sentimental, or inflammatory. But be very cautious of inflammatory.) Of course, you can always do a call to action in your post as well and request that the video get reposted.

> Please, let's get the word out. Repost this video to your wall—tell your friends!

PARTICIPATING IN THE CONVERSATION

After you post your original status message, you may also want to occasionally participate in the follow-up conversation by posting in the comment stream and liking comments from your fans.

When you like a comment, the person who made the comment gets a message that their comment has been liked! It closes the loop on the conversation and makes them feel good. If you are the administrator of the page and they see you liked their comment, it makes them feel especially good. So like lots (but not all) comments. Like the comments you really like. If you like them all, it may trigger Facebook to recognize that you are trying to game the system. Be genuine. Be real. Use these tips to generate real interaction and conversation, not to game the system.

We strongly encourage you to allow your customers to freely comment and post to your walls. You have the ability to delete comments, but this function should be used sparingly. Specifically, delete only:

· Spam
· Inappropriate language
· Unfair or attacking comments.

Some conversations can get heated. We like to stay out of those conversations and allow them to burn themselves out. We are not here to fight or argue with our customers or to convince our customers to think like we do about every issue. If two customers are arguing with each other and keep posting comments, think of how you must have convinced Facebook that they really like spending time on your page. We bet they count every single comment as a deep and abiding interest in your status updates.

If a user is spamming or otherwise behaving inappropriately, you can remove the comment, ban the user, mark the comment as spam, and report the comment as abusive as seen in Figure 18.2. To do this, click on the X that appears when you hover over the upper right corner of the comment.

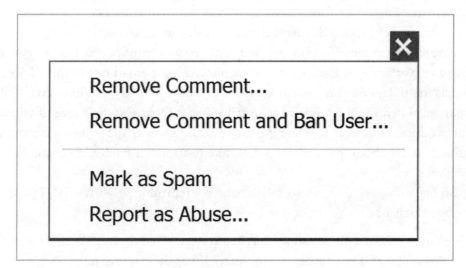

FIGURE 18.2–Dialogue to Report Abusive Comments

Syndicating Your Status Updates

It is possible to directly reference people, pages, events, and groups in your status updates. If you are responding to someone in a comment or posting a status message to someone who has "friended" you, put the @ character before you type the user's name and you will have the opportunity to turn that name into a link to the user's profile. The message will also be posted on that person's home page, visible to the user and his or her friends.

If you reference another page, event, or group in your status message, you can also place the @ character in front of the name of the page, event, or group, and those names will become links in your message to the page, event, or the group you referenced. In that way, your status update will appear on the wall of that page or group.

This is a powerful method of syndicating your status message to multiple walls all at once. However, it should be used with care so that you are not perceived as spamming. Use this feature:

· when you want to respond directly to a specific comment by a specific person, and
· when you want to have your message appear on the wall of another group or page.

Harvest Spontaneous Testimonials

Testimonials are your greatest friends. People are dramatically moved to action by testimonials. This effect is why testimonials are so frequently faked and why many governments are cracking down on the use of testimonials in advertising.

Give someone scientific evidence that your product helps people lose weight, and they yawn as their eyes glaze over. Have a hot, young woman testify that "I lost 15 pounds in 10 days on this diet, and I loved it," and suddenly you have everybody's attention. When users of your page post messages featuring their love of you and your products, it is clear to everyone that a real person is speaking—not a canned testimonial. Facebook page testimonials take testimonial credibility to an entirely new level.

So encourage your users to talk about your products. To testify! Try status messages such as:

· Press "Like" if (your product) has helped you. What do you like most about it?
· Press "Like" if you love (your product). What do you love most?
· Press "Like" if you use (your product). Why did you choose us?

- Press "Like" if you've ever recommended (your product) to a friend. What did you say?
- Press "Like" if you are a customer. What product do you like most?

Not only do these messages elicit conversation, they also deliver great insights into how your customers are thinking about your products and services. Of course, there is a little risk associated with asking this type of question—you may receive negative feedback as well. However, negative feedback is important for you to hear, too, so you might as well hear it now. Plus, you control the delete button!

If a customer leaves an especially great testimonial, send them a private message asking for permission to repost the testimonial on your website and in your outside marketing literature. You now have a nice, clear record for where the testimonial came from and how it was solicited in case anyone ever asks.

Commenting on Other's Walls—Another Reason to Have a Page

Facebook allows pages to behave, to some degree, as if they were users. If you are the administrator of a Facebook page, you may select to "'Use Facebook" as that page. If you select that option, you receive "likes" for the page and "notifications" for the page as if you were a normal user.

If you are using Facebook as your page and you post a comment or a status message on another page's wall, then your post includes your page name, your page thumbnail, and links back to your page.

It is perfectly reasonable to identify 50 to 100 additional, active pages whose visitors may also be interested in your page. You may post comments on these pages from time to time that add to the conversation on that page and complement your page's offerings. Spend some time reading each page and learn what types of comments are common and well-received. Your goal is to blend into the conversation and to occasionally say something so interesting or insightful that readers of those other pages decide to click on your profile and learn more about your page, too.

This is a great way to generate some free publicity for your page. However, be careful; your posts should actively add to the conversation of the page you are visiting or that page's administrator may mark your post as spam.

Some people simply don't pick up on subtle social clues as to what is proper behavior and what is rude behavior. Rude behavior is likely to get you marked as a spammer and abuser on Facebook, and it may kill your ability to syndicate messages.

So here's some frank advice: If you are the type of person who talks loudly on your phone in a restaurant or in a coffee bar, then you probably should not be posting on other people's pages. You are not good at picking up on subtle social clues as to what is proper social behavior and what is rude, and you should not be trying to execute this strategy. We are totally serious.

Keeping Up With Comments on Your Page

People may make comments on new and old stories all over your Facebook pages, in old status messages, and on other tabs such as discussions.

If users are making comments in a discussion, it can be easy for you to miss them. However, if you "Use Facebook As Your Page," you can select to receive a notification email that a user has posted a new question or comment to your page, even in an obscure discussion section. You can then click on that notification and go directly to the point where you need to respond to your user's comment or question.

You may also elect to have these notifications sent directly to your email. If your users are asking questions on Facebook, your support team can be very responsive without actually having to log into and look at Facebook. Given how distracting Facebook can be, this is a real win. You can respond in almost real time to customer questions and comments, creating an active community feel to your Facebook page without having to be actively scanning your page.

UNBLOCK AND MANAGE YOUR OWN NEWS FEED

On your Facebook homepage, Facebook has placed your incoming news feed. The messages you receive automatically every day from status updates posted by friends, family, groups, and pages you have "Liked" go into this news feed.

May I suggest you manage your news feed instead of letting Facebook manage it? If you like pages that are important to you but those pages only infrequently post messages, you may still want to get those messages. Don't let Facebook decide whether or not to show them to you.

At the very bottom of the news feed page is an option marked "Edit Options." If you click on this link, you find settings for "Show posts from:" Change this setting from the default of "Friends and pages you interact with most" to "All of your friends and pages" as seen in Figure 18.3.

This will allow you to be the editor of your news feed. If a friend or a page you like posts too many messages, then simply block that page or friend yourself. You can always unblock them from this same location later.

FIGURE 18.3–Censor Your Own Messages

PAGE INSIGHTS

Facebook has created page "Insights" to provide you with summary information about how your pages are being used. Check on your insights every few days to look for unexpected trends.

To find this information, click on a link called "Insights" on your Facebook page or in the ad manager.

Then click around in the insights reports. There are a lot of interesting hyperlinks and controls on these reports that do not necessarily look like hyperlinks and controls. So click on everything!

Insights on page visitors include:

· New and lifetime likes
· Daily, weekly, and monthly active users
· Unique page and post views
· Likes and comments on posts
· Page fan age and sex demographics
· Page fan country and city geographics
· Page fan language
· Total tab views
· External referrers.

Insights on posts include:

· Impressions
· Feedback percentage

Insights also provide nice trending graphs on page use and trending activity such as the Daily Active Users Graph seen in Figure 18.4.

The labels "Daily Active Users," "Weekly Active Users," and "Monthly Active Users" on this graph are controls. Clicking on the label "Weekly Active Users" turns that part of the graph on or off.

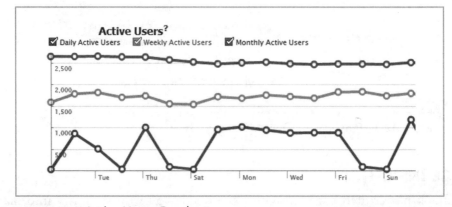

FIGURE 18.4–Active Users Graph

Chapter Nineteen

A Laser-Guided Missile for Your Marketing

BLOWHARD ON THE FRONT PORCH

If you really understand what it means to sell on the front porch, you will treat ad fatigue as a friend and a signal, not as a problem.

Imagine stopping by the front porch for a casual conversation and you meet someone who, at first, seems interesting but quickly monopolizes the conversation. You suddenly realize you have been standing there for 15 minutes and haven't been able to say a single word. This is not a conversation, it is a lecture, and you are the student.

> *"Any subject can be made interesting, and therefore any subject can be made boring."*
>
> —Hilaire Belloc

In 15 minutes you have already learned everything you ever wanted (and didn't want) to know about ancient Greek pottery, the speaker's passion, and your passing interest. But seriously, after 15 minutes, you don't really want to learn more about Greece.

The speaker still doesn't change the subject, so you make an excuse and leave the porch.

The next time you stop by to chat that person is still there and picks up on the pottery conversation again. Another 15 minutes of Greek pottery conversation.

Another 15 minutes with you unable to get even a word in the mix. Again you make an excuse and leave the porch.

The next time you walk by, you skip the porch entirely. You've had enough of ancient Greek pottery.

People who think ad fatigue is a problem want to yak about pottery forever. Their problem isn't ad fatigue. Their problem is they are boring their customers to

---

A SIGNAL TO CHANGE THE CONVERSATION

I have a simple ad I really like. It features a happy woman giving the thumbs-up sign.

Homeschool Advantage

Thank you. I signed up for a 1-month free trial and my daughter is loving it!

She is looking directly into the camera, has a beautiful smile, and is clearly enthusiastic. The body text comes directly from a status update a fan posted on Facebook.

It received 3.8 million impressions in 90 days. The reach was 138,000 and the frequency was 27.

Of course the ad fatigued eventually—but it never failed.

It worked!

It was an amazing success delivering thousands of clicks for a reasonable price. So what does it mean when the users stop clicking?

The people are telling you they need to hear or see something else. So what will it be? Here is a secret. Ask them!

---

death. They are talking on and on about Greek pottery and don't get that it's time to change the conversation.

Your ad that fatigued didn't fail. It was an amazing success.

It is just time to move on to another topic.

MISSILE ENGAGED—MOVING THE CONVERSATION FORWARD

Ad fatigue is your prospects of way of saying they want to change the conversation, so what do we do? We're selling on the front porch, so we do not need to be doing direct sales as seen in most Facebook ads. We can actually have a front porch conversation.

It turns out that Facebook has provided us with a wonderful tool to change the conversation. And it can be used in many different ways. The tool?

Facebook events.

You can advertise a Facebook event to your fans (see Figure 19.1). Advertise an event after a group of your ads have fatigued in order to change the conversation.

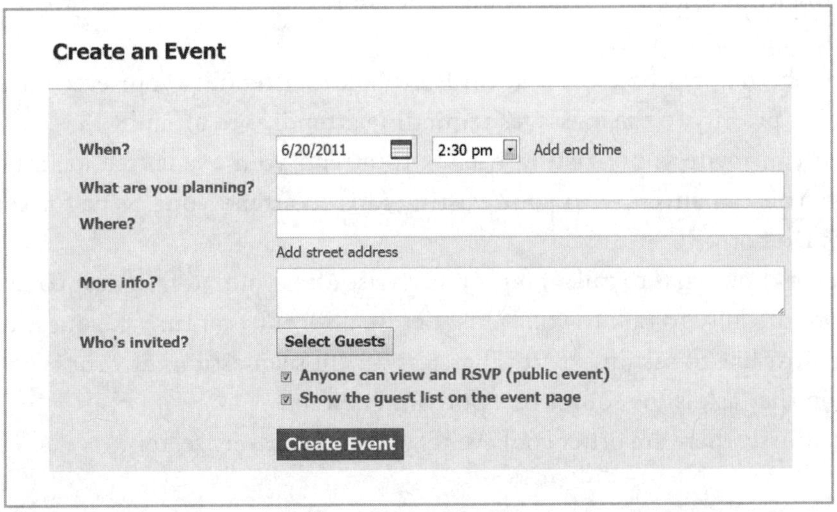

FIGURE 19.1–Interface to Create a Facebook Event

Facebook events appear as destinations that you can select in the "design your ad" section of the ads manager. You can target the advertising for your event just like any other ad. They are simple, powerful, guided missiles.

Once people confirm that they are "attending," Facebook does all the work required to remind them of the event.

An event is a great way to engage your user in additional conversations. And events don't fatigue—they happen.

"Ask Campaign" as a Facebook Event

When you run out of things to talk about on the front porch, see if your visitors have something they want to talk about. Allow them to initiate the next conversation.

One way to do this in Facebook is to launch an "ask campaign." In an "ask campaign," simply ask your fans, "What is the one question you would most like to ask an expert?"

Let your fans tell you what is on their minds!

To make the campaign more interesting, launch an event where you will commit to answering the most common and most interesting questions—LIVE. Answer questions in a free teleseminar, webinar, or even a live-in-person event.

An ask campaign is a guided missile designed to reconnect you to your target audience. Learn the questions they want to ask. Then be, or find, the expert to answer their questions.

The questions your fans ask are guaranteed to contain right angle marketing terms you can use in your next ads. Let the fans help your write your ads! Host an event and learn what needs they want to be addressed.

Yes. This really works.

Even better, if people commit on Facebook to attending your event, Facebook gives high priority to the messages reminding attendees to attend.

You can invite your existing friends to attend your event free in limited size groups. You can advertise to your existing fans to attend your event for very little money. Do both.

Don't know what to talk about or advertise after your ad fatigues? Great. Use it as an opportunity to talk to your fans! Set up a form to capture the questions they would most like to ask an expert. Then answer those questions at your event! Every question they ask is the source of a potential new ad.

Of course, there are other cool events you could advertise, too.

Throw a Party

If you hold a special sale at your store, throw a summer picnic for your church, or produce a teleseminar for your consulting firm, then advertise your special event to those who specifically liked your page.

By the way, does your place of worship have a Facebook page? IT SHOULD.

For pennies per person, you can get out the word about your special event to your fans and to the community as a whole by advertising it on Facebook.

The "Is Facebook for Me" test gauges your Facebook friendliness in part based on how event-driven your business is. The more event-driven the business, the better your presence on Facebook because Facebook is all about new, novel, different.

Make your business more Facebook-friendly and destroy ad fatigue by creating and advertising events.

- Offering a special on customers' favorite product for one day only? Make it an event.
- Having a picnic or front porch barbeque? Make it an event.
- Giving away cupcakes this coming Tuesday at a Facebook friends' party? Make it an event.
- Bringing in special speakers or musicians? Make it an event.
- Sponsoring a visiting author? Make it an event.
- Hosting a book club, music club, fantasy football club, any club that features a strong psychographic interest in your fans? Make it an event.
- Putting on a show that features local heroes or even celebrities? Make it an event. You'd be amazed how many celebrities—even famous actors and actresses—are, uh, looking for work right now. Perry knows one guy who hired a very well-known NFL player to endorse his mortgage business for one year for $5,000. Big Ass Fans hired William "Refrigerator" Perry to come to all of its trade shows–and it was rockin' successful. You can read all about it and see a picture of the huge line at the trade show booth at www.perrymarshall.com/marketing/big-ass-fans/.
- Struggling with ad fatigue? MAKE UP AN EVENT!

Events can be anything you can specifically schedule and invite people to attend. They should be something people would find fun or interesting, but they do not have to be complex or elaborate. Anything that connects you to your fans.

A restaurant with amazing pies can have a taste of pie event–a single day a month where anyone ordering a regular dinner gets a free slice of pie. It is simple to do, easy to track and measure the results, and simple to discover if the net impact is increased traffic and increased sales of pie.

It is also fun.

Everybody coming into the shop can sign up to be reminded of the event. And everybody who likes the Facebook page can be invited to attend the event by a very affordable ad.

EVENTS DON'T FATIGUE—THEY HAPPEN

Everyone advertising on Facebook complains about ad fatigue. "I built an ad on Google search and it runs and runs and runs," they report. "I write an ad on Facebook, and after a week or two it stops getting clicks."

"I'm giving up, I can't fix this problem."

Unfortunately, there is a fundamental flaw in their thinking.

They think they have a problem.

They do not.

What they describe as a problem is the fundamental nature of Facebook. Facebook is a different beast. It is not search. It will never be search. To unlock Facebook's true potential, to take your advertising to a different level, stop seeing ad fatigue as a dragon, as something to be defeated by better armor or the latest sword.

Ad fatigue is not a problem; it's an opportunity.

It is not a beast to be slain, but information to be processed and used to your advantage.

Ad fatigue is the launch signal for you to send out a guided missile—a Facebook event. Facebook provides the missile. You need to press launch. Create an event by pressing the "Event" button on your homepage.

FIGURE 19.2–Events Button

Host an event a month, listen to your customers, and learn how to blow apart the competition.

THE NEXT MISSILE IS FACEBOOK DEALS

Facebook is actively developing other additional advertising tools to reach your customers beyond just traditional ads. Facebook Deals, where you can offer your fans specific short-term deals and discounts, is being test launched in several cities as this book is written.

Deals is implementing a powerful shopping model of offering large discounts to entice new customers and spread the word of your business. It has powerful viral tools for sharing and liking the deal. It offers additional discounts when they buy the deal with a friend!

A deal will live on your main Facebook Page, making it easy for current fans to see and share your special offers. In fact, there are eight ways Facebook helps spread the news of your deal:

1. The Facebook homepage

2. The deals page

3. Sponsored units

4. Personal messages and wall posts

5. News feed stories

6. Onsite notifications

7. Deals tab

8. Emails

Facebook also understands their service is fundamentally different from search. As a result, expect them to create powerful new advertising options over the coming years to fully take advantage of the unique social graph they have created. These tools will change the way you reach customers for years to come. Start adding fans to your Facebook page today and take advantage of these amazing new ways to reach customers.

Chapter Twenty

And in the Facebook Bind Them

FACEBOOK DOESN'T STOP AT FACEBOOK ANYMORE

The amazing social graph of people and relationships Facebook has assembled is too big and too important to reside only in Facebook. Amazingly, Facebook agrees and has extended the Facebook social graph outside of and beyond Facebook.com. As a result, your website can incorporate Facebook's social experience directly on your pages by using Facebook Connect.

Facebook Connect services allows your users to "experience" Facebook social features directly on your website. It presents an absolutely amazing opportunity for you to leverage Facebook's gigantic social web directly into your products and services.

Facebook Connect accomplished very quickly and quietly what other larger corporations have been trying to do for years—provide users with a single user name and password to log into millions and millions of websites.

> "*T*hree Rings for the Elven-kings under the sky,
> Seven for the Dwarf-lords in their halls of stone,
> Nine for Mortal Men doomed to die,
> One for the Dark Lord on his dark throne
> In the Land of Mordor where the Shadows lie.
> One Ring to rule them all, One Ring to find them,
> One Ring to bring them all and in the darkness bind them
> In the Land of Mordor where the Shadows lie."
>
> —J. R. R. TOLKIEN, LORD OF THE RINGS

If you support Facebook Connect on your website, Facebook users may log into your services using their Facebook ID with a simple press of a button (see Figure 20.1). They do not have to create a new user name or password because you seamlessly support their existing Facebook identity.

FIGURE 20.1–Allow People to Register for Your Web Service Using Facebook

As a Facebook Connect supporting site, you access the real identity of those logging on to your site. Facebook tells you who your visitors are and that they can be trusted. Facebook users who log into your site can seamlessly bounce back and forth between you and Facebook.

In addition, when your users connect to your site via Facebook Connect, you can request additional Facebook information about them. You can potentially see their

· full name,
· profile picture,
· demographic information,
· real email address,
· friends,
· interests and activities,
· pages.

You can send them

· Facebook messages,
· emails
· status updates.

Actually, you can do so much more it is mind-boggling. But we will start you on the easy stuff.

If you have a really compelling site that people want to join, ask for all of this information and more. And people will provide you access. However, be warned, the user has control. They see the amount of information you are requesting in advance and have the ability to stop the connection process if they feel you are requesting access to too much of their Facebook data.

Facebook puts the users in the driver's seat. They see in advance what information you are requesting, and if they feel you are being too nosy, they may just walk away.

It Is Insane to Advertise on Facebook and Not Offer a Facebook Connect Login

It is insane not to offer your visitors Facebook Connect login if you advertise on Facebook. It has fewer steps than a traditional login, provides more information, and seamlessly integrates your website with the familiar Facebook experience.

On your opt-in form you could demand your prospects type in their name and email address yet again, or you could offer them the opportunity to provide their name and email address with a simple click on a log-in button. Facebook requires you to offer both options to your visitors.

Another benefit of using Facebook Connect is that you can access your prospects' Facebook listed email address. This is likely a better email address than what many people enter into a form. More and more people use second or third email addresses that are not their primary email addresses when they fill out opt-in forms.

In addition to Facebook Connect buttons, you can offer on your opt-in page other rapid connection options such as OpenID, an open standard used and provided by many large websites including Google, PayPal, and LiveJournal.

So how much information and control should you ask for? Split test multiple settings and see how many prospects drop out if you ask for more information. Unless you know what you are planning to do with that information, don't be too greedy if you see a high dropout rate. Even if you collect minimal information, you will still know more about your prospects than you would have using a traditional two-field, opt-in form. At the very least, you have harvested a real email address and not one created just for a response form.

Facebook Connect allows users to move across different websites with a single ID and password, and with a single manager of their privacy settings. The user sets their profile and privacy settings and manages their personal data all on Facebook, and those settings are automatically honored on Facebook Connect websites.

For example, if you change your profile picture on Facebook, it is updated automatically on all sites you access using Facebook Connect.

FACEBOOK PLUG-INS LINK YOUR WEBSITE TO THE SOCIAL GRAPH

Facebook Connect allows you to do much more than just a rapid login. Facebook has extended an entire series of social services directly into your website.

Facebook intends for users to be able to easily reuse their data (profile, name, email address, friends, likes, and interests, etc.) across the internet while still controlling the content and access to that data.

Facebook provides a method for website developers to read and understand your data. They refer to this method as the "graph API" (application programming interface). This allows for formal requests to Facebook for user data. Facebook also provides a series of simple methods to embed the social graph into your pages, too.

Your Website Pages Can Be Facebook Pages Too

Facebook has implemented a protocol to allow you to embed "open graph" tags on your own web pages. This means your own web pages can become the equivalent to a Facebook page in terms of people being able to "like" the page. That is, your individual web pages can become known to Facebook, and when they are liked, those likes will appear in the visitor's status messages and statistics.

It is even possible, when the user likes your page, to provide an optional comment. Facebook says that if the user does add a comment, then "the story published back to Facebook is given more prominence."

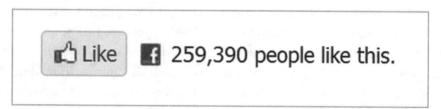

FIGURE 20.2–Facebook Button Allows Users to Like Your Web Pages

This feature is really amazing. It allows you to extend Facebook social credibility and news feed messages to pages on your website. If Facebook is the source for a lot of your leads and traffic, then making some of your pages Facebook pages and obtaining likes for them should absolutely become a part of your long-term site strategy.

You can target ads to people who like your content!

Likes for Your Facebook Page from Your Website

I strongly encourage advertisers who create a Facebook landing page to get likes on that page in addition to getting the user to opt in to an email follow-up campaign.

But what if your split tests showed that you lost too many users asking for a like first? No problem. Facebook comes to the rescue with the "Like Box" social

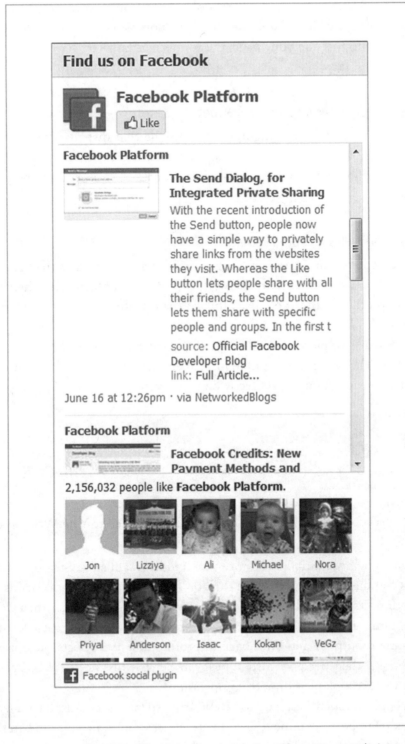

FIGURE 20.3–Like Box—Like Your Facebook Page from Your Website

plug-in. This device lets you put a Facebook Like button on your website where your users can like your official Facebook page. The box, as seen in Figure 20.3, contains the most recent posts on your page, the number of fans you have, and thumbnail pictures of your fans.

A Pile of Friends' Faces on Your Web Pages

Facebook provides a social plug-in called Facepile that displays the faces of users who have liked a page or signed up for a website. It provides a feeling of comfort and social credibility to your site by showing the faces of other Facebook fans and members.

Facebook Comments on Your Website

Facebook's wall is that section on a user's profile where users and their friends post messages. When people post to the wall, they do so publicly, with their full user name and profile picture and a back link to their profile. The date and time of the post is also displayed.

The post is also placed into the news feed and may be sent directly to multiple users' feeds. The wall is an example implementation of Facebook comments. You can have Facebook comments directly on your website, as seen in Figure 20.4.

FIGURE 20.4–Facebook Wall-Style Comments Can Be Added to Your Web Pages

Comments most socially relevant to each individual user are featured first. This includes comments from very active threads, friends, and friends of friends.

If your users add Facebook comments to your page, they transform a static page into a dynamic, open forum. User comments come complete with their pictures, like and comment buttons, and links back to profiles. If a user selects the option "Post to Facebook," then her post also appears in her friends' news feeds. Yet another example of Facebook providing free impressions.

Facebook comments are easy to defend from spam. Users must have a legitimate Facebook ID to post a comment. If someone abuses your wall, you can ban that user once on one page, and he is banned everywhere on all your pages.

If you have pages on your website with articles, products, information, video—really any content you can think of—you may want to support Facebook comments on those pages.

Streaming Comments on Your Website

If you have an active website or are hosting live conference calls or events from a page on your website, Facebook provides a live, streaming comment window that you can easily plug into your site.

This allows for a real-time chat window that displays live, streaming comments of Facebook users.

Recommendations on Your Website

This plug-in is almost spooky. A visitor to your website can see personalized recommendations on your specific URL based on pages that other Facebook users have liked. Your visitors receive these recommendations whether or not they are logged into your site.

The plug-in reviews the social interactions Facebook users have historically had with your URL. It then highlights specifically the objects the users' friends have interacted with. Personalized recommendations provided by the social graph. Social credibility provided instantly by Facebook directly for your site.

Facebook Provides Analytics About Your Facebook Connect Users

Facebook provides analytics that describe how users share information from your website. If you implement Facebook Connect, use the "insights" reporting feature to see data on usage and behavior tracked to your specific web domain.

DON'T BE A DIGITAL SERF

It is possible for your business to build its entire online presence around your Facebook pages, events, and groups.

Don't.

This is a profoundly bad idea. It is akin to digital sharecropping where you till the soil and grow the food, but somebody else owns the land.

Sharecropping is a time-honored tradition vastly superior to starvation. However, the label "serf" is not exactly something to aspire to. A serf is always subject to the whims of the king and may be thrown off the land tomorrow. Make no mistake, your Facebook page is on Facebook's land.

Build your entire business around a Facebook page and one day Facebook might decide that it does not like the name of that page. A Facebook ruler declares from the royal throne, "Your page violates our terms of service. Haven't you read the King's pronouncements? You are in violation of the King's hunting rules. Begone from our kingdom!"

Page gone.

Fans gone.

Business gone.

That is what it means when you are a digital sharecropper. It can happen to you.

A real company I know of built a large and successful fan page with more than 50,000 fans. One day, a day company representatives happened to be publicly speaking at a large conference, they tried to demonstrate the fan page. It was gone.

Gone.

What would you do? There is no one to call at Facebook to report the problem to. No way to know if it was intentionally deleted or if it is was a terrible glitch. No way to know, if it is a glitch, when it might be fixed.

This is what it means to be a digital sharecropper. Somebody else controls your destiny; they live in the castle, you live in a hovel in the muck, and you may not even be able to get an audience with them.

In the case of my friend, whose 50,000 fans disappeared overnight, it was, thankfully, a temporary problem. Facebook fixed it a few days later. The page and the fans came back. The incremental loss was minimal. Still, it reminded this company of who is king. And it is why company representatives don't want the company or the page mentioned here by name—don't risk pissing off the king.

Keep sharecropping. It is a great way to use Facebook to get leads. But please, buy your own fields. No matter how important Facebook becomes for your business, continue to maintain your own site and your own list of customers.

WHITE HAT

I've intentionally left unsaid secret or exploitative hacks that could be used in Facebook, Facebook Connect, and Facebook apps. Anything that is generally considered less than ethical—"dark hat" tactics—should be avoided.

These tactics can and do work. But if your own personal ethics do not prevent you from going there, perhaps a little additional information may encourage you in the path of righteousness. There is something you should know about companies like Facebook—they are worse than Santa Claus. Santa sees you when you're sleeping and knows when you're awake. Facebook knows everything else.

Facebook records everything.

You leave a unique trail of everything you do on the internet directly traceable back to you. Facebook staffers know who you are, they know what you are doing, they know how you interact with their system. They likely know every keystroke you ever typed on their site. Heck, they probably know how long it takes you to press each letter on your keyboard.

You may be able to exploit secrets or hacks for days, weeks, months, and sometimes even years. But eventually, Little Brother will catch up with you. One day you will wake up and discover a steel door you used to drive a truck through has been slammed shut and welded closed. In some cases, this shuts down your entire business.

We suggest a "white hat" approach. Be the good guy. Treat people the way you would want to be treated and use Facebook tools in a manner even your mother would be proud of.

Facebook is likely to be a very important advertising platform for years to come. Be one of the good guys. There is a fortune to be made using Facebook for selling legitimate, high-quality products and services. So do it.

Chapter Twenty-One

A Brief History of Google Advertising—and Some Predictions about Facebook

 THE SMART STUDENT OF ANYTHING IS ALWAYS A STUDENT OF HISTORY FIRST

When you understand the history of Google, not only will you position yourself to avoid a bunch of mistakes in Facebook, you'll also be able to seize very big opportunities. Vast treasures are buried in the shark-infested waters of internet advertising.

Hint: You often find these treasures in sunken sea vessels.

I started using AdWords when it was little more than one month old, and today my books on Google AdWords are the most popular in the world. I've had a front-row seat to Google's zero-to-tens-of-billions smash business success story.

> "*T*hose who don't know history are destined to repeat it."
>
> —EDMUND BURKE

I knew exactly what was going on long before Google went public at their audacious opening price of $85. I've witnessed the birth and growth of the biggest and most successful advertising machine in history, and it's been flat-out amazing.

Along the way, I also consulted with thousands of people in hundreds of industries. I have close, personal connections with hundreds of solo entrepreneurs and Roundtable members who have grown businesses from zero to millions of dollars of sales.

Not only have I observed the pay-per-click industry evolve, I've also watched business owners fight their way from zero to raging success. I've walked with them through their personal struggles and victories.

This is a vitally important chapter for you to read and understand, first and foremost from a Facebook perspective, but more broadly for perspective on any kind of online advertising. Even for forms of internet advertising that we never discuss in this book. Please pay close attention.

FROM GOTO.COM TO OVERTURE TO GOOGLE

The first time I ever heard of pay per click, I thought it sounded perverse. *You're going to sell search engine listings to the highest bidder? Only whores would do that. How are you going to have any kind of honesty with that kind of system?*

I gave it little thought beyond that. It didn't occur to me that the highest bidder is often the company that does the best job of giving lots of people exactly what they want (which is why most large shopping malls have Sears and JC Penney and every city has a Walmart).

That was probably 1999 or so. GoTo.com had started a bidding system, which it then syndicated to search engines like AltaVista, Yahoo!, and MSN. I was scarcely aware during the next two to three years that it was fast becoming a billion-dollar company.

GoTo.com changed its name to Overture and continued making money hand over fist.

My mentor, Ken McCarthy, encouraged me to attend his "System Seminar" in April, 2002. He said his colleague Jon Keel had actually figured out how to make pay per click work.

Jon gave a stunning presentation, explaining Overture's system in detail—the psychology of keywords, the importance of tracking conversions—and he revealed what to me was a bombshell revelation: the Overture inventory tool. It displayed what search terms people were typing and how frequently.

Tools like this are pretty familiar today, but then it was earth shattering. It was like peering behind the internet curtain for the very first time: seeing exactly how many people were searching for paintball or plumbers or airline tickets to Philadelphia; having the ability to endlessly explore human desires and eavesdrop on the conversation inside peoples' heads.

INSIGHT NUMBER 1. The cornerstone of all internet advertising is market research. Everything starts with understanding a market. In online marketing you *never* just sling mud against the wall to see if it sticks. You always start with at least some knowledge of what's already going on—otherwise you'll get killed.

(Dr. Glenn Livingston offers an excellent free series of tutorials for online market research at www.LivingstonReport.com.)

INSIGHT NUMBER 2. The internet is all about *rifle shots not shotgun blasts*. This is especially true if you're new. Keyword research tools have been telling us that for 10 years. Facebook likes and interests tell you the same thing. The more narrow your focus, the easier it is to speak to your prospect in the exact language she wants to hear. Selling to large audiences with broad interests is a game for ninjas—not beginners.

In Jon Keel's seminar presentation, he explained the huge difference between two keywords that amateurs might assume are similar: "weight loss" and "bariatric surgery," a procedure that shrinks your stomach.

Jon explained that "weight loss" is very general; it's something people search for when they're just looking around on the internet. "Bariatric surgery" is a much more serious term for people who have something very exact in mind. It converts to sales much better, and it's a lot more expensive.

Even back then, Jon was painstakingly measuring sales from clicks. He was years ahead of everyone else. Jon insisted that if you weren't tracking conversions you might as well drive down the expressway at 85 miles per hour and fling $100 bills out the window.

At this time, AdWords had existed in its current form for only a month or two. I went home and decided to try AdWords instead of Overture. It only took a day or so for me to become hooked. Most people weren't using Google yet, but I thought it was a great search engine. I quickly discovered that Google had built the coolest direct marketing machine ever.

> *F*or a free Google AdWords Cheat Sheet and ongoing updates on Google's system, visit www.perrymarshall.com/google/

Overture simply gave the top listing to the highest bidder. AdWords had an extra twist—Google multiplied the bid price times the click-through rate (CTR). It favored advertisers who wrote better ads, because an ad that doesn't get clicked on doesn't make Google any money. It also doesn't serve the advertisers, and it doesn't serve the end customer, either.

This was a stroke of genius on Google's part.

Google execs had another rule: ads had to achieve at least 0.5% CTR or they would get disabled.

Eventually Google replaced the 0.5% rule with more sophisticated mechanisms. But at that moment, this rule meant AdWords was only easy for people who were good at writing copy. It added a barrier of entry that favored people like me who already understood direct marketing.

Google had four other major advantages compared to Overture.

1. *It allowed you to split test ads.* I'll never forget—I created an ad and noticed the "create a new ad" link was still there. I clicked on it again and made a new ad, different from the first one. I went to Google and searched for my keyword and hit refresh a few times. Sure enough, the ad flipped from A to B and back to A. And yes, sure enough, Google gave me statistics for both ads!

   Dang. I can now test copy as easy as clicking a "submit" button!

   And I discovered that even tiny differences made *huge* differences in response.

   ### Get the Ethernet Basics
   Simple Tutorial on Ethernet, TCP/IP
   5-Page Paper, Free Instant Download
   www.bb-elec.com
   0.2% CTR

   ### Ethernet Basics Guide
   Handy Tutorial on Ethernet, TCP/IP
   5-Page Paper—Free PDF Download
   www.bb-elec.com
   1.2% CTR

   WOW. What a tremendous advantage for Google! They gave advertisers incentives to write better and better ads, pulling eyeballs from the left side to the right side. A copywriter's dream. I was in heaven.

   Overture did not have this feature. You could only run one ad at a time.

   Massive disadvantage for Overture, as time would tell.

2. *Google ads showed up instantly; Overture's took three days to get approved.* When you submitted a Google ad, it started showing right away. You could submit more ads, run them against each other, and three days later on Google you might have a winner out of four ads you'd tested.

   Meanwhile your first ad was just getting started on Overture. And you couldn't test.

   This advantage accrued compound interest over time. In a month, you could test 10 things on Overture, but could test 100 on Google because it provided so many more feedback loops than Overture.

This meant that Google's revenue engine was improving its effectiveness daily and Overture's was not. It also meant that the innocent endeavor of managing a Google AdWords account became an adventurous, addictive, profitable game of human psychology.

Massive disadvantage for Overture.

3. *Most people didn't know this then, and most still don't today, but Google applies the same culture of testing to everything they do internally.* Not only do they give their advertisers immense ability to test things, they test everything themselves.

The standard size of a Google ad? It's the result of billions of clicks of testing. The colors, fonts and images of the Gmail sign-up page? Exhaustively tested. Google researchers probably tested 47 shades of green. At Google, every dispute is settled by testing.

Overture did much less of this than Google.

Once again, *massive* disadvantage!

4. *Overture's interface was clunky and hard to use.* Google's was easy and intuitive. Add that to all of Google's other advantages, and it was hard to see how Overture could possibly stay in the lead. Overture's customers begged for better tools. Overture ignored them.

Later, Yahoo! bought Overture. And it still ignored its customers. In only two to three years, Google became a juggernaut and beat its competitors by miles. Google left Yahoo! in the dust.

Why am I telling you this? Because in any form of online advertising, you're going to succeed for the same four reasons:

1. Testing
2. Speed
3. Testing
4. Ease of Use

As you experiment with different ads, landing pages, and offers, you will find it's devilishly difficult to predict what people want. Heck, I've been indulging in the sport of direct marketing for 15 years. But when I try to guess winners on A/B tests, I still get only 50% of the answers right. Even with all my experience, I just don't know.

You don't guess, you test.

One more thing about speed. The reason YouTube passed up Google Video and all other video sharing sites—and the reason why Google eventually had to buy YouTube for $1.65 billion in 2006—was because Google Video was slow just like Overture.

It took three days to get videos approved. YouTube was instant. Again, more feedback loops and more opportunities for addictive behavior on the part of content providers.

My friend, if you're online, you gotta' strip the bureaucracy out of whatever you're doing and build your business for speed.

SITE DOMINANCE—NO WAY TO CATCH UP

On the internet, once a site establishes dominance, it's very difficult for rivals to catch up. Sometimes impossible.

Why? Because size gives you more speed, speed gives you more size, size attracts audience, audience builds size, and a snowball effect always kicks in.

FROM AN EMAIL I SENT IN 2006

How Google Kicked Yahoo! in the Ass

A few weeks ago, a very large Wall Street investment firm with many hundreds of millions of dollars invested in Yahoo!, and Google called me to schedule a consultation.

They wanted me to help them understand "how the sausage is made" and share my views on Google and Yahoo's long-term prospects for growth.

Back in the day, GoTo (oops, I guess they're called Overture now. Oops, I guess they're called Yahoo! Search Marketing now) had the tiger by the tail.

They built the world's first pay-per-click money machine and they had it made in the shade. They organized all the chaos of the internet and started selling clicks. Now search engines could finally start making some money.

And baby, did they ever make money. They thought they were making a lot.

But then Google came along. Google showed 'em how it should REALLY be done. I'm not sure any company in the history of the world has ever made so much with such apparent ease.

FROM AN EMAIL I SENT IN 2006, continued

You can ask any guy on the street why Google has done so much better, and they'll tell you it's 'cuz Google is just a better search engine. And that's true, but that's only half the story.

The other half of the story is that they designed AdWords to maximize the amount of money they make on every search. Advertisers have great incentive to lure people from the left side of the page to the right side to click on those paid ads.

And yes, this has a LOT to do with you, as I shall explain shortly. If you're going to succeed in this game, you're going to succeed for the exact same reasons Google succeeded. So pay close attention as I tell you what I told the guys at the big investment firm.

You may know that Yahoo! just changed the size of their ads from 190 lines of description to 70, just like Google.

Know why they did that? Because Google figured out before Yahoo! did that they'll make more money showing 10 little ads than 3 or 4 big ones. Yahoo! finally figured it out, too.

How did Google know that? By testing.

Yahoo! didn't test. Shame on Yahoo!. (Shame on everyone who doesn't test, for they shall share the same fate.)

Well then there's the click-through-rate formula. You should know by now that Google multiplies your bid price times your click-through rate to figure out where you belong on the page. Yahoo! doesn't do that. Which means Yahoo! ads that get clicks don't rise to the top, and Yahoo! makes less dollars from every single search than Google.

Now let's say they make 10% less. Does that mean they get 10% less business? NO, it's worse than that, because they have syndication partners (MSN, Alta-Vista, etc.) and thousands of individual sites who share the profit.

FROM AN EMAIL I SENT IN 2006, continued

If their partners get a piece of the action, they make 10% less, too. Which means they'd rather run Google ads than Yahoo! ads. Which means Google gets more clicks and Yahoo! gets less. The 10% disadvantage becomes 25%.

But it gets still worse: If you've got 25% less traffic, advertisers are 25% less interested, which means there's fewer of them. So the bids are lower and now you're 40% behind not 10%.

In the real world of business, 10% is really 40%.

(You should write that on a piece of paper in big fat magic marker and tape it to your wall.)

I'm not done yet. Yahoo's software is 5 years old, it's clunky and horribly bureaucratic. Every time you want to change something, it takes 3 days and it's a nightmare.

I told my friends who manage those hundreds of millions of dollars that heads should have been rolling at Yahoo! a LONG time ago, because this should not be news to anybody!

Heck, I knew this back when Overture was still ahead of Google.

Sad. Very sad.

To our friends at Yahoo! Search Marketing—who will no doubt see this email—I say: You better accelerate your plans to fix your stupid broken system, because you're losing ground every single day.

I say this as someone who has not the slightest interest in the Wall Street side of this equation. I own no Google stock (that would create a conflict of interest, given the work I do). I own no Yahoo! stock. What I'm interested in is me and my customers getting the most bang for our advertising buck. And I know that pressure from Wall Street just makes it tougher on advertisers.

Plus I'd like there to be at least one company besides Google who doesn't have their head stuffed in a cloud. I want just ONE good PPC alternative to Google. How about you?

FROM AN EMAIL I SENT IN 2006, continued

(Need I mention that MSN has a program in beta right now? Yahoo!, you'd better watch out, Bill Gates is coming to plunder your house.)

OK, all this Wall Street stuff is fine for analysts and pundits. But what does this have to do with YOU?

A LOT. The lesson here is: 10% is really 40%. 20% is really 100%.

Because there's always a feedback loop. What goes around comes around. How effectively you use every single click on your Google ads, your website, your emails, your upsells; how well you're able to pay your affiliates or JV partners—multiplies and multiplies. On tiny hinges, big doors swing.

A 10% improvement on your sales page today may very well be the difference between you being number 1 or number 2 in your market one year from now, or being totally out of business.

I am not exaggerating. And folks, we can all point fingers at Yahoo! for being number 2 instead of number 1. That's easy to do. Next weekend at the Super Bowl, the winner will take it all and the loser will slink away in shame.

But this is your website and your business, and you're not an armchair quarterback. You are THE quarterback. Woe be unto you if you fail to apply to your own business the lesson that Yahoo! is learning right now—that every one of those clicks count, and they don't just add up, they multiply.

Also, please notice that it's not about "first mover advantage." It's about speed and testing advantage. Most of the "coulda, woulda, shoulda" stories are about internet companies that couldn't get out of their own stupid way.

SPEED SPAWNS ANOTHER JUGGERNAUT—AFFILIATE MARKETING

I wrote the first edition of *The Definitive Guide to Google AdWords* in the summer of 2003. At this point, AdWords hadn't quite caught on, but then a young surfer dude named Chris Carpenter wrote a book called *Google Cash*.

Google Cash explained how you could sign up for an affiliate program, sign up for Google AdWords, give Google five bucks and start sending traffic through your affiliate link. You could be an invisible traffic broker, pocketing the difference between your click cost and your affiliate commission.

All you had to do was find a combination of keywords and affiliate programs that was profitable and you had an instantly profitable business. You were now an invisible traffic broker.

Google Cash caught on like wildfire. Within six months, hundreds of thousands of people all over the world were bidding on every conceivable word and phrase in the English language—and quite a few other languages—and driving traffic to eBay, Amazon, ClickBank, and thousands of other sites.

It was a massive, underground gold rush.

The thing about it was, it *worked*.

Honestly, I thought it was stupid at first. (Remember, I also thought pay per click was perverse, too. I was wrong.) To me it was just too simple.

Well it *was* too simple, as I shall explain later. But actually it was too simple *not* to work. Some percentage of the time, it was bound to succeed. A lot of people were making a lot of money with this, and there were a lot of keywords available for 5 or 10 cents.

This is what made Google go supernova. Because after a while, no matter what you typed into Google, you saw ads. Every company president, every marketing and sales manager, every webmaster saw somebody showing up on Google, and it wasn't them.

This sucked 'em into Google AdWords against their will. Ya think clicks should be free? Too bad. Cuz your competitors are buying space where you ought to be showing up. Google hit the tipping point and exploded. I had customers making $100,000 a month brokering clicks.

The genius of *Google Cash* was:

> *You have zero commitments. It's way easier to go find another product to promote than it is to own a product or change your own product. Or even change your website, for that matter. The name of the game is speed and testing.*

Google cashers embraced speed and testing overnight. So a new, billion-dollar industry—pay-per-click affiliate marketing—sprang up out of nowhere. At light speed.

THIS IS THE HISTORY LESSON, RIGHT HERE

The history lesson has everything to do with Facebook and pretty much anything else you do in marketing or advertising. Because this speed/testing combo was like crack cocaine. It was addictive, and it was shallow. It created lots of problems, including the following:

- *An invisible affiliate business is extremely fragile.* It's very easy to knock off. (Within a year or two, people started selling software that helped you detect and copy successful affiliate campaigns.)
- *You own zero assets in a business like that.* A $1 million-per-year direct-linking affiliate business is equivalent to building a mansion on the side of a hill in Sao Paulo, on rented land. The next rainstorm could wash that mansion away in a mud slide. You have nothing to show for it.
- *Invisible affiliates often have no ethics.* Some of them promote horrible products.
- *Thousands of affiliates all do exactly the same thing at the same time.* They have no advantage over each other; they just drive bid prices up.
- *Affiliates cluttered the internet with all kinds of lousy offers.* Sometimes you'd search for something and 10 people were all promoting the same thing at the same time. It took a while for Google to eliminate duplicate offers from their search results, but they did.
- *Content is king, and most affiliates create no content.*
- *Click for click, the most profitable offers are generally overpriced, over-promised products.* In the short term, "edgy" offers with unrealistic claims, obnoxious websites with pop-ups and no back button, and abusive return policies make twice as much money as sane, honest offers.
- *Websites like* The New York Times *don't like "edgy" advertisers.* Neither does Google, nor Facebook. In the early days, edgy advertisers were all they had. They accepted the money for a while, but as soon as sites like Facebook or Google have enough legitimate advertisers, they kick out the edgy ones.
- *From the perspective of Google—or Facebook—affiliates are disposable.* "Thank you, Mr. Affiliate, for your giving us so much money for these last few years. Now that you've helped us attract 'real' businesses, we're done with you. Happy trails, you poor, pathetic scumbag."
- *Google and Facebook don't like affiliates all that much.* Not usually. After a couple of years, Google started tightening the screws on affiliates. Facebook will, too.

Please understand that some affiliates are really cool and very likeable. At the same time, average, unsophisticated, garden-variety affiliates are the trailer trash of the internet. Just tellin' it like it is.

So with that in mind, I'd like to offer you 10 tips on how you build a robust, stable, long-term, internet business.

1. Build a presence over time that's difficult or impossible to knock off. Any business that can be replicated with "cut and paste" is the online equivalent of a shantytown. A trailer park in Tornado Alley. You want original content, extensive sales funnels, and a unique selling proposition that's hard for others to attain.

2. Build assets: email lists, snail-mail lists, unique products, unique processes, unique experiences. You want your business to run on systems that you own, not rent. You want to build a brand. Better if there's more to those systems than meets the eye. By the way, you can do all of those things as an affiliate. You can build a website, and content, and systems. All those things are hard, tangible assets. Intellectual property. Technology. Patents. Things that aren't easy to replicate. Amazon is nothing more than a sophisticated affiliate for probably 25% of the things they sell. All those product reviews on Amazon are a *huge* asset.

3. Consider the value of your product. Google's staff who manually review websites use this criteria: "Would I send my grandma to this site?" Your criteria should be: "Would I sell this to my grandma? Or my sister-in-law?"

4. Use a different style than everyone else. You are *always* developing and sharpening your USP.

5. Sell different things than everyone else.

6. Create great content.

7. Remember that solid, dependable, and honest beats edgy every time—in the long run.

8. Make your product something other sites, including Facebook, would feel proud to advertise. Every shopping mall in the country would be delighted to have Nordstrom as their anchor store; become Nordstrom for internet sites.

9. Do not look like, taste like, or smell like an affiliate—even if you are an affiliate. You should add value to the equation.

10. Understand how media companies tighten the screws on affiliates and "thin" advertisers. I shall explain this concept in the next section.

W-a-a-a-y back in 2004 (how many internet dog years has that been?) I recorded a now-famous teleseminar called "Jet Fuel for Google Cash." Everything in it applies to Facebook advertisers, too. As an owner of this book, you can get the seminar as a special free bonus at www.perrymarshall.com/fbtoolbox/. I strongly suggest you listen to it.

The thrust of *Jet Fuel for Google Cash* is that affiliate marketing is just a way to test new markets. It's not a permanent place to camp out!

As pay-per click grew more sophisticated, Google started erecting hoops for advertisers to jump through. It created something called a "quality score" (QS), which was both an automatic and manual index of your site's quality.

If your QS was 1, you had to bid a minimum of $10 per click for your ads to get shown. Which was just another way of Google saying "get lost." One day without warning, Google threw the switch, initiated quality scores, and instantly shut out tens of thousands of advertisers.

Google also made it impossible for more than one ad to show at one time in any search result for a single website. This eliminated duplicate affiliates. Only the highest paying one got a spot.

It even started penalizing AdWords accounts that *had at one time* promoted affiliate offers that Google now (not then) decided it didn't like.

Google didn't explain what it was doing; many times it did not warn people. Google representatives wouldn't accept phone calls, and even if you were spending $10,000 per month they wouldn't talk to you. You're just dead. End of story.

Facebook can—and will—do the same thing. And it will probably take action based on an algorithm. Do you think Mark Zuckerberg is any more compassionate than Larry and Sergey?

Algorithm-based bans trigger a lot of collateral damage, but Facebook and Google seldom care. As long as they're right three-fourths of the time, they're happy.

Oh, and by the way they will also pay people in India and the Philippines $2 per hour to judge the quality of your $20,000 website, and you may have no recourse. One time Google banned my site. A Google rep from India sent me an email that said, "Also please stop scams."

Please understand, I'm not trying to discourage you. And if you run an honest, straightforward business you probably won't have any problems. But you must recognize these things can and do happen, and companies like Google and Facebook have no qualms about "thinning the herd."

Google and Facebook want their users to have the highest-quality experience possible. They do not ultimately consider their advertisers to be their customers. They consider their users to be their customers. Never forget that.

You need to study the above list of 10 tips very closely. And here are some more:

· You need to make sure that you're absolutely straightforward with customers about things like recurring billing and charge amounts. Nothing will get you in hot water faster than charging peoples' credit cards without permission. That will get you thrown out of Facebook. It will get your merchant account canceled, too. It will also get you slapped with fines and lawsuits by the attorney general of some state somewhere.

- The claims on your site need to be true, they need to be verifiable, and they need to be reasonably realistic. No fake testimonials. Readers should be able to find the people or companies who say they liked doing business with you.
- You need transparency. That's what social media is all about in the first place, right? You have a Facebook page where real people interact; you have an email address; you have a phone number. You have real people who can fog a mirror and answer questions.
- Some categories are automatically suspect: make-money opportunities, weight loss, medical products, alternative medicine, drugs, gambling, real estate, marketing techniques, stock trading, securities, and adult websites—all attract more than their share of riffraff and are heavily scrutinized. Some such sites are highly regulated. Some markets are filled with vermin. (These categories are also very profitable for ninjas.)
- "Boring" categories seldom have problems. If you sell barcode readers or packaging machines, if you own a local insurance agency, or if you market sewing supplies, you have very little to worry about.

BID PRICES: THE TREND IS USUALLY UP

Let's say you're buying clicks for 60 cents and you're profiting an average of 40 cents on each click. Congratulations—you're a successful online marketer!

You need to expect that those clicks are going to get more expensive. 62 cents . . . 70 cents . . . 85 cents . . . a buck.

You need to test and track so that the following can happen:

- Your ads get better and better CTRs (thus counteracting the upward pressure of bid prices).
- You convert more and more visitors to buyers, pushing your profit margins up.
- You sell more in each transaction.
- You sell more after the first transaction.

In every market—and in every form of advertising—bid prices will tend to rise until most advertisers are breaking even acquiring a new customer. They're not making money on new customers, only on repeat business.

If you enter a market and find that you're making money hand over fist—and you don't even have a sophisticated sales funnel—then you need to stay ahead of the pack and build that sales funnel out. Cuz the competitors are coming, I promise.

On the other hand, if you're building and cultivating an email list, if you sell products at a wide range of price points, if you have cross-sells and upsells, if you connect to your customers in multiple ways (email, chat, in person, live events, brick and mortar), you grow your roots deeper. Your business becomes stable.

Once you get ahead of the curve, your job of staying ahead becomes much less tiresome. It is frankly much easier to be number 1 in your market than to be number 4 or number 5 and fighting over the scraps. And once you get to number 1, momentum is on your side. Because you can test more things faster than your competitors.

YOU MUST DIVERSIFY

For years I've told my Google AdWords students: if one year from now you're still getting 100% of your traffic from Google, I have failed to do my job. Same with Facebook. You might get started on Facebook. For the next six months all your traffic may come exclusively from Facebook.

But once you start figuring out the formula, as soon as you start selling, you need to expand into other paid (not necessarily free) media, including:

- Google AdWords display network
- Google AdWords search
- Yahoo!, Bing
- Affiliates
- Banner ads
- Retargeting
- Paid insertions in email newsletters
- Print advertising
- Radio
- TV

Of course there's also free media, such as the following:

- Search engine optimization
- Viral Facebook traffic
- Twitter
- YouTube
- Newspapers and magazines
- Blogs
- Publicity

Any business that works with one of these mediums will probably work with several of them. Your business begins to diversify as your traffic diversifies.

Your goal is for none of these to represent more than 20% of your business. Once you achieve that, it becomes very unlikely that any one disaster will tank you.

WHAT I LEARNED FROM INFOMERCIALS

Some people watch infomercials; some buy from them. Some don't.

I for one have never bought a single thing from an infomercial. I'm not "an infomercial buyer."

In general, I don't even care to watch them all that much, even though they are extremely educational for sales people. (Tip: If you want to see a sales pitch that has been scientifically proven to work, just watch an infomercial that's been on the air for three months. I can guarantee you, it's making money. Take notes and look for ideas you can borrow.)

But anyway, in 2002, when I first began using pay per click, I almost instantly knew how the entire AdWords market was going to develop. Even though it was virgin territory, it was undeveloped, and nobody understood it.

I knew that in 10 years it would become a fiercely competitive, dog-eat-dog marketplace and there would be certain things you HAD to do in order to win, and I knew that because I had studied infomercials.

You can make the exact same predictions about Facebook.

What does Facebook have to do with infomercials?

Back in the '80s, broadcasting laws changed, and it suddenly became possible for TV stations to sell extended slots to advertisers. You may recall that 30 years ago, most TV stations went off the air at 1 A.M. or 2 A.M., saying, "We'll be back at 6 A.M."

So people started making 30-minute commercials.

I remember when I was a kid, turning on the TV one night and seeing an infomercial shot at a Holiday Inn meeting room. It was a single camera pointed at an overhead projector and some guy was pitching information on how to get rich in real estate.

When infomercials were new, the airtime was incredibly cheap. You could actually shoot a cheap video at a seminar, air it, and make money.

Then companies started discovering that this worked. And the bid prices went up.

Today if you want to test an infomercial you're going to spend a minimum of $75,000 to $100,000 to put a show in the can and test it in a few markets. It's going to have to be professionally produced and superbly scripted; otherwise it doesn't even stand a chance.

Most of the players in the infomercial biz are companies who specialize in this and do hundreds of millions of dollars of business. The largest such company is Guthy-Renker, whose sales are about $2 billion.

The barrier to entry is now very, very high.

I knew that pay per click would be a microbusiness version of the same thing, on the internet. And as online advertising matured, I always knew what was next. I knew history repeats itself so I studied history.

Here are some factoids about the similarities between infomercials and Facebook that I would like you to think about.

- It used to be said that infomercials were the most competitive place you could possibly sell anything, because the customer's hand is always on the remote control and she can change channels if she gets bored for two seconds. That's even more true online: People have 12 windows open, and the entire internet is only a click away.
- Sales funnels get more sophisticated as media prices rise. A few years ago, a simple long-form sales letter did the trick. Now, many products require well-scripted, well-shot video. A few require a carefully engineered webinar. Extremely sophisticated marketers build carefully engineered webinars into timed automated email sequences, total systems that Rich Schefren calls "Evergreen Event Driven Marketing." Because I'm in a very sophisticated market, I've built several of these with Rich's help and they're a key to our success.
- Barriers to entry go up. Good for you if you're an insider, bad for you if you're an outsider.

One last comment about internet media companies:

They favor their existing advertisers over new ones. New advertisers are a "credit risk." If companies are going to take space away from an existing, profitable advertiser and give it to a newcomer, they're exposing both the customer and their bottom line. So they'll only serve ads a little bit at first.

You can expect the formulas Facebook uses to determine ad serving to become more sophisticated and more automated all the time.

The good news is, as you crawl inside the machine and experience it, you'll develop an intuitive feel. It will no longer be formula, it will be natural to you. That's how you will know you're achieving mastery.

Chapter Twenty-Two

Mind Your Business

"ONE LONG SHOT AND THREE FISH IN A BARREL"

Every Friday, Tom Hoobyar, and I (Perry) have a chat. He, a salty dog, old enough to be my father; me, a Gen X marketing punk. We coach each other. The two of us in the trenches every day make a good team.

> *"Hell, there are no rules here—we're trying to accomplish something."*
>
> —THOMAS A. EDISON

A few years ago, he left his post as CEO of a Silicon Valley biotech firm, trading "INC" style small-company entrepreneurship for lone-wolf entrepreneurship. Big shift. Suddenly, he found himself where I was when I started my present business; he's also had about 10 times as many careers as I.

As he described one of his projects, I recalled a formula that helped me keep the income steady when I was getting started. But before I explain that formula, we've got to address the matter of taking risks and matching them to your risk tolerance.

Every dollar and every minute you spend buying Facebook traffic or any other kind of traffic is a risk and investment of your time.

Invest wisely, and your business will prosper. Invest poorly, and you'll be divorced and stocking shelves at Walmart. That's why the last chapter of this book is about *managing risk*. My friend and mentor Dan Sullivan, founder of Strategic Coach, says, "Entrepreneurs aren't more honest than everybody else. They just get punished a whole lot faster for lying to themselves."

It's difficult to imagine a career track with a higher failure rate than the music circuit. Drummer Mike Portnoy is one of my personal fave musicians. Someone once asked Mike, "Did you have a backup plan (alternate career), just in case?"

His answer: "I never gave myself an option. As soon as you have a 'backup plan,' you will be likely to fall back on it the minute the times are tough. Succeeding requires 100% dedication and perseverance, which means you have no choice but to keep trying and moving forward. And to be honest, I never *thought* about making music my career . . . it kinda just happened because it is what I 'did'."

When Mike was trying to make it, he was delivering Chinese food for a living and had no family to support. For me it was different—wife and 3 kids, a mortgage and car payment. Being "out on the street" was the number-one item on the "unacceptable outcomes" list. Destitution was more unacceptable than failing in business. I had to have a backup plan.

Risk, Paranoia, and the Burning of Boats

People have wildly different reactions to risk. For me, having a backup plan does not necessarily mean that I'm going to yank the parachute lever when the going gets tough. (If anything, I'm prone to taking a long, circuitous, "challenging" route when an easier way is sitting right there in plain sight.) Knowing that I *do* have a backup plan is reassuring because I'm less fearful. The trapeze artist takes bigger risks when she knows there's a net to catch her if she falls.

Other people may need to close off all exits. The famous story of Cortés burning his boats before conquering Mexico comes to mind—except I researched that story and found out it's a legend.

Cortes didn't burn his boats at all. He had 12, ran 9 into the sand (to keep enemies from using them against him) and kept 3—and a master shipbuilder among his crew. According to *Fast Company* and John Coatsworth, dean of the School of International and Public Affairs at Columbia University and an American scholar on Latin America, "Cortes beached the ships to prevent anyone from heading back to Cuba to report to the Spanish nobilities that he was engaged in an utterly unauthorized and illegal expedition. He was running for cover."

So much for Cortes motivating his men.

ser·en·dip·i·ty (sĕr'ən-dĭp'ĭ-tē)

1. The faculty of making fortunate discoveries by accident.

2. The fact or occurrence of such discoveries.

3. An instance of making such a discovery.

Serendipity will bring you from where you *thought* you wanted to be to where you *should* have been all along. I don't know about you, but very few things I've ever done turned out exactly the way I envisioned them at the beginning—sometimes much different.

It's usually just plain dumb to "burn the boats." I've long lived by the phrase "never burn a bridge," which normally means, *Do NOT get all uppity and tell somebody off. Even if you're "sure" you'll never ever need anything from that person in the future, because you probably will, anyway.*

I've rarely violated that rule and have never been sorry for *not* breaking it.

Which brings me back to my story about Tom. He was describing the simultaneous launch of three or four different products, and in some cases building a new prospect list from scratch in order to launch them. His plans were thorough, as they normally are with Tom. Still, a little warning bell went off in my head: "Too many long shots at one time" feeling about launching that many products simultaneously.

When I went out on my own, the first order of business was to secure enough monthly retainer income from active consulting projects (*hunting*) to cover my nut. Then and only then would I embark on a much lengthier process of building a list, selling information, and being a published author (*farming*).

For several years I had three to four consulting clients who collectively more than paid the bills. So I could afford to invest in developing a robust information business. Once the consulting business was in place, I stopped taking new clients, tightened my belt a little, and invested in list-building and product development. The product income slowly matched and then replaced the consulting income, giving me more options.

The consulting was kind of like shooting fish in a barrel. For the most part, any particular project was a slam-dunk—writing a white paper or magazine article or press release or building an opt-in page, suddenly getting my client 15 leads a day instead of one or two—that, for me, was easy. (And sometimes a little boring.) My clients got the results they were after, and I got paid.

So here's what I related to Tom. A real nice formula for building a prevailing business with minimal risk is: *One Long Shot and Three Fish in a Barrel.* One big project that is long-term and speculative with huge upside potential, and two, three, or four small games you know you can easily win, that will definitely pay the bills, and eliminate the panic factor from your decisions.

When people are consumed with fear—and possibly shame because they're running out of money or whatever—they make bad decisions. Fear alone is *always* a bad foundation for decision-making.

Why It's Hard to Hire a Good Marketing Consultant

Many marketing geniuses are on the rise, and the good ones do outstanding work. Problem is, if they're really good, they're only available to do project work for a window of time, typically a couple of years. Here's why.

A gal does crackerjack consulting work—she's the "rainmaker" for her client. Eventually, she has the following conversation with herself:

"Self, you boosted your client's sales by $1.5 million this year."

"By golly, I think you're right."

"They made $350,000 of additional profit, and they paid you $30,000 in fees. Oh, and the CEO's got heartburn about the $15,000 bonus he's supposed to pay you at year's end—you know, the 1% of sales growth thing. He wants to trim that back to 0.5% for next year. But he says we can easily expect another $3 million growth for next year, and he feels a $15,000 bonus is real good for a gal your age."

"You mean I futzed around with that 'marketing communications manager' for eight months and pounded all those changes through their bureaucracy, we *still* grew sales 1.5 million, and he's complaining? Self, I'll find a product some place and we'll sell it all by ourself, thank you very much, and I won't have to deal with these tight-fisted morons anymore."

"Gary Halbert was right, clients *do* suck."

She takes fewer and fewer clients at higher and higher fees, only accepting deals that match her growing list of requirements, and eventually she does no client work at all—because she went to a trade show and found a Korean tent manufacturer and now she's distributing that stuff online and taking a 70% gross margin.

The Korean guys don't have the slightest idea how to replicate what she does, and she's got a little blue notebook with seven other promising projects a lot like this one. She can eventually have all of them running in tandem, if she wants. Suddenly those $15,000 bonuses are chump change. Not worthwhile if it takes a fight to get 'em.

The upshot of all this is that she's going to be available for two to three years, and after that she's unavailable. She's doing her own thing.

One time I got into a tiff with a client, and I was feeling intimidated. I asked John Carlton for some advice; after I explained the situation to him, he said, "Perry, you're not just a mouth in the food chain, you *are* the food chain. Listen up—if the CEO's hand isn't shaking when he writes you the check, you're not charging enough."

If you know how to research markets, understand groups of people, buy clicks from Facebook and sell—then you can write your own checks.

"Three Fish in a Barrel" Can Take Many Forms

At my *Dilbert* cube job, we worked furiously for four years and the owners sold the firm to a publicly traded company for $18 million. I left with a check. That happened because of the *long shot*—we'd invested $2 million (mostly borrowed from angel investors) in product development and created a digital communications chip that people in our industry needed.

But that long shot chip was still not even selling yet, and the whole project was only possible in the first place because the company's bread and butter was something else. We were distributing communication boards from three European companies in the United States and Canada. Buying them, marking them up, and reselling them.

We gained great insights from selling and supporting these products, which helped us design our chip. The margins kept the lights on. It was a natural transition from one to the other—in fact the new chip was designed to be interchangeable with the old computer boards.

Remember that when you buy a product from Germany or Sweden and resell it in the United States, you turn your money around a *lot* faster than if you spent two years and $2 million designing a chip. But even that distribution business was bootstrapped by another business when it was new. At first *that* business was a long shot. So while we were getting that distribution business in place, with sub-distributors and reps all over the country—a process that took a couple of years—we were doing hardware/software consulting projects.

A company would come to us and say, "Hey, can you write this software for us?" and we'd do it. Hand-to-mouth consulting projects. Shooting fish in a barrel. Putting food on the table in the short term.

People sometimes think they're above doing simple things that pay the bills because they're enamored with the romance of their long-shot deal. Not only do they underestimate the task of making the long shot happen, they often don't recognize that the lesser, related business will teach them many important things they still need to know.

A *long shot* is anything that involves building a list slowly from scratch, extensive and expensive product development, investment of big dollars, slow accumulation of assets.

Shooting fish in a barrel is anything where there's existing, pent-up demand for something you can easily assemble or convert from existing resources, "will-work-for-food" opportunities that pay on an hourly or per-job basis, affiliate or joint venture situations where an existing set of customers can be matched to a new offer.

Again, all of these situations come with a side benefit of giving you a view into situations you wouldn't otherwise be privy too. Sometimes we can be totally blind to things that are happening right in front of our eyes.

One guy merely lays bricks; another builds a wall; another builds a cathedral. There are always easy opportunities sitting right in front of you that you haven't seized yet.

Multiple, Multiple Backup Plans in Your Shirt Pocket

Doing consulting work was at the top of my list of "shooting fish in a barrel" options, but it was by no means the only thing on that list. There were a bunch of other options on my "B" list, like writing content for industry magazines ("stringer work"); being a Chicago sales rep for one or more companies; actively soliciting consulting projects through direct mail, magazine publicity, and ads in trade magazines; starting a new publishing venture with my buddy Heather in Toronto.

I was prepared to do any and all of these things.

When you've got a backup list that long, and you're in the middle of a tough negotiation, all you have to do is remind yourself that you've got that big, long "B" list to fall back on and you can easily maintain your composure.

SELL EARLY, SELL OFTEN

Many entrepreneurs are building startups from the ground up. An interesting question I (Tom) hear is "When should I start advertising?"

Most people wait waaaaaay too late.

Here is my suggestion. Start waaaaaay too early.

Start on day one.

On your first day, put up a simple web page with a description of what you are trying to do and a form for someone to give you their name and email so you can tell them when you are ready to launch.

Don't wait.

Each day you work on your start-up, add more to your web page and add ways for people to send friends to your page.

Don't wait.

Every week or two, mail out to your list of prospects the progress you are making and how the idea is growing. Offer a forum for them to make suggestions.

Don't wait.

If you are building software and are unfunded, try to release a beta version of some minimal working functionality as soon as possible—hopefully within two months of starting the business. Release software when it is too early and have people look at it and try to use it. Their feedback is priceless.

Don't wait.

If you are building software, or any service, try to get someone to pay for it while you are still embarrassed to ask for money. Someone paying for your product or service is the best indication you are not delusional in your start-up idea.

Don't wait.

If you've never failed, you've probably never really pushed yourself hard enough.

Fail at something. It is good for the soul.

Don't wait.

—*Thomas Meloche*

HORTON HEARS A WHO

Dr. Seuss wrote the story of Horton the elephant who, while splashing in a pool located in the Jungle of Nool, hears a small speck of dust speaking to him. Turns out the speck is a tiny planet, home to a city called Who-ville. Microscopic inhabitants known as Whos are led by their courageous mayor.

Horton can't see them, but with his large ears he can hear them. The mayor asks Horton to protect them from harm. Horton happily agrees, proclaiming throughout the book that "even though you can't see or hear them at all, a person's a person, no matter how small."

The other animals force Horton into a cage for believing in something that they're unable to see or hear. Horton tells the Whos that, lest they end up being boiled in "Beezelnut Oil", they need to make themselves heard to the other animals.

The Whos orchestrate themselves and in the end a "very small shirker named JoJo" makes enough of a peep for the jungle animals to hear the sound. Finally everyone agrees, "A person's a person, no matter how small."

When you operate a small, online business, you are a Who.

Large animals in the jungle can't hear you. Or if they do, they ignore you. Here's an example: in 2011, the state of Illinois created a new law. The law dictates that if an affiliate in Chicago generates a sale to a customer in Ohio, shipped and fulfilled by Amazon in Kansas, the customer in Ohio has to pay 8% Illinois sales tax.

How much sense does that make?

What if the buyer lives in Seattle where Amazon's headquarters are, and buys through an affiliate link from the woman in Illinois? Does Amazon pay sales tax to both states? Well, the whole reason mail-order companies don't pay sales tax is to keep states from hindering interstate commerce with ridiculous tariffs. You can easily imagine how this could escalate out of hand.

It's probably unconstitutional, but that didn't keep from Governor Patrick Quinn from signing it into law . . . which meant Amazon and Overstock and a bunch of other companies had to terminate their affiliate programs in the state of Illinois.

The hundreds or even thousands of letters and emails to the governor didn't help. A whole bunch of Whovilles, snuffed out.

I'm not telling you this to gripe. I'm just telling this so you know, there's pros and cons to being an invisible business. And one of the cons is that some huge beast can flick its tail and push you out of the way.

I started this chapter talking about managing risk, and this is just another example. Maybe you solve this problem by getting only a portion of your revenue from affiliates. Maybe you incorporate in a different state. Maybe you have multiple sources of traffic. Maybe you have a fallback position in case one of your product lines doesn't work out.

The other thing you need to do is band together with other Whos. Let me tell you how a different group of Whos escaped the wrath of the state of Illinois.

This picture shows what happened in the Illinois state capitol when the state threatened home-schooling parents with regulation.

My friend, what you see here is only the *overflow*. This is the part of the crowd that spilled out of the main auditorium. Thousands of home-schooling parents took a day off work and drove down to Springfield, Illinois, (that's 3.5 hours south of Chicago, a long, boring drive). Considerable inconvenience.

Then for hours, legislators heard about how home-schooled kids are in the 80th percentile and are courted by major universities, while kids in the Illinois public schools can't even read. *No thanks, State of Illinois, we don't need your "help" educating our children.*

The state legislature *quickly* backed down.

This is the second time I've seen this happen, by the way. Several years ago I went to a hearing about a similar bill. About 50 very resolute individuals spent 2.5 hours making sure lawmakers heard loud and clear that we did not want them meddling in our affairs, and we do an excellent job without any of their red tape.

They heard it again, and again, and again. Finally the person running the meeting said, "Uh, OK everyone, we get the point and we realize that the original legislation will not achieve the objective it was originally intended to accomplish."

My friend, those guys will definitely think twice before trying again to regulate home schools.

My point is this: "virtual" is great most of the time. But being REAL—in person, breathing and fogging a mirror, showing up and confronting a lawmaker—*that* is how you get counted in the affairs of the brick-and-mortar world, government or otherwise. Being an invisible noncitizen won't get you any representation at all.

This brings up the whole issue of online marketers as a community vs. being a vast sea of invisible, faceless people hiding behind their computers. If you've been around Planet Perry for a few years, you'll notice I've stepped up my delivery of seminars in the last couple of years.

Why?

Because a community of people who never meet each other really isn't much of a community.

Google advertisers had to band together when Google started "slapping" them left and right.

Facebook advertisers will likewise need a voice, because your friendly Facebook rep in the Philippines may be just another "Who" at Facebook.

Many, if not most, online marketers can find some way to physically connect with their customers *in person*. You included. Surely there's a way.

There certainly is such a thing in Planet Perry. I invite you to register for the free bonuses for this book at www.perrymarshall.com/fbtoolbox and try our Facebook club membership when you get there. You'll get email updates about Facebook's system and information about what other successful Facebook marketers are doing.

BIG CHALLENGES, DARK FEARS, AND THE S-T-R-E-T-C-H-I-N-G OF COMFORT ZONES

I (Perry) just got back from the Upper Peninsula of Michigan, 450 miles north of Chicago, where my daughter and I went on a daddy-daughter camping trip.

No running water, no electricity, cabin in the woods, swimming in the river, and being close to nature. It was great. Good for our relationship, too, and not a moment too soon. She's my oldest and she's halfway grown up already. College years are approaching fast, and every minute is precious.

One of the things we did was pole climbing and rope climbing, with harnesses and mountain climbing gear and all that stuff. One day we climbed this contraption of ladders and ropes, built on a tower 50 feet high.

I'm sure I appeared composed and seemed to be doing just fine, but halfway up that thing I was desperately wanting to be anywhere else. I'm struggling to get a toehold; I'm hanging by my fingers; my hands are sweaty; I'm 25 feet in the air swinging back and forth. And all of my normal instincts are screaming *get us down from here right now, Perry! Like, now!*

I don't know about you, but all my years of living on planet earth have conditioned me to feel safe only when my feet are on ground that isn't moving. Even though I had a big cable attached to my chest, even though I could have let go and only fallen six inches—even though I was actually completely safe—I didn't *feel* safe.

At that point you can only do one of two things: Go up or go down. Finish the climb or quit.

I took a 10-second break and collected my thoughts, and what ran through my mind was, *Hey, Perry, this is just like every other significant thing you've ever done in your life— as scary as all get out, risky, totally unnatural. And it made you nervous because . . . because it mattered.*

Insignificant things don't feel that way. Watching TV, eating pizza, and drinking beer—those things don't make you feel nervous and scared. They don't shove you out of your comfort zones.

I was talking to one of the girls at the camp and told her, "When you feel that nervous, 'let's get out of here right now' feeling, it either means (a) you really shouldn't be doing this at all so you'd best go right back down to the ground where you came from, or (b) you feel nervous because it matters, because it is important, because you *should* be doing it."

Which is to say, if you don't feel scared every now and then, you're not doing anything important.

Life is too short to not go ahead and get totally terrified every now and then. It's a sign that your soul is still alive and kicking.

I'm guessing it took me five, six, maybe seven minutes to climb that 50-foot rope ladder. But then about a half hour later I watched two of the camp counselors race to the top on a bet. First place, 40 seconds, second place 45 seconds. Young, wiry guys. They practically sprinted up that thing, better than a foot a second.

Watching them I realized that people can get used to, and even quite comfortable with, climbing at dizzying heights and doing things that are totally abnormal and terrifying to most people.

Not only that, but everything I've gotten really good at—everything you've gotten really good at in life—was a lot like rope climbing or mountain climbing. Once you've acquired a certain level of skill, whether it's climbing a 10,000 foot peak or making a million dollars a year, it isn't such a big deal. On a good day, you might not even break a sweat.

It's usually the first 50 feet—making that first dollar of actual profit—that deters most people. Get past that point and the competition thins dramatically. Soon you find you're not only comfortable with it, but enjoying it. That's how the serial entrepreneur is born—so addicted to the adventure he or she can't stop.

My friend, I've come to recognize that feeling of terror, that icy sensation of exposure and fright, is a signal that what I've just begun is important. That it *ought* to be done. The fear is a signal that it's worthwhile.

Yes, you might feel fear when you've begun something totally foolish. But you'll also feel that fear when you start a new enterprise, when you seek to repair a broken relationship, when you pick up the phone to make that important phone call. Nothing that matters happens until you do it.

The winner takes all, and the winner is you—when you decide to conquer fear and make it your ally.

—Perry Marshall

Index